EMDR

in the Treatment
of Adults Abused
as Children

. . . .

Laurel Parnell, Ph.D.

W.W. NORTON & COMPANY

New York | London

For information about permission to reproduce selections
from this book, write to Permissions,
W. W. Norton & Company, Inc., 500 Fifth Avenue,
New York, NY 10110

Composition by Paradigm Graphics
Manufacturing by Haddon Craftsman

Library of Congress Cataloging-in-Publication Data
Parnell, Laurel, 1955–
EMDR in the treatment of adults abused as children / by Laurel Parnell.
p.   cm.
Includes bibliographical references and index.
ISBN 0-393-70298-7
1. Adult child abuse victims—Rehabilitation.   2. Eye movement
desensitization and reprocessing.   I. Title.
RC569.5.C55C367   1999
616.85'822390651—dc21   99-21288   CIP

W. W. Norton & Company, Inc., 500 Fifth Avenue, New York, N.Y. 10110
www.wwnorton.com
W. W. Norton & Company Ltd., 10 Coptic Street, London WC1A 1PU

5 6 7 8 9 0

That which haunts us
will always find a way out.
The wound will not heal
unless given witness.
The shadow that follows us
is the way in.

Rumi

Contents

Introduction

My introduction to eye movement desensitization and reprocessing (EMDR) came in May 1991 at a yoga retreat in the Southern California desert, where a colleague enthusiastically described how EMDR had dramatically changed the way she did psychotherapy. She told me that her clients were improving more rapidly than ever before, that the changes were lasting over time, and that EMDR seemed to *transform psychological memory to objective memory*. As I described in *Transforming Trauma: EMDR* (1997a), after this glowing recounting of the wonders of EMDR, my friend demonstrated EMDR's power by working with a man at the retreat who had decompensated and was acting in a bizarre manner during the yoga sessions. The day after her EMDR work, the man rejoined his peers, doing the yoga appropriately. Impressed with the results, I signed up for Francine Shapiro's Level I training in Sunnyvale, California, three weeks later.

I had a firsthand experience of EMDR's power during the training practicums. Working on a relatively uncharged childhood memory, I found myself transported to an earlier time when my two-year-old child-self felt like she was about to be killed by her angry father. I experienced a full-blown abreaction with intense heat flashing through my body, rapid shallow breathing, and a racing heart. My child-self was terrified! From this experience I really understood that my childhood experience was frozen in time, with the thoughts, feelings, and beliefs I had had as a small child. I also learned the importance of riding the waves of the abreaction, letting the feelings gain in intensity and then subside, without stopping the processing. As a result of the practicum experiences, I felt encouraged to enter my own EMDR therapy and work on early abuse incidents. Subsequently, I experienced changes in my internal structure and core self-beliefs, which altered my relationship patterns. I ended an unhappy marriage and met and married a more compatible mate. My relationship with my father, which had always been strained because of the early abuse, transformed, and is now friendly and loving—a change I never before would have imagined possible!

I completed the EMDR Institute's Level II training in 1992, and later that year became a facilitator. Immediately upon completing the Level I training I began using it with many of my clients. In addition to the EMDR Institute trainings, I attended a weekly case consultation group of EMDR-trained colleagues and a monthly peer consultation group with other EMDR facilitators. These groups were very valuable, helping me to develop confidence in the method and its potential to heal. In my weekly consultation group I learned about using inner child work, which I integrated into my work with clients.

EMDR has come a long way since Francine Shapiro's famous walk in the park. Many of us who were trained by her in the early years took this powerful method and used it with our clients, adapting it for their specific needs and discovering new applications along the way. The early view of EMDR as a quick fix changed as we used EMDR with more challenging clients with complex diagnoses—particularly those with histories of childhood abuse. We found that their processing did not always simply go down the track to a resolution of the traumatic memory. We often found ourselves stuck, with the processing not moving and the client in distress. We tried different things—some worked and some did not—and we shared our discoveries with one another as EMDR evolved.

Through teaching EMDR, facilitating at EMDR Institute trainings, and providing consultation to EMDR-trained therapists, I have found that EMDR practitioners need detailed information on how to work with the complex issues presented by adults who were abused as children. The available literature to date does not yet offer sufficient preparation to help EMDR therapists deal effectively with the complex issues of this group of clients. Some therapists consequently either don't use EMDR or are unable to integrate it well into their psychotherapy practices. For the past several years I have taught the material in this book as a specialty presentation at the EMDR Institute's Level II trainings, at EMDR International Association conferences, and in my own EMDR courses.

EMDR in the Treatment of Adults Abused as Children offers practical information about the use of EMDR in a typical clinical setting and presents innovations that build upon the information in Shapiro's 1995 book. It not only teaches many practical techniques that help the therapist when a therapeutic impasse is reached but also provides a selection of treatment choices. Case material is used throughout the book to illustrate the techniques described and to provide the therapist with a deeper, more grounded understanding of different kinds of abuse cases. Included are suggestions I have used with my clients and collected from other sources over the last eight years. Many friends and colleagues have shared their insights and discoveries, and new ones can be expected as EMDR continues to evolve.

It is my hope that this book will help you to navigate the difficult terrain of the heart and mind as you work with EMDR. I do not pretend to know all the different paths processing can take. Everyone is so wonderfully different. Your attuned compassionate relationship with your client is most important, along with your training and clinical experience. Stay open and listen to your intuitive voice. Try what it tells you—if it doesn't work, try something else. *Always* check with your client. Be creative! The more open and courageous the therapist is, the more inspired the client will be.

My original intent was to write about using EMDR with adult survivors of sexual abuse, but I later widened the focus to general abuse, because so many of the issues for emotional, physical, and sexual abuse are the same. The principles outlined in this book apply to all types of abuse. I also want to emphasize that I have *not included work with dissociative identity disorder.* That disorder entails a much more complex treatment and involves special training. I leave it to my EMDR colleagues to write on dissociative disorders.

Therapists should be fully trained in EMDR and have experience employing the standardized protocol as outlined in the EMDR basic text (Shapiro, 1995) before working with multiply traumatized adults or employing the modified protocols outlined in this book. This book is a complement to the training and the textbook, not a substitute.

MY BACKGROUND

I have had a wide range of training and experience and have worked with adults, adolescents, and children in long-and short-term psychotherapy. My psychotherapeutic orientation is both pragmatic psychodynamic, which includes a developmental/ego-psychological and self psychological perspective, and Jungian, which takes into consideration the archetypal realm, with an appreciation for and sensitivity to unconscious symbols. I have worked with dreams, imagery, and active imagination for many years. I have received training in hypnotherapy and relaxation techniques. I also have 26 years' experience with various meditation practices, including Vipassana meditation as taught by Joseph Goldstein (1976) and Jack Kornfield (1993) and Tibetan Buddhist visualization practices (Yeshe, 1995). My work has also been influenced by the non-dual advaita teachings of Jean Klein (1988) and the mindful body-work he taught. Since my training in EMDR I have been more sensitive to clients' beliefs and body experience, including their emotions, energy changes, and physical sensations. In the EMDR work I do, I am directed by my sense of what the client feels both emotionally and physically as well as what he or she reports to me. I typically pay a lot of attention to the somatic aspect of the processing.

CONVENTIONS USED THROUGHOUT THIS BOOK

All of the identifying details of the cases have been changed in order to protect the the clients' privacy. I have changed names, professions, family constellations, races, and specific life events; some cases represent composites of more than one client.

Instead of *patient,* I have used the word *client,* a term I prefer. All clients are referred to by first names, which I feel creates a more personal sense of the people whose lives I describe. Most of the case examples in the book are my clients, although some are from EMDR colleagues.

In my EMDR work I use eye movements directed by a light bar and hand passes, as well as alternate tapping on the hands or knees. In the book's transcripts you will see the "►◄►◄►◄" sign, which indicates a set of reprocessing stimuli that may take the form of alternating eye movements or alternating auditory or kinesthetic stimuli. Unless otherwise indicated, assume that the client was directed by the therapist to focus on whatever material had just come up, and that at the end of bilateral stimulation the therapist asked the client a question like, "What came up for you? or "What do you get now?" to elicit information about the client's experience during the set of bilateral stimulation.

Acknowledgments

I want to offer my heartfelt appreciation to the many wonderful people who have inspired me and contributed to the creation of this book. First I want to thank my clients, who had the courage to face their greatest fears and with a leap of faith trusted me and EMDR to help them heal their traumatic past. Their healing process taught me so much about EMDR, which has made it possible for me to share my discoveries with others.

I appreciate Francine Shapiro for developing EMDR and encouraging the creative enhancement of the method to meet the needs of different kinds of clients. Her courage and determination to bring EMDR to the world are inspiring.

Many EMDR therapists contributed to this work. I want to express my gratitude to my friend Linda Cohn for providing case material, helpful brainstorming, and expertise about integrating art and imagery with EMDR. I am grateful to Brooke Brown for her friendship and support at all stages of this project, particularly for her help in creating a structure for the book and her editing skill. Thanks to Landry Wildwind, an EMDR pioneer, for her use of EMDR in ego strengthening with complex cases; Margaret Allen for her precious friendship and very helpful feedback; John Prendergast and Richard Miller for their friendship and support through the years, and for teaching me about inner child work and the development of inner resources; Curt Rouanzoin for his input and enthusiastic support of this book; Christie Sprowls for the use of interweaves on Ecuadorian train derailments; Mark Dworkin for the Humphrey Bogart resource installation; A. J. Popky, Sandra Foster, Jennifer Lendl, Debra Korn, Maggie Phillips, and Andrew Leeds for their contributions to using EMDR for strengthening positive resources.

I want to thank my sister Cherie Vandenburgh for our time of sharing and writing in Sedona and for her feedback on Chapter 12. My appreciation to Jean Pumphrey, who has supported my writing since childhood, and my parents, Helen McDonald and Dean Parnell. Thanks to Sheryl Fullerton, my literary agent, for her guidance on this project and to Susan Munro, my editor at Norton, for her support and recognition of the value of this book.

I want to acknowledge my sons, Catono and Etienne, and I especially want to thank my husband, Pierre-Antoine Blais, for his love and encouragement, which have sustained me with such warmth.

EMDR
in the Treatment of Adults
Abused as Children

Part I

. . . .

Treating Adults Abused as Children with EMDR

Chapter I

The EMDR Model

This chapter is meant to refresh your memory and understanding regarding EMDR, thereby providing the background and foundation for the more complex and challenging information that follows.

EMDR'S Discovery and Development

The use of eye movements to affect psychological disturbances was discovered serendipitously in 1987 by Francine Shapiro, then a psychology graduate student. While walking through a park in Los Gatos, California, disturbing thoughts plagued her; then suddenly she noticed that the thoughts were disappearing. She recalled them, but they were not as valid or distressing. Intrigued, she began to closely watch her thought processes and noticed that when a disturbing thought came into her mind, spontaneously her eyes began to move very rapidly. The eye movement seemed to cause the thought to shift out of her consciousness. When she made the thought resurface, it had lost much of its negative charge. Then she began doing this experiment deliberately. She thought about things that bothered her and moved her eyes in the same way. Again the thoughts went away. Further experimenting, she tested this process with some older memories and some present problems. They all reacted the same way. Curious to know if this discovery would work on other people, she tried it on her friends. She found that most of them couldn't sustain the eye movement for any length of time, so she began to direct them to follow her fingers with their eyes.

After testing this process on about 70 people, Shapiro came to believe the eye movements were causing a desensitization of the disturbing material and she developed it into a more refined method. She called it eye movement desensitization (EMD). (In 1990 she expanded the name to EMDR to include the concept of reprocessing. Further experience with the method convinced her that the eye movements reprocessed traumatic memories into something more adaptive and functional.) In 1988 Shapiro tested her new method in a research study conducted in Mendocino, California, with with 22 volunteers: Vietnam vets, victims of rape, and victims of sexual abuse. All were suffering from symptoms of PTSD, including nightmares, flashbacks, intrusive thoughts, low self-esteem, and relationship problems. All were experiencing persistent traumatic memories. At the initial session, the volunteers were divided into two groups and measured on their symptoms, as well as on their anxiety and beliefs about the traumatic event. Volunteers in the treatment group had one EMDR session ranging from 15 to 90 minutes. Those in the control group did not get EMDR but instead were asked to describe their traumatic experiences in detail. After a single EMDR procedure, the treatment group showed a marked decrease in anxiety, a more objective assessment of the trauma, and a reduction in symptoms. The control group showed no or minimal changes. For ethical reasons, those in the control group were then given an EMDR session, and they too experienced a significant decrease in their symptoms. One and three months later the treatment group was measured again. Shapiro reported that EMDR led to significant and enduring positive behavioral changes, as rated by the participants and their significant others (Shapiro, 1989a).

Since Shapiro's initial efficacy study, EMDR has had more published case reports and research to support it than any other method used in the treatment of trauma. Positive therapeutic results with EMDR have been reported with a wide number of populations, including: previously resistant combat veterans (Daniels, Lipke, Richardson, & Silver, 1992; Lipke & Botkin, 1992), persons with phobias and panic disorder (Goldstein, 1992; Goldstein & Feske, 1994; Kleinknecht, 1993), crime victims (Baker & McBride, 1991; Kleinknecht, 1992; Page & Crino, 1993), victims of grief and loss (Puk, 1991; Solomon & Shapiro, 1997), traumatized children (Greenwald, 1994; Lovett, 1999; Puffer, Greenwald, & Elrod, in press; Tinker & Wilson, 1999), sexual assault victims (Cohn, 1993a; Parnell, 1994, 1997a, 1998a; Puk, 1991; Spector & Huthwaite, 1993; Wolpe & Abrams, 1991), burn victims (McCann, 1992), victims of sexual dysfunction (Levin, 1993; Wernick, 1993) and dissociative disorders (Paulsen, Vogelmann-Sine, Lazrove, & Young, 1993; Young, 1994), as well as a wide variety of diagnoses (Marquis, 1991).

At this point there are more controlled studies on EMDR showing significant treatment effects than on any other method used in the treatment of post-traumatic stress disorder (Boudewyns, Stwertka, Hyer, Albrecht, & Sperr, 1993; Carlson, Chemtob, Rusnak, Hedlund, & Muraoka, 1998; Levin, Grainger, Allen-Byrd, & Fulcher, 1994; Marcus, Marquis, & Sakai, 1997; Pitman, Orr, Altman, Longpre, Poire, & Macklin, 1996; Rothbaum, 1997; Shapiro, 1989a,b; Scheck, Schaeffer, & Gilette, 1998; Silver, Brooks, & Obenchain, 1995; Solomon & Kaufman, 1992; Wilson, Covi, Foster, & Silver, 1993; Wilson, Becker, & Tinker, 1995; Wilson, Becker, & Tinker, 1997).

One of the most significant EMDR research studies was done by

EMDR-trained researchers Sandra Wilson, Lee Becker, and Robert Tinker (1995). Wilson and her associates sought to replicate the findings of Shapiro's original study while improving the research method to address issues raised in critical reviews (Acierno, Van Hasselt, Tremont, & Meuser, 1994; Herbert & Meuser, 1992; Lohr et al., 1992). In order to address the issues raised, a large and diverse sample was employed (N =80); participants were randomly assigned to treatment or control conditions and to one of five EMDR-trained therapists; evaluations were conducted by an independent assessor using objective and standardized measures; subjects participated in no other therapy while in EMDR treatment; PTSD diagnoses were objectively made; and all subjects' treatment was monitored by the principal investigator. The participants were 40 men and 40 women with traumatic memories. Very few of the participants had heard about EMDR before the study. Their traumas occurred from three months to more than 50 years prior to the beginning of the study. The volunteers were suffering from anxieties, phobias, sleep disturbances, intimacy problems, and depression and had been experiencing these symptoms since the traumas had occurred. Participants were randomly assigned to either a treatment or a delayed treatment group. All of the treatment subjects were given a pre-test, three EMDR sessions, a post-test, and a follow-up test 90 days later. The non-treatment group was given the pre- and post-tests and follow-up test without any treatment.

The results were very impressive. Those in the EMDR group showed significant improvement in all areas and maintained relief from their symptoms over the 90-day period. No improvement was observed in the untreated group. After these delayed-treatment participants received their EMDR sessions, they also improved on all measures.

Fifteen months after the EMDR therapy, another follow-up study was conducted, which demonstrated that the volunteers continued to benefit from the treatment. Many of the participants said their self-confidence had increased and the positive treatment effects had generalized into other aspects of their lives (Wilson, Becker, & Tinker, 1997).

These EMDR efficacy studies (Shapiro, 1989a,b; Wilson et al., 1995), which studied EMDR's effectiveness with people suffering with PTSD symptoms, included in their pool of subjects adults abused as children who, along with the others, experienced an amelioration of their symptoms.

Scheck, Schaeffer, and Gillette (1998) studied the efficiacy of EMDR with 60 traumatized young women between the ages of 16 and 25, 90% of whom reported being victims of childhood physical or emotional abuse. After pretesting, participants were randomly assigned to two 90-minute sessions of either EMDR or an active listening control. Following the two sessions a post-test assessment was done. A follow-up interview was conducted 90 days after the post-test assessment. Significant improvement was found for both groups and a significantly greater post-test change was found for the EMDR subjects. The largest effect size difference was for the Impact of Events Scale, the measure that was most trauma specific. The improvement of the EMDR treatment subjects placed them within normal range relative to the symptoms and self-concept they reported.

These results are quite impressive given the subject population and the brevity of the EMDR treatment, although it could be that the subjects who participated were not representative of the general population of traumatized young women. The participants remembered their early traumas and could provide a narrative account of what had happened to them, and they were stable enough to show up for the sessions and provide post-session feedback. Many abuse survivors do not have narrative memories of the abuse and require time in therapy to establish a trusting relationship with the therapist before beginning EMDR processing. There are also no data to show that the observed improvements continued. The findings, however, are encouraging, demonstrating that EMDR can produce results in reducing symptoms of traumatic stress in a very brief time with young women with traumatic histories.

To date two studies have focused on the effectiveness of EMDR on healing sexual abuse in particular. In a controlled study of rape victims, Rothbaum (1997) found that after three EMDR treatment sessions 90% of the subjects experienced a decrease in their PTSD symptoms. Datta and Wallace (1996) did a controlled study testing the effects of three sessions of EMDR for adolescent sexual perpetrators who had been sexually abused and were incarcerated in a treatment program for sex offenders. The participants were randomly assigned to EMDR treatment; the results were compared to those obtained with individual and group treatment. The group that received EMDR treatment showed significantly better results than the other group. There was a reduction in anxiety and distress related to their trauma, an increase in the sense of cognitive control, and an increase in empathy for their victims. (See Chambless et al., 1998; Feske, 1998; Shapiro, in press; Spector & Reade, in press, for more research reviews.)

Therapists who use EMDR find it to be more effective than other therapeutic methods. Success rates with previously difficult cases has been quite high, and clients are getting better much faster. In a survey of 445 EMDR-trained clinicians who together had treated more than 10,000 clients, 76% of the respondents reported EMDR to be more effective than other treatments they had used, and only 4% found it less effective (Lipke, 1994).

EMDR has come a long way since Shapiro's 1987 walk in the park. Thousands of therapists have been trained worldwide, EMDR courses are being taught in psychology graduate school programs, there has been increased acceptance by managed care companies and HMOs (Kaiser Hospital in California), and there is an international EMDR professional organization (EMDRIA). Further, in 1995 the American Psychological Association Division 12 (Clinical Psychology) initiated a project to determine the degree to which extant therapeutic methods were supported by solid empirical evidence. Independent reviewers (Chambless et al., 1998) recently placed EMDR on a list of "empirically validated treatments," as "probably efficacious for civilian PTSD." EMDR practitioners who have used EMDR extensively in their clinical work have expanded it beyond Shapiro's original protocols and have developed protocols and procedures for working with a wide range of client populations. Those of us who have used EMDR with clients with complex issues and multiple childhood traumas have found that Shapiro's original protocols weren't always enough for successful healing. So we have taken the basic EMDR premises and added guided imagery techniques to increase the efficacy. Additional sophisticated interweaves have been added to those described in Shapiro's (1995) book.

Theoretical Model for Understanding EMDR Processing

TRAUMA MEMORIES RELIEVED WITH ACCELERATED INFORMATION PROCESSING

In its broadest definition, a trauma is an experience that causes one to develop limiting and sometimes erroneous beliefs about oneself or the world. For example, a child who is molested may come to believe she is bad and the world isn't safe. These experiences also become fixed in the body-mind in the form of irrational emotions, blocked energy, and physical symptoms, and measurable changes in brain functioning (van der Kolk, Burbridge, & Suzuki, 1997).

Shapiro describes two types of traumas: minor traumas, which she calls "small t" traumas, and major or "big T" traumas. The "t" traumas are those experiences that give one a lesser sense of self-confidence and assault one's sense of self-efficacy. Like a perceptual filter, they cause one to develop narrow and limiting views of oneself and the world, keep one from living to one's full potential, and cause suffering. An example of this kind of trauma is a woman who sought therapy because she was suffering from chronic depression. She traced her very low self-esteem to her childhood. She had been fat as a child and had been teased mercilessly by her schoolmates as well as criticized by her family. She had developed a deep negative belief about herself, a belief that she wasn't good enough, and her depressed feelings were associated with these childhood experiences. Despite years of talk therapy and much insight, she couldn't shake this feeling and negative self-concept.

The "T" traumas are those that affect one dramatically, such as rape, childhood physical and sexual abuse, disasters, accidents, and losses. They jolt one out of one's usual perspective on life, causing one to question oneself and the order of one's world. These traumas often lead to debilitating symptoms of PTSD, like nightmares, flashbacks, anxieties, phobias, fears, and difficulties at home and work. Like the "t" traumas, they also affect one's sense of self-confidence and self-efficacy.

It seems that when a person experiences a trauma, either a "t" or "T," it becomes locked into its own memory network as it was experienced—the images, physical sensations, tastes and smells, sounds, and beliefs—as if frozen in time in the body and the mind. Consequently, a woman who has been raped may develop a fear of going out alone. She may avoid places that in any way remind her of the assault. She may develop a fear of men who share characteristics of the perpetrator, such as age, race, or stature. Reminders of the assault trigger an emotional response, because all of the memories related to the assault are locked in her nervous system and she has been unable to process them. Internal or external reminders of the rape will cause the experience to flash into her consciousness in its original form.

Ordinary daily events seem to pass through us without leaving a mark. Traumatic events, however, often get trapped and form a perpetual blockage. Like a broken record, they repeat themselves in our body-mind over and over again. Nightmares may actually be the mind's attempts to process this trapped information, but the trauma memory always lasts beyond the dream. Perhaps this mechanism that freezes traumatic events was an adaptive device in early humans, helping to protect them from repeating mistakes. But now it has become maladaptive; rather than protect us, it obscures our perceptions and emotions. For example, a young girl who is sexually abused by a man may fear all men when she is an adult. This fear can impede her ability to form a close relationship with a mate, prevent her from having male friendships, and cause problems for her with male bosses in the workplace. Her anxiety around men may be very high, and she may have no idea why.

In theory, just as the body has a natural healing response to physical injury, the brain has an information-processing system that works to keep one in a balanced state of mental health. The body automatically goes into action to heal a wound; but, if the wound is blocked, it will fester and resist healing. When confronted with a trauma, the nervous system gets stuck—like a blocked wound in the body—causing an ongoing array of PTSD symptoms.

In EMDR, clients are asked to focus on a "target" related to the trauma, such as a person; a memory or dream image; an actual, fantasized, or projected event; or a part of the experience like a body sensation or thought. Through this target we attempt to stimulate the memory network where the trauma is stored. Simultaneously, the eye movements or other bilateral stimuli appear to trigger a mechanism that restores the system's information-processing abilities, enabling it to draw on information from a different memory network where the client will find insight and understanding. In what is called *accelerated information processing* (Shapiro, 1995), a type of rapid free association of information between the two networks occurs. Each set of eye movements further unlocks the disturbing information and accelerates it along an adaptive path until the negative thoughts, feelings, pictures, and emotions have dissipated and are spontaneously replaced by insights and an overall positive attitude.

Therapists' experience using EMDR with thousands of clients have shown that EMDR clears locked-in damaging information from both the body and the mind *without removing anything that is useful or necessary.* A molestation victim, for example, may no longer be plagued by nightmares and flashbacks of the traumatic events, but she will not forget that it happened. Instead of believing that no one can be trusted, she comes to know that some people can be trusted. According to Shapiro (1995), "When the information is positively integrated, and adaptively resolved, it is available for future use. EMDR doesn't take away anything that's supposed to be there and it doesn't give a person amnesia." A basic principle of EMDR is that basic health resides within all of us. What EMDR does is remove blockages caused by negative images, beliefs, and body sensations, allowing one's natural state of well-being and emotional balance to come through.

WHY DOES THE EYE MOVEMENT WORK?

EMDR is a complex, integrated form of psychotherapy. There are many theories about different components of EMDR (see Shapiro, 1995), but it is not known precisely how eye movement achieves therapeutic effects. In theory traumas leave unprocessed memories, feelings, and thoughts that can be reprocessed or "metabolized" with these eye movements. Similarly to the way rapid eye movement (REM) or dream sleep works, the eye movements help to process this blocked information, allowing the body-mind to release it.

Dreams each night cleanse the body-mind of the day's residues. It seems that some particularly strong dreams that are related to past events are the body-mind's attempt to heal. The problem is that during disturbing dreams the eye movements are often disrupted and one wakes up, thus not allowing the REM sleep to complete its job. With EMDR, different from dreams, the therapist keeps the eyes moving back and forth and guides the client into focusing on the traumatic event. This allows the event to be fully experienced and reintegrated.

EMDR clinicians have found that hand tapping and bilateral sounds are also effective in stimulating the reprocessing of material. Perhaps rhythmic, alternating stimulation of the two hemispheres of the brain causes the reprocessing effect of EMDR. There is also a theory that the eye movements may serve a function in facilitating the hippocampus in consolidation of memory. Another theory is that the dual attention the client maintains with EMDR, focusing simultaneously on the inner feelings and the eye movements, allows the alerted brain to metabolize whatever it is witnessing.

I have heard anecdotal accounts of eye movements being used for hundreds of years by yoga practitioners to calm the mind. It may be that Shapiro not only rediscovered a basic biological mechanism for clearing the body-mind of present-time disturbances but ingeniously made the leap to linking the eye movements with stored psychological material.

NEUROBIOLOGY OF TRAUMA AND RECENT BRAIN RESEARCH

It is useful to know something about the neurobiology of trauma when working with adults abused as children. In the past ten years there has been an explosion of research that has greatly increased our understanding of how trauma affects the brain and human behavior. One of the preeminent researchers in this area is Bessel van der Kolk, whose edited book, *Traumatic Stress* (van der Kolk, McFarlane, & Weisaeth, 1996) contains much of the research cited below. This new knowledge has been made possible by the development of neuroimaging devices, including the SPECT scan, which allow us to view the brain under different conditions. This very exciting information has revolutionized the way we view the process of encoding traumatic memory and the long-term consequences of trauma. The new realization is that trauma, particularly during the early stages of brain development, impairs mental and emotional functioning and affects physiology far more than we realized and for a much longer time. Trauma memory is stored differently than ordinary memory—in the right hemisphere in fragmented, unintegrated form, separate from the brain's language center—which explains why traditional talk therapy is inevitably limited and inadequate to effectively resolve early trauma.

Memory Development

When we are born we have *implicit* memory. This emotional, behavioral, somatosensory, perceptual, and nonverbal memory is stored in the right hemisphere of the brain. The infant has no concept of time. When he is hungry, he wants to be fed; when he is wet, he cries. There is no concept of past and future. There is also no self-concept. The locus of *me* or *I* has not yet developed as a concept that is experienced as ongoing over time. Focal attention is not required for encoding of this memory. Sensorimotor schemas are developed in early childhood that form a template of schemas for the self and world.

Later we develop *explicit* memory. Explicit or narrative memory is semantic and autobiographical. One has a sense of self in time—"I did this," and "I felt that." In explicit memory, which requires conscious awareness and focal attention, there is hippocampal processing. Information is consolidated into working memory and then moved to long-term permanent memory.

From birth to three years the hippocampus is not mature, so memory is left in implicit form in the right hemisphere and not encoded into explicit memory. This is referred to as "infantile amnesia." People can remember early childhood events implicitly with somatic responses but not explicitly in a narrative (Siegel, 1998). For example, the smell of warm milk might elicit feelings of happiness and comfort with no narrative memory accompanying them.

Psychological Trauma in Childhood

Psychological trauma causes *disassociation of hemispheric processing*. The left hemisphere, which is responsible for verbal and motor control, the manipulation of words and symbols, and the sequential processing of information, is locked out, and memory is encoded only as implicit memory in the right hemisphere. Memory remains in fragmented form as somatic sensations and intense affect states and is not collated and transcribed into personal narratives. It appears that terror blocks the hippocampus, so that information does not go to explicit memory. Researchers have found that there is diminished hippocampal volume in chronic PTSD (van der Kolk et al., 1997). If a person is triggered by something in her life that activates her implicit memory, it feels "timeless," like it is happening now. This is what we find so often when using EMDR with adults traumatized as children. The feelings aroused in their bodies feel current, and clients lose the sense that what they are experiencing now comes from something that happened in the past.

Early abusive experiences are stored in the right hemisphere of the brain separately from the language centers of the left brain; the right side of the brain holds the negative affective states. Early trauma causes what Schore (1998) calls "synaptic pruning" in the orbital frontal cortex and creates a disturbance in the sympathetic-parasympathetic systems that results in hyperarousal, the misreading of external cues, and difficulty with self-soothing or calming. Children who have been abused have problems with affect regulation. They become easily overstimulated and have trouble calming themselves. They also have difficulty coping with stress. Early trauma creates a predisposition to the development of posttraumatic stress disorder. Synaptic pruning also affects the ability to experience positive emotional states and predisposes individuals to depression (Schore, 1998). When there is excessive pruning of the synapses in the orbital frontal cortex, it affects attachment, empathy, and the capacity to regulate body pain. People with childhood trauma *do* hurt more.

Trauma and the Brain

Traumatic memories lodge in the brain in different ways from other memories. During the trauma, the pieces are not put together: Trauma freezes the integrative process, and the information is not integrated into schemas like ordinary memory. Trauma interferes with the evaluation, classification, and contextualization of experiences. Memory remains as implicit memory stored in the back of the brain in the limbic system, which is responsible for fleeing, fighting, feeding and reproduction. In the limbic system the *amygdala* attaches emotional meaning to incoming information. It passes the information on to the *hippocampus,* which is the brain's early warning system, telling it whether information is dangerous or not. The hippocampus filters out irrelevant information, evaluates what stays, and files it.

In traumatized people, because the amygdala to hippocampus connection is disrupted, the information is not integrated and filed. Information is left in fragmented form. The different fragments include visual, affective, tactile, olfactory, auditory, and somatosensory information.

When a person experiences a trauma, the left anterior frontal lobe, known as Broca's area (the language part of the brain), is deactivated. This deactivation of Broca's area causes "speechless terror" for many traumatzed people; they can't talk about or understand their experience with words. They feel intense emotions without being able to put a label on what they are experiencing. Although they may be feeling intensively, they are unable to communicate what they are experiencing (van der Kolk et al., 1997). In working with traumatized people, we must activate the right side of the brain where the trauma is stored. Art, EMDR, movement, and sandplay work activate the right hemisphere.

The following are important things to keep in mind when working with traumatized people:

1. *People with PTSD don't attend to neutral stimuli: their brains are geared to traumatic stimuli.* Their lives are fixated on the trauma; they live in the past. Because their brains don't attend to neutral stimuli, they don't take in new information. Real life loses its meaning on a daily level; they only process and pay attention to threatening stimuli. This results in a lack of engagement in the world (McFarlane, Weber, & Clark, 1993).

2. *People with PTSD have more active limbic systems, and ordinary talk psychotherapy doesn't decondition the limbic system.* The part of the brain that holds the traumatic memory continues to be triggered, acting as if present-time nonthreatening internal or external stimuli are dangerous, even if the person *understands* that the stimuli are not dangerous and not the cause of his or her responses. He or she still has the same somatosensory or emotional responses to the old cues. You can't reason the body out of reacting to stimuli that cause a reaction in the limbic system. Stimulation of this part of the brain causes a nonverbal response that is impervious to intellectual understanding. The limbic system continues to respond as if there were present dangers (van der Kolk, 1994). This is why so many clients who have been abused as children or traumatized as adults do not change their behavioral responses to triggers even after years of insight-oriented psychotherapy.

3. *With PTSD there is a loss of the capacity to analyze and categorize arousing information.* People with PTSD cannot talk about their experience. The left hemisphere is locked out. Reason is absent, and there is an increased emotional response (van der Kolk et al., 1996).
4. *People with PTSD are not able to utilize language to gain distance from the offending stimulus.* Therefore, therapies that depend on language are not able to help traumatized clients (van der Kolk et al., 1996).
5. *Fragmented or misclassified sensations are reactivated in state dependent form with PTSD.* Traumatized people are "triggered" by internal or external reminders of the original trauma (van der Kolk et al., 1996).

According to van der Kolk (1998), part of the treatment for PTSD is to teach clients to pay attention to nontraumatic stimuli as a way of deconditioning the limbic system. It appears that mindfulness training, which I describe in more detail in Chapter 4, can help activate the frontal lobes and enhance the left hemisphere. In conjunction with mindfulness practices, EMDR may help people process specific traumas and integrate memory fragments by activating the frontal lobe, thus moving memory from implicit to explicit. After the fragmented memory is transformed into a narrative and the traumatic event successfully processed with EMDR, the person can tell the story of what happened.

Van der Kolk's SPECT Scan Study Pilot Study

Van der Kolk, Burbridge, and Suzuki (1997) conducted a pilot study using EMDR with indiduals who had experienced a single incident trauma and were suffering from PTSD. The six subjects' PTSD scores were measured by the CAPS pre- and post-EMDR. SPECT scans were done of each subject's brain as a script was read to him or her of the traumatic incident. Each subject then received three sessions of EMDR, after which another SPECT scan was administered as the trauma script was read. Four out of the six subjects showed improvemement in PTSD as measured by the Clinician Administered PTSD Scale (CAPS), with an average decline from 84 to 36. (It was later discovered that the two subjects for whom there was no significant drop in PTSD had multiple traumas that had not been initially reported [Francine Shapiro, personal communication, 1998].) Prior to the EMDR treatment, there was high activation of the amygdala and deactivation of the frontal lobes. After treatment, for those subjects showing improvement there was increased activity in the anterior cingulate bilaterally and increased activation of the right prefrontal cortex. The anterior cingulate is the part of the brain that puts together affective and cognitive elements. According to van der Kolk et al. (1997), these findings suggest "that the recovery from PTSD may depend on the capacity of higher brain functions to override the input from limbic structures charged with the initial appraisal of the degree of threat posed by incoming sensory stimuli" (p.

106). Subjects were able to take in new information (the script) and appreciate it as nonthreatening. In other words, although the old script may sound like trauma, it is an *old* script—*it is not happening now.* The subjects were able to distinguish between current and past experiences because their filtering system was activated. The study's results are consistent with what we observe in our clients after successful EMDR threatment: Clients become conscious and are no longer triggered by old trauma reminders. They are no longer run by their unconscious reactions.

Review of Basic EMDR Protocol and Procedures

EMDR therapy typically begins with a client's desire to heal from a trauma, overcome a performance problem, or deal with a troubling aspect of life. There are eight phases of EMDR treatment, which Shapiro has outlined in *Eye Movement Desensitization and Reprocessing: Basic Principles, Protocols, and Procedures* (1995). Therapists should use that book as a basic text, since various cautions and issues are not repeated here. The first two phases are *history taking* and *preparation* for EMDR processing.

It is essential that before EMDR processing begins the therapist take a thorough history. This enables him or her to establish hypotheses about the origins of the presenting problem, so that the appropriate clinical interventions can be used, safeguards established, and the best targets for EMDR processing selected. Also, during this time the therapist and client are establishing a therapeutic relationship within which the reprocessing work can take place.

During the preparation phase the therapist gives the client specific instructions about what he or she will be doing during EMDR processing, along with a summary of the theory about trauma and what the eye movements or other bilateral stimulation seem to be doing. The therapist lets the client know that it is important to give accurate feedback about what he or she is experiencing during the processing and to let whatever happens happen without censoring it. The therapist tells the client that there are no right or wrong feelings and that everyone processes things differently. Clients are told that they are in control and that they can stop the processing whenever they feel a need to. A signal for stop, like raising a hand or closing the eyes, is established. This is an important part of the client instructions, especially for adults who have been abused as children and who experienced themselves as helpless and without control at the time of the abuse.

An important part of the preparation for many clients, especially those with a history of early childhood abuse, is to establish an safe inner place where they can go if they want to stop the processing and take a break or to close the session. I will discuss the use of the safe place in more detail in Chapter 5.

It is essential that a feeling of connection, caring, and safety be established between therapist and client. The client is ready for EMDR processing when there is a feeling of safety and trust established in the therapeutic relationship, the client understands what the processing entails, and both the therapist and client feel prepared. Later in this book these first two phases will be described in more detail, particularly as they pertain to adults abused as children.

Phase three is the *assessment* for the EMDR processing session. Ninety minutes or longer is the usual length of time for a session, especially if an early childhood abuse memory is to be processed, because there is often strong emotion expressed and it takes longer than usual to complete sessions. The first step in an EMDR processing session is to help the client to identify and focus on a target related to the trauma. The therapist asks the client, "What picture represents the worst part of the incident?" A woman who is working on an abuse memory might choose as her target the image of being fondled by her brother while she was in bed at night. Next, the client is asked for a *negative cognition*—a life-limiting, self-referencing belief associated with the incident that has carried over to the present. She might be asked, "What words best go with the picture that express your negative belief about yourself now?" Her belief might be "I am not safe." Because this negative cognition has an emotional charge, it affects her everyday life. The therapist then asks what she would like to believe about herself when she brings up the image. In this case such a *positive cognition* would be "I am safe now." The therapist then asks the client to rate the validity of the positive statement on a scale from 1 (completely false) to 7 (completely true). "When you bring up the image of your brother touching you in your bed how true does 'I am safe now' feel to you on a scale of 1 to 7, where 1 feels completely false and 7 completely true?" This is called the VoC or validity of cognition. (As will be detailed later in Chapter 8, the positive cognition may need to be modified or postponed with adults abused as children.)

Next, the therapist asks the client what *emotions* she feels when she brings up the picture with the negative cognition. "When you bring up that incident and those words 'I am not safe,' what emotions do you feel now? In this example, the client might report fear and anxiety.

At this time the therapist takes a SUDS (subjective units of disturbance scale; Wolpe, 1991) reading to determine the degree of disturbance. A SUDS reading is taken at different times during the processing to measure progress. "On a scale of 0 to 10, where 0 is no disturbance or neutral and 10 is the highest disturbance that you can imagine, how disturbing does it feel to you now?" In this case the client may report that she feels it is an 8.

The therapist then asks the client for the *location of the body sensation.* "Where do you feel the disturbance in your body?" She may feel tension in her stomach and a knot in her throat.

Phase four is the *desensitization*. The client is asked to bring up the disturbing image, together with all of its emotions, body sensations, and the negative cognition, and to follow the therapist's fingers with her eyes, letting whatever comes up come up without censoring it. The goal is to stimulate the network in which the memory is locked so that its various components can be reprocessed. "I'd like you to bring up that picture with the words *I'm not safe* and notice where you are feeling it in your body—and follow my fingers." The eye movements are begun slowly, increasing to a pace that is comfortable for the client. After about 24 saccades (one saccade is equal to one left–right eye movement) or when there is an apparent change, the therapist stops and instructs the client to "let it go and take a deep breath." The therapist asks, "What do you get now?" or "What are you noticing now?" Clients may experience images, body sensations, a range of emotions, insights, ordinary thoughts, or nothing much at all. After the client reports her experience, the therapist says, "Go with that," or "think about that," and begins another set of eye movements.

It is important that therapists pay close attention to their clients' experience and be present with them. The therapist keeps the client's eyes moving until there is an indication that the client has finished processing a piece of information. If clients are very emotional, the therapist may keep their eyes moving until they become calm, allowing them to fully clear a part of the traumatic event. Each client prefers a different speed and number of eye movements. Some do best with only 10 or 15 saccades at a time, whereas others like to go on for hundreds. After each round of eye movements the client is asked "What is happening now?" or "What do you get now?" The client reports his or her experience and then may continue with more eye movements.

Some clients like to talk during the EMDR processing. For many, this is very useful for keeping them in contact with their experience and allowing the therapist to track their experience. During the eye movements clients go through a multidimensional free association of thoughts, feelings, and body sensations. Some people go through an enormous range of experiences, including intense sensations, horrific images, strong emotions such as homicidal rage, overwhelming terror, grief, love, and forgiveness; possible memories, including descriptions attributed to prenatal and infancy experiences; and dream-like imagery rich in detail and symbolism. Throughout all of these experiences clients may be told to "stay with that," "let it all just pass through," and are reassured that "this is old stuff." Therapists can use the metaphor of riding in a train and tell the clients that their inner experience is like passing scenery.

Many clients experience a kind of witness awareness or observing ego, which enables them to observe their experience as if they were watching a movie. It is as if they are both in the experience and *observing* it simultaneously. For clients who lose their observing ego and become overwhelmed by the old traumatic memories, it can be helpful for the therapist to encourage and strengthen the observing part.

This process of eye movements and check-ins continues during the session, with the therapist occasionally rechecking the original image and measuring the SUDS. It is important to keep the processing from becoming too dispersed. Some clients go down many different associated channels, getting further and further from the original issue or memory. In these cases it can be helpful to return to the target image and check in. For example, the therapist might ask, "When you bring up the image of your brother fondling you in bed, what comes up for you now?" This check-in gives the therapist an indication of how much of the reprocessing has been done. If in this case the client responds, "I feel angry now when I see the picture," then the therapist knows that things are processing (note: the client began with feelings of fear). The therapist says, "Go with that," and directs the client to move her eyes again.

When the client returns to the image and reports that it doesn't disturb her anymore, the therapist does a SUDS reading. "Bring up the original incident. On a scale of 0 to 10, where 0 is no disturbance or neutral and 10 is the highest disturbance that you can imagine, how disturbing does it feel to you now?" When the client feels free of the emotional charge, reporting a SUDS of 0 or 1, it is time to proceed to phase five: the installation of the positive cognition. With the installation, the positive cognition is linked with the original memory or incident along with the eye movements or other bilateral stimulation. First the client is asked to bring up the original image and then to recall the positive cognition she came up with at the beginning of the session (in this case, "I am safe now") and check to see if it still fits or if there is another positive statement that she feels is more suitable. She might, for instance, stick with "I am safe now," or choose "I did the best I could with what I knew at the time," or "It is in the past." The VoC (validity of cognition) is then checked. "Think about the original incident and those words 'I am safe now.' From 1, completely false, to 7, completely true, how true do they feel to you now?"

If the client reports that it feels completely true—6 or 7—the therapist installs the positive cognition by asking the client to hold that statement with the previously distressing event (the image often changes by becoming smaller or dimmer, black-and-white rather than color, or less threatening in some manner) and do a few sets of eye movements. The therapist then again checks the VoC to see if it has remained the same or changed. Sometimes new material emerges that needs to be reprocessed; a new associated memory network may have opened. If so, the therapist can either try to clear it in the same session, if there is time, or make a note of it and return to it next time, making sure to close down the client as much as possible before ending the session.

If the client reports a VoC less than 6, there are several things the therapist can do. First the therapist can check the appropriateness of the positive cognition. Perhaps the cognition just doesn't fit the situation. Maybe the client is holding a blocking belief that that needs to be addressed and possibly reprocessed. The client may have additional memory links that keep the positive cognition from being completely true. Often abuse survivors are not able to feel a 7 on "I am safe now" if there are more memories of abuse to be reprocessed.

The sixth phase in EMDR is the *body scan,* which the client does after a memory or incident has been reprocessed and the installation of the positive cognition has been completed. In this case the client would be instructed to "Close your eyes, bring up the incident and the thought 'I am safe now,' and mentally scan your entire body. Tell me where you feel anything." If the client reports any sensation, she does more eye movement. If it is a positive sensation, the eye movements will strengthen the feeling. If it is a sensation of discomfort, the therapist should reprocess until the discomfort clears. The body scan can alert the therapist to unprocessed memories. In our example, the client may find that in doing the body scan she is constricted in her throat. This could be a body memory linked to another abuse incident or part of the current incident that was not completed. If there isn't time left in the session to reprocess this, the client should be properly closed down and debriefed. The therapist notes that this body sensation remains and may return to it in the next session.

The seventh phase of EMDR is *closure.* If the processing has cleared the disturbance from the original incident, the closure is rather simple. The therapist and client may talk for a while about the processing session and the insights that emerged. The therapist advises the client that the processing of material may continue on its own between EMDR sessions and that any new material that arises between sessions can be worked on in the next session. Clients can help to facilitate this natural processing by recording their dreams and insights in a journal, as well as drawing, painting, or engaging in other kinds of art. To help clients cope better with stress between sessions, it is useful to teach them meditation and stress reduction techniques. The client is told that she can call the therapist if she needs to.

Often the problem is not cleared during the EMDR processing session, and the session is incomplete. The client still feels upset, or the SUDS is above 1 and the VoC is less than 6. If this is the case, the positive cognition is not installed and the body scan is not done, especially if it is obvious that there is still material to be processed. There are a variety of methods to close down such a session. First, the therapist asks the client how comfortable she feels stopping the session because they are out of time. The therapist gives the client encouragement and support for the effort that was made and the work that was done. It can be helpful to close by doing a meditation or relaxation exercise, or returning to the safe place. Interweaves can also be used during closure. Creating a sense of closure is crucial for clients' well-being, because EMDR brings up highly charged material that can leave them open and vulnerable. Some people should be advised to walk around the block before driving and perhaps not to return to work for the day.

The eighth phase of EMDR treatment is *reevaluation*. When the client comes in for the next session, the therapist inquires about anything of importance that has come up related to the issue that was worked on in the previous session. The client may have had dreams, insights, memories, thoughts, flashbacks, or new physical sensations. The therapist asks the client to check the target that was worked on in the previous session to see if anything new arises. For example, the client may have a memory associated with the one that was cleared that now feels upsetting. The therapist and client then choose the next target for EMDR processing, considering what has come up during the week.

RATIONALE AND APPLICATION OF INTERWEAVES

There are times when using eye movements and following the client's process are not sufficient to keep the information flowing to a positive resolution. Clients sometimes enter into cognitive or emotional loops, repeating the same images, thoughts, emotions, and body sensations without a reduction in the SUDS level. This looping is like a broken record, with the client stuck in a groove going over and over the same material.

Processing can also be blocked without the high emotional intensity of looping. There is no change, and the disturbance isn't being processed. At these times the therapist can use creative means called "cognitive interweaves" (Shapiro, 1995) to continue the release and reprocessing of the trauma. Cognitive interweaves are a proactive EMDR strategy that serves to jump-start blocked processing by introducing information from the therapist, rather than depending solely on what arises from the client. The statements the therapist offers weave together memory networks and associations that the client was not able to connect. Interweaves introduce a new perspective, new information, or information that the client "knows" but does not have access to in the state of mind that is activated. Traumatic experiences often seem to be stored in one part of the body-mind without being affected by more current information. Interweaves bridge the parts of the client's mind that have been separated. After an interweave is introduced, eye movements are added and the processing begins to flow again. Interweaves are particularly effective with adults traumatized as children, who often seem to relate to the experience completely from the child perspective, without the observing ego and/or adult perspective. Types of interweaves and interweave strategies will be presented, along with case material, in Chapters 9–12.

Chapter 2

Primary Treatment Issues and Symptomatology

This chapter is a reminder to therapists to be mindful of certain treatment issues, such as safety, responsibility, choice and control, boundaries, interpersonal relationships, body awareness/image, sexuality, self-esteem, strong affects, defenses, nightmares and flashbacks, body memories, panic and anxiety, and depression when working with this client population. Awareness of these things is important because, although some clients wish to specifically address the abuse they suffered as children, at other times the abuse surfaces during treatment ostensibly undertaken for another reason. These treatment issues are important for the clinician to keep in mind, so that he or she can listen for targets and limiting beliefs. Often a client's processing halts because of unconscious blocking beliefs or blocking images. The therapist may need to then use appropriate cognitive interweaves, to facilitate movement.

Treatment Issues with Adults Abused as Children

Considering that one of four girls and one of seven boys are sexually victimized by the time they reach 18 years of age—and these figures may be an underreporting—it is quite likely that EMDR therapists will have such clients. Further, if one adds other types of abuse—emotional, verbal, and physical but nonsexual—those numbers swell horrendously. The term "abuse" covers a broad spectrum of behaviors, which range from a child being struck a few times to being fondled by a stranger to full-blown incest from infancy to young adulthood.

Adults who were sexually abused as children comprise a unique population and as such present specific challenges to the clinician. Consequently, it is imperative that the therapist be alert to potential pitfalls and be sensitive, all the while, to the continual needs of each client—needs that may not be obvious during initial presentation. Working with this population requires finely honed sensitivity and alertness, so that the clinician does not inadvertently rewound the client by unconsciously reenacting childhood traumatic dynamics. As adults abused as children, these clients often present with a wide array of symptomatology. On measures of distress, adult survivors of abuse generally score higher than the rest of the population in the areas of insomnia, depression, anxiety, anger, drug addiction, self-mutilation, and suicidality. They may have learning disorders, tics, or other nervous reactions. Adults sexually abused as children may engage in promiscuous behavior or other activities that place them at risk. Somatization, dissociation, and abuse are significantly associated.

Clients who were abused in childhood enter into treatment with a range of presenting problems. Actually, it is not always apparent or known at the onset of treatment that abuse had occurred in childhood. Clients may come to a therapist because of relationship or work difficulties. Or, they may have somatic complaints of unknown origin. Many clients are plagued by anxiety or depression or suffer from eating disorders. *It should be underscored, however, that no adult symptom pattern should be taken as a definite sign of childhood abuse. There is no way of knowing exactly what happened without present corroboration* (see Shapiro, 1995).

Although not in the *DSM-IV*, the term "complex PTSD" is now in the vernacular and refers to the resultant symptomatology suffered by persons with characterological issues who have suffered major trauma. Often, they have undergone repeated victimization. According to van der Kolk (1996), children who have been abused are prone to a spectrum of psychiatric disorders, including borderline personality disorder, somatization disorder, dissociative disorders, self-mutilation, eating disorders, and substance abuse. Dissociating is a defense learned by many children who are abused physically or sexually, and people who dissociate as children have a higher incidence of PTSD as adults (van der Kolk & Fisler, 1995).

Affect dysregulation is another issue that therapists should bear in mind. The chronic hyperarousal experienced by many abused children compromises their ability to modulate strong emotions. Consequently, these children may grow into adults who, among other errant behaviors, act out or withdraw socially. As a result, the impairment in this emotional area engenders problems with self-definition.

When defining PTSD for the *DSM-IV*, the research committee clustered various core symptoms as tentative criteria for "disorders of extreme stress not otherwise specified" (DESNOS). These symptoms fell into five categories: alterations in regulating affective arousal, alterations in attention and consciousness, somatization, chronic characterological changes, and alterations in systems of meaning. The committee found in the *DSM-IV* field trials that adults who were abused at an early age tended to have problems in *all* of these categories. The shorter the duration of abuse and the older the victim at the time, the more likely that the victim developed only the core symptoms of PTSD. However, damage was more pervasive in individuals who were younger during the abuse, endured the trauma for a longer time, and had less protection. It is unclear as to which comes first: the characterological problems or the trauma; in either case, the clinician *must be mindful* that he or she is working with a person with complex (Axis II) issues.

SAFETY

First and foremost is the matter of safety. At the time of the abuse, the child was *not* safe. The child's nervous system then locked in that experience of danger, and belief that the world is not safe. It is essential that the therapist create a safe container in which the client may work. If the client does not feel safe, it is both futile and potentially harmful to proceed. Because the child nervous system is activated in the EMDR work, the client may regress, experience severe abreactions, and feel threatened by the transference when in that child state.

In the realm of sexual abuse, the matter of safety raises the distinction between incest and molestation by a stranger. In the incestuous family, the child likely never felt safe because of the proximity of the abuser. For this child, safety was in being alone rather than in relationship. This may undermine or stress the ability of the client to trust the therapist, and the therapeutic alliance is critically important to establish before proceeding with this client. Moreover, working with such a client may prove challenging for the clinician when it comes to the development of a safe place.

Many such clients have maintained total secrecy regarding abuse they suffered as children. Initially, they may have been coerced to do so by the perpetrator's threats. Later, when the threats no longer had power over the "adult," he or she may have refused to break the silence because of the shame bred by carrying such a secret.

For other clients abused as children, safety may be more situational. Specifically, if a child was abused by a stranger, that child may be able to remember places or people who provided safety and refuge. Nevertheless, at the time of the abuse the child was at the mercy of the abuser and as such was *not* safe.

The therapist's gender, race, or appearance may pose a hurdle for some clients if the therapist resembles the perpetrator. The therapist must be vigilant for such a possibility, because it may impede the establishment of trust in the therapeutic alliance. Furthermore, even when the alliance is strong, the client might experience the therapist as a perpetrator during processing if the therapist were to unwittingly transgress boundaries, such as by using unannounced knee taps or hand-tapping, or if the client were to experience a flashback transference, which can occur during EMDR or other therapy (see example of Melanie in Chapter 5).

In addition to client safety within the therapeutic hour, the matter of client safety after hours is important to keep in mind. Sometimes clients who were abused as children recreate the old traumatizing situation within present-day situations. For example, a man abused in his family of origin may repeat the abusive situation in his adult sexual relationships with a partner. Or a man who was raped as an adolescent may engage in sadistic and/or masochistic adult relationships in which he assumes the roles of victim and sometimes of abuser.

On occasion, as in any form of therapy, a client's self-loathing escalates during treatment and sparks self-injurious behavior and self-mutilation. While this mutilation may not be motivated by suicidal ideation, it can nevertheless be dangerous. It is imperative to listen and watch for such signs while taking the client's history.

Also, previously suppressed material may surface after and outside of sessions and seriously frighten the client. This may mean that the client needs to be on medication during the processing and monitored by a physician. One must also ask whether the client has a sufficient support system to provide out-of-session containment.

RESPONSIBILITY

Abused children often decide they must be bad to deserve such pain and therefore are responsible for the abuse. Perhaps a client went somewhere her parents had told her not to go; thus, she might feel she was responsible for the ensuing molestation. Or a client might feel it had been her duty to please her father in whatever ways he demanded because her mother had been unable to do so. In any case, by deeming themselves bad, they can maintain the fiction of having "good" parents, which is a strong psychological need.

Often, the abuser tells the victim that he or she is to blame—and the child accepts and internalizes this belief. The child's lack of discernment results in misinterpretation of events, leading to a dysfunctional self-narrative or "story," which then reinforces and repeats the original wounding many times—at least internally. Most children want and enjoy attention, and in some cases the child may have been seduced by the perpetrator's attentiveness. Then, when the child's body responded pleasurably, she/he interpreted that forbidden physiological response as badness. Simply, the natural desire for attention is confused with responsibility for the abuse.

In addition to feeling responsible for the abuse, many persons who were abused as children feel responsible for myriad other problems over which they had no control. This profound—and misplaced—sense of responsibility interferes with their ability to place responsibility where it appropriately belongs. These clients may even feel responsible for the therapist. This may manifest in processing sessions as eagerness to please, as the client tells the therapist what he/she thinks the therapist wants to hear rather than that nothing has changed. For example, the client may have difficulty telling the therapist that there has been no shift after a couple sets of eye movements because he/she doesn't want to suggest the therapist is inept and a failure. In other words, the client feels a need to take care of the therapist.

CHOICE AND CONTROL

At the time of the abuse, whether once or chronically, the child was powerless; the child did not have any control over his or her body, the perpetrator, or the circumstances. The child's powerlessness in that moment is frozen in psychological time and continues into adulthood. Consequently, in numerous situations the adult feels like a victim. The adult may not feel that he or she has any choice or control over his or her body. In truth, the child did not have any control, but once the negative cognition thaws, the adult *can* make choices.

The fear engendered by feeling a lack of control can be terrifying, especially when pain accompanied the child's lack of control. For this reason, it is essential that the therapist emphasize to the client that she or he is in control of what transpires in the session. Client empowerment is a critically important piece of this work.

Akin to the feeling that the person does not have any control over circumstances, *autonomy may be an alien concept.* In other words, the idea that the client is entitled to base her actions and beliefs on what she needs or wants is totally foreign. That she can say "no" or "yes" or that she has choices in her life is hard for her to believe, because as a child she was neither listened to or believed. Not surprisingly, she may doubt that anyone would accept or heed her words.

This belief might appear in an EMDR session in the following ways. It could be that the therapist is moving his/her fingers too near to or too far from her face, but she will not volunteer this information. This may also manifest in the transference as her having difficulty telling you that she doesn't want knee taps—or does—or wants longer/shorter sets. Quite possibly, the thought or option that she could say "no" to a therapist request might never cross her mind. Particularly for an incest survivor, a core issue may be learning that she can exercise choice in any situation.

Some clients—who do know what they want—have difficulty asking for it. They may have been punished as children for asking for anything from their parents, or had their requests ignored. In either case, they experienced the futility of asking, not receiving, and feeling helpless. Enabling a client to overcome long-term feelings of powerlessness is a valuable—and essential—aspect of therapy with this population. Clients needs to reclaim their ability to discern what is appropriate for them and to trust their sense of what is right. By identifying and voicing their needs and experiencing their power within the EMDR session (learning that you respond positively to their needs), clients can experience major healing.

BOUNDARY ISSUES

The client who was sexually abused as a child experienced invasion and violation of her personal boundaries, possibly repeatedly. Because of this, she may not have a clear sense of self.

Clients who are prone to dissociating may have a hard time knowing what their personal boundaries are. Because they feel outside of their bodies, they don't know what feels physically bad or invasive. Feeling—being present in their bodies—enables them to discern right from wrong in relationship and to say no.

On the other hand, a client may have walls around her to keep everyone, including the therapist, out. Even being asked yes/no questions may feel intrusive. Personal space may be an important issue—the client may not want the therapist to sit near her/him, and the client may not want to be tapped on her knees or hands. I have had some clients who have wanted me to sit quite a distance from them so that they would not feel I was intruding on their personal space; in these cases I've used the light bar to lead the eye movements. In fact, two women asked me to sit across the room from them. At that distance they would direct me when to start and stop the light bar.

Without an internal sense of appropriate boundaries, a client who is desperate for nurturance and acceptance may disregard her own needs in an attempt to please the therapist. Because the child grew up without developing boundaries, the adult client manifests this legacy in such ways as calling the therapist at home or thinking nothing of demanding appointments after hours or on holidays.

INTERPERSONAL RELATIONSHIPS

Because it is likely that communication in abusive families is ineffectual or, at best, meager, adults abused as children frequently present initially in therapy with relationship difficulties as their primary complaint. Because of the dysfunctional environment during childhood, these clients never learned skills for healthy relationships. Commonly, these clients' world-construct is that it is not a safe place, that other people are not to be trusted—a belief that inhibits building intimacy—and that they cannot trust even their own sense of things. Often, these clients predicate their lives on the erroneous belief that they are "damaged goods" and for that reason no one would want them.

Projective identification may occur in interpersonal relationships. Clients unconsciously project unto others negative attributes that they refuse to recognize in themselves, which the therapist finds him or herself feeling or enacting. This dynamic may cause clients to despise and act hostilely toward people in their environment. These clients may also be cruel to and victimize others as they reenact their childhood trauma. Sometimes, they may assume the role of a victim in a relationship.

Adults who were chronically abused may be overly dependent on external sources to protect and support them. Thus, interpersonal relationships may be characterized by various forms of victimization, such as when a client continues to stay with an abusive partner. Some clients might remain in such an unhealthy situation because they lack initiative, a common characteristic of adults who were victimized as children. Other clients don't deem a situation as abusive because they don't believe they deserve any better.

Betrayal looms large in the psyches of many abuse survivors, particularly incest survivors who were betrayed by a person close to them whom they had trusted. For this reason, the therapeutic alliance needs to be continually assessed. Although a client may say that she trusts the therapist, she may actually be terrified of relationship and feel incredibly alone. The inability to trust others is extremely common in this population, and it may take a great deal of courage for these clients to turn to a therapist for help.

Because they suffered an early betrayal of trust, adults abused as children may also struggle with a deep-seated fear of intimacy. Multiple traumatic incidents may have left clients with major breaches in their development, thus handicapping them when it comes to knowing how to even trust themselves. The distinction between caring and sexuality is particularly blurry for incest survivors, leaving them open to exploitation. Additionally, the abused child may have missed the normal developmental stage when an individual learns how to cope with competition and to negotiate and how to develop intimacy. Consequently, as an adult, the client's life may feel shallow and meaningless.

The tenor of a client's interpersonal relationships can provide a clinician with valuable information. Although some clients present with complaints of difficulties forming relationships, the clinician might do well to remember that a client's tendency to form intense relationships with people too quickly may also indicate early childhood abuse.

BODY AWARENESS/IMAGE

The abused child learned very quickly that one's body was not a place of safety. Commonly, the adult client displays a lack of awareness of bodily sensations and may, at an intense point in the session, suddenly "leave" his or her body. Teaching this client to connect with and identify body sensations helps him/her to define a clearer sense of self. In this very concrete way, the client learns what is and what is not oneself.

As a clinician, note that a history of dissociation may point to childhood abuse. Likewise, be aware that numbing is a major coping mechanism used by this population. Numbing oneself blankets one in dullness, so that one does not feel anything and is thus safe from pain. Clients who feel endangered by their bodies might choose to hide their "selves" under layers of fat or obscure their bodies from others' view by wearing shapeless, dumpy clothes.

Self-mutilation, such as cutting, often occurs in response to social isolation and fear. Van der Kolk, Perry, and Herman (1991) found a highly significant relationship between childhood sexual abuse and self-cutting and self-starving behaviors in adulthood.

SEXUALITY

When sex is inflicted on a minor, that person is not likely to grow up to see sex as an activity of mutual sharing in which concern for the needs of both partners is important. Respect and trust may be absent in any sexualized relationship. Promiscuity, sexual acting out, predatory behavior, and objectification of the other are part of the legacy of sexual abuse.

Furthermore, it is not uncommon for clients to be disgusted by sexual feelings. They may, on the one hand, deny that they have any sexual feelings or, on the other, appear oversexualized. There is no telling which extreme might dominate. Two sisters abused by their father might, in later life, pursue polar extremes, such as prostitution and a religious life.

Children who gained parental attention through sexual behavior may continue such behavior as adults. On the other hand, other clients disavow any sexual behavior and shield themselves from attracting sexual attention by purposely appearing unattractive. They may be markedly overweight and dress frumpily or as inconspicuously as possible. They may feel that drawing any sexual attention to themselves puts them at risk.

Unsurprisingly, many persons who suffered sexual abuse as children have poor marriages. Many have a specific sexual dysfunction, while others go to great lengths to avoid having sex with their partners. The belief that sex and love can go together is untenable for many of this population, and they can feel that if they want sex, they are "dirty" or "disgusting." Certain sexual acts may trigger memories of early abuse. For example, as simple a gesture as stroking a woman's cheek may upset her. Sometimes kissing her triggers her intense anger or panic. Her rage may erupt if her spouse acts sexually toward her. One woman told me that when her husband desires sex with her, she wants "to kill him!"

Because of the adult's transgression of boundaries, lack of respect for the child, and assault on the child's self during its formative years, the matter of sexual orientation as an adult can be problematic. This issue is extremely common for male survivors of sexual abuse.

SELF-ESTEEM

The client may have a severely negative self-image. Self-hatred, worthlessness, and feelings of incompetence figure prominently in verbal self-portraits of adults abused as children. These negative feelings color interactions with other people and often drive these clients to socially isolate themselves and to avoid intimate relationships. Other clients may be able to relate more easily but carry deep-seated feelings of inadequacy and of being an impostor.

Abusers often tell the child he or she is bad because she "liked it" or "asked for it." Consequently, the child carries shame, guilt, and an inappropriate sense of responsibility for the abuse into adulthood.

A child who is beaten or otherwise abused tries to make sense out of what is happening to him or her in the same way we do as adults. However, a child's self is the center of his or her world, whereas we, as adults, have a broader awareness of the world around us and interpersonal dynamics. Thus, the child will try to assign a self-referential reason for his or her abuse, such as, "I am bad," or "I am stupid." This is particularly the case when the child is the scapegoat within a family. The likelihood of building healthy self-esteem is slim in that situation.

In *Trauma and Recovery* (1992), Judith Herman writes, ". . . the child victim takes the evil of the abuser into herself and thereby preserves her primary attachments to her parents. Because the inner sense of badness preserves a relationship, it is not readily given up even after the abuse has stopped; rather, it becomes a stable part of the child's personality structure" (p. 105). Consequently, many of our adult clients are self-contemptuous, highly self-critical, and extremely harsh on themselves. Because they may disdain the inner child, the therapist would be well-advised to assess early in the work the client's attitude toward this inner figure.

Other clients may present as a driven achievers. A client may have a long list of awards he or she has won for community service or achievements within a corporation. However, the client may be unable to internalize good feelings from these accomplishments and ensuing praise because she/he feels like an impostor. The client may be convinced that others simply have not seen how bad and worthless she is. Anything that might increase positive self-esteem is ego-dystonic; the client feels she is simply good at obscuring her badness and inadequacy.

Impaired self-esteem may go hand-in-hand with a client's feeling guilty for having done something bad—to the point of feeling guilty for simply being alive! Such clients may experience your asking yes/no questions as demanding their accountability and, consequently, may feel you are blaming them in some way. Likewise, a client with impaired self-esteem might interpret your moving your chair back (because your shoulder is getting sore and you are attempting to better angle your arm for conducting the eye movements) as rejection.

It is not surprising that the development of healthy self-esteem is thwarted in an abused child who learned that his or her needs were not as important as the adult's. For instance, a child who was admonished by her father not to tell her mother what he was doing to the child because the shock would kill her mother is not likely to place importance on her own worth as a person. The fact that halting the abuse, which might well be experienced as life-threatening to the child, does not matter as much as someone else's needs undermines the child's development.

STRONG AFFECTS: FEAR, ANGER, SHAME, GRIEF

At the time of the trauma, extremely strong affect is "frozen in time." When that affect is triggered in the present, it is very compelling. The client believes, "Because I feel this so strongly, it must be true." For example, when a client is feeling absolutely terrified, she will believe there is good reason, whether or not the situation warrants that response. If the client feels strongly ashamed, he will believe he must have done something to feel that shame. If she experiences deep feelings of badness, she equates the feeling with "truth": "I must be bad or else I wouldn't feel this way."

The abuse situation is stored in the brain's architecture, perhaps in a separate ego state. This happens when children are not helped by their caretakers to move out of an agitated, troubled state to one of calm. What this means in therapy with the adult who was abused as a child is that anger and rage may well be a part of the work. Sometimes rage is part of the client's presentation and must be worked through; at other times, the client grapples with getting in touch with his or her anger. Often, the work entails the client's realizing that a person may be both good *and* bad, a concept that expands the client's perspective.

When the abuse was sexual and the child's body responded with pleasurable feelings, the child's sense of shame and badness resides in the mind until it can be cleared. Although the adult client may agree that such a physical response is natural, the child then would not have known that. Consequently, the child grows into an adult who carries feelings of badness and guilt and possibly feels she or he was betrayed by his or her own body.

Along with fear, anger, and shame, grief is a profoundly felt emotion. During therapy many adults who were abused as children begin to feel the irrevocable loss of their childhood. They mourn the loss of their innocence, the developmental gaps that occurred because of the abuse, the loss of their "life" and/ or "self." Often, whether age five or fifteen, these clients felt out of sync developmentally with their peers; many clients remember always feeling older than their classmates. As children, these clients felt as if they were outside of time—that they did not inhabit the same world as other people around them.

They lament the absence of deep interpersonal relationships, relationships they were never able to form because of their wounding. They may bemoan the lack of education or meaningful work in their lives, again areas where they were handicapped by the abuse.

DEFENSES: REPRESSION, DISSOCIATION

Abused adolescents studied in the *DSM-IV* field trials denied that the abuse they had suffered had impacted their lives. Nevertheless, many of these adolescents had abusive relationships with peers, used substances, and engaged in other high-risk behaviors. This demonstrates the prevalence of repression as a defense.

During the initial evaluation or early sessions, nondisclosure of early abuse or disguised presentation might manifest as part of a posttraumatic response (avoidance/dissociation). Sometimes, delayed recall is the case. At other times, a client might speak of herself in the third person. Also, clients abused as children may have numerous psychosomatic complaints, such as headaches, insomnia, gastrointestinal disturbances, and hysterical conversion symptoms.

Dissociation covers a spectrum of situations, and the therapist is well-advised to consider in what way—if at all—dissociation is part of a client's repertoire of defenses. All the while, remember: Clients learned to dissociate to minimize their pain. Van der Kolk and Fisler (1995) differentiate between four types of dissociation. The first is the sensory and emotional fragmentation of experience that occurs in the brain. The hippocampus gets blocked and cannot process the traumatic experience; consequently, the trauma automatically is stored in an unintegrated form in the brain. The second type entails depersonalization and derealization at the moment of the trauma. Third, there is ongoing depersonalization and spacing out in everyday life. This person removes him or herself from the scene in present time, repeating what he or she did at the moment of the initial trauma. In an EMDR session, this might mean that when stimulating the target memory, the client remembers dissociating at the time of the initial trauma, and suddenly, when you start talking about something distressing, the client immediately dissociates. In this case, the client is not leaving because of the memory but rather because he/she has adopted this defense as his/her ongoing coping style. The fourth type of dissociation entails containing the traumatic memories within distinct ego states, as in dissociative identity disorder. Working with clients with DID is beyond the scope of this book.

FLASHBACKS AND NIGHTMARES

In a flashback, a client reexperiences the original abuse. Frequently, the flashback is visual, but it may also be auditory or somatosensory. In any case, flashbacks are unbidden and engender hyperalertness and vigilance in the client.

Talking about one's own children—memories of doing things with them—may trigger a flashback to one's own childhood. The therapist might get a clue that this is happening if a client substitutes the word "I" for another person's name when relating a story about that person. A fleeting image of someone is sufficient to stimulate a flashback for some clients.

Panicky and vivid dreams of rage, violence, or threats—among myriad other themes—often plague clients who suffered abuse as children. Consequently, they commonly may have sleep difficulties. Some clients without a history of sleep disturbance may experience such dreams during the early stages of therapy, and the therapist should attend to these dreams as an integral part of the EMDR work.

BODY MEMORIES

Often, a client has no visual memories; rather, the memories arise out of the somatosensory system. Those memories may be triggered by hearing someone else tell a story of abuse. For example, a client may suddenly experience nausea and discomfort when hearing a woman talk of being beaten as a child. Additionally, body memories may arise during bodywork sessions or when clients are undergoing medical or dental procedures.

PANIC AND ANXIETY

Panic and anxiety are quite familiar to most adults who were abused as children. Feelings of not being safe in the world, an inability to trust one-self or others, and a history of victimization relate closely to the panic and anxiety that drive many individuals into our offices.

Abandonment and exploitation fears are prevalent in this population. Clients may be anxious around such things as your taking a vacation, being able to reach you during the week, or your safety. Some clients may harbor deep anxiety around the thought of your death—even though you appear to be in good health and are totally reliable in keeping appointments! The transference may have an intense, life-or-death quality. Not only does it reflect the client's degree of terror, but it mirrors the client's feeling of helplessness.

A client's fear of abandonment may drive her to conceal sexual arousal from you. She may not report feeling such arousal—toward you or anyone else—because she fears your opinion of her.

When male clients shift into allowing themselves to feel their suppressed emotions, they may become anxious because this behavior is in direct opposition to what they were taught as children. Specifically, many men were taught as children to handle their emotions "like a man," which meant alone and in a way devoid of outward signs that might suggest any "weakness." It was unacceptable for a boy to admit to being confused, afraid, or sad.

Male clients who were sexually abused as children by men may harbor tremendous anxiety because of societal pressure to avoid homosexuality. (Male children, for this reason, often refrain from informing authorities of any molestation.) So, in therapy, when needing to describe the trauma and their attendant feelings, they become increasingly anxious. Happily, EMDR allows the processing of many memories without a detailed description by the client.

Clients may also experience an upsurge of anxiety or panic at times of life markers. Specifically, a woman may give birth and then experience free-floating anxiety that does not abate. Anxiety may increase around the illness or death of a parent or close relative, possibly because that person played an important role in the child's life at the time of the abuse.

DEPRESSION

When you consider that depression is often anger turned inward, it makes sense that adults who were abused as children and have not been able to release and process the trauma have a high incidence of depression. According to Pynoos, Steinberg, and Goenjian (1996), early childhood abuse affects brain chemistry and predisposes a child to depression. As adults, many clients who were abused as children suffer from chronic depression, which seems unrelated to any specific events. The depression may seem intractable, and the client may experience deep-seated feelings of passivity and helplessness. Often, the depression manifests in somatic complaints, which cease when the causes underlying the depression are processed and cleared. For many clients, their depression stems from grieving their lost childhood or from unresolved feelings of betrayal by those loved family members closest to them.

Nearly all survivors grapple with some degree of guilt—albeit undeserved—and depression accompanies the struggle. Suicide attempts, self-mutilation, compulsive eating, drug abuse, and alcoholism are some of the manifestations of this deathly duo of guilt and depression.

Some clients who have numbed themselves in order to survive their depression cut themselves so they can *feel* something, whereas other clients will tell you they feel only an inner void—a hole in their stomach or an empty space in their chest. Yet other clients defend against this depressed emptiness by overeating or other addictive behaviors, such as overworking, exercising overzealously, or acting out sexually.

Not surprisingly, many people who suffer from depression self-medicate with alcohol and other substances. In fact, there is a much higher incidence of childhood abuse and neglect among populations marked by substance abuse than in the general population (van der Kolk, 1996). ·

Therapist Attitude

It is essential that the therapist recognize his/her own attitudes, values, and beliefs concerning the myriad aspects of abuse. Consultation and peer supervision may be critically important while working with these clients for several reasons: vicarious traumatization, burn-out, and transference/countertransference issues. Depending on the therapist's history, overidentification with the client could be problematic. As well as having bizarre dreams and feeling incompetent or overwhelmed, the therapist is at risk for burnout if he/she does not have the support and guidance of consultation and/or personal therapy.

It can be challenging to hold one's therapeutic ground when one's client displaces his or her anger at the perpetrator to the therapist. This can play out in a scenario of a client raging at the therapist for not healing the client. Challenges in the therapeutic relationship may appear as a client repeats highly charged emotional and traumatic events that have been repressed for many years.

Another area of critical importance is the therapist's stance. Therapeutic neutrality is important for the therapist, who by role occupies a position of power in the relationship and must not have a political or emotional agenda. Rather, the therapist's job is to bear witness to the client's struggle and rebirthing of self while processing and clearing the trauma from his/her body-mind. At the heart of the therapeutic challenge is the empowerment of the client.

Chapter 3

Important Considerations in Using EMDR with Adults Abused as Children

The EMDR therapist treating adults abused as children can expect to deal with stabilization issues, challenges to one's competence, powerful abreactions, the need to adjust the length of therapy, the isolation of the adult's child self in its memory network, symptom relief rather than memory retrieval, and transference issues. These issues are highlighted to set the stage for the following chapters, which go into more treatment detail.

Early Childhood Abuse and Alterations of the Standard EMDR Protocol

STABILIZATION NEEDS

Many people who have been severely abused as children had unstable or chaotic relationships with their primary caregiver, which led to characterological impairments, oftentimes borderline personality disorder, or attachment disorders. Therefore, for many clients it is necessary to spend a considerable period of time preparing for EMDR processing by working to stabilize them, creating a strong therapeutic relationship where they feel safe, cared for, understood and attuned to, and developing and installing internal resources. This will be discussed at length in Chapter 5.

CHALLENGES TO THE THERAPIST'S COMPETENCE

Working with adults who suffered various types of childhood abuse requires considerable experience and clinical skill on the part of the EMDR therapist. This work can be very challenging to even a seasoned therapist.

One enters quite deeply into the inner world of the psyche, where fantasy and reality are not clearly delineated and intense emotional experiences are relived. The therapist must be comfortable working with clients when they are having intense emotional experiences in regressed child states and adept at closing down incomplete sessions. As therapist you must have confidence in EMDR and the importance of acting as a facilitator for your client's process. To best help your clients, you must let go of your own beliefs about how much healing is possible for someone hurt as a child and allow your client's own healing to unfold.

If you are an adult survivor of abuse, it is essential that you work on your abuse with an EMDR therapist. Even if you have already done years of conventional therapy, EMDR can clear remaining pockets of pain. In this way you will understand from the client's position what EMDR can do and what it feels like. You can work on your own potential triggers so that you will be less likely to limit your clients' healing or be triggered yourself by their process.

WORKING WITH STRONG ABREACTIONS

Therapists working with adults abused as children should prepare their clients for the possibility of strong emotional responses. Therapists should be comfortable with intense emotional releasing, know how to keep their clients moving through the material, and be familiar with a number of interweave strategies for unblocking stuck processing when clients are looping (see Chapter 9). Because adults abused as children often expend considerable psychic energy keeping the disturbing memories at bay, when these memory compartments are opened up during EMDR processing and the images, emotions, and body sensations are released, the intensity of the affect can be shocking and overwhelming for both therapist and client. Since the memories are held in the physiological and nervous systems, EMDR processing can bring out early physical body responses. In some cases of severe childhood abuse, clients might scream, cry uncontrollably, convulse and/or contort their bodies, feel like vomiting, and writhe on the floor or couch. Anya, described in Chapter 11, regularly had very intense abreactions, during which she would convulsively jerk her upper body, scream, and breathe rapidly in a state of terror. It was essential that she not be stopped in the middle and that she be allowed to process the disturbance to its completion. Both of us were exhausted by the end of the sessions, but she felt considerable improvement in her symptoms, was not traumatized by the experience, and was motivated to do more EMDR.

ADJUSTING THE LENGTH OF THERAPY

This is usually not short-term therapy, particularly if the abuse was severe, committed by a close relative, and extended over a period of time. Oftentimes clients believe EMDR is a quick-fix panacea that will erase the abuse in a short period of time. It is important to inform them that EMDR can accelerate the therapy, making the overall time involved much shorter than by traditional methods, but that it *may still take time,* depending on the client and the abuse involved. EMDR is but one tool within a comprehensive treatment that respects the pacing most appropriate for each client. Clients should be informed that EMDR processing begins only after therapist and client have developed a strong therapeutic relationship, the therapist has an understanding of the client's issues and needs, the client has the internal ego resources needed to handle the processing, and the client is stabilized. It is a collaborative, interactive, client-centered therapy.

Sometimes I have seen clients who have had many years of traditional talk therapy and know themselves well. However, their insights have not changed their irrational beliefs, behaviors, and body memories. In many of these cases, the groundwork has been done, and EMDR processing is able to clear the life-limiting symptoms in a few months. Because these clients do not have character disorders or early attachment issues, it is fairly easy to develop a therapeutic relationship in which the processing work can occur. In some of these cases clients easily develop and clear targets because they clearly remember the abuse. These clients typically have high affect tolerance because of their earlier work and so do not fear strong feelings.

WORKING WITH THE CHILD SELF

During EMDR with an adult who was traumatized as a child, the "child self" becomes activated and the adult client may feel like a child. The client may feel like he or she has a child-sized body, and thinks, feels, and perceives things with the child's mind. This can be disorienting—even frightening—for the client and confusing for the therapist. What has happened is that the child memory with all of its associations has been activated. It is like the memory compartment in the body-mind that stores the childhood experiences has been opened and the client has stepped into it. Generally, the adult self will be simultaneously aware of the child and act as a kind of witness to the memory processing. Sometimes, however, the adult self is temporarily lost or seemingly overtaken by the power of the child self's experience. This can be scary and disorienting for the therapist and/or client. Clients can feel totally regressed and lose touch with their adult power and capabilities. It becomes the therapist's job to maintain the sense of balance and adult perspective.

This child self coexists with the adult self, seemingly occupying a separate memory network. The child self will still hold simple self beliefs that accompanied specific traumatic events. Often life events will trigger the child's memory network. The child self may then cause the adult to act in ways that seem quite irrational. For instance, the sound of a man's loud, angry voice may cause an otherwise strong, powerful woman to feel helpless and frightened, as she did as a child with her alcoholic, abusive father. She may lose contact with the adult information that she can take care of herself now. Things like movies or medical procedures can also trigger strong emotional responses like fear, anxiety, flashbacks, and nightmares. These irrational feelings can feel frightening and confusing to clients who may fear that they are "crazy."

The child self thinks in simple black-and-white terms, good and bad, right and wrong. For most there are no shades of gray. This is exemplified in early negative beliefs like "I'm a bad girl." Developmentally there is a split in the self and in the object. Clients can think of themselves as all good or all bad, the same with the perpetrator—all good or all bad. Often the "good" self and the "bad" self are in separate memory compartments. Likewise, the perpetrator is remembered as all bad or all good, without a sense of both good and bad residing in the same person. These splits do not necessarily mean that these clients have character disorders. They may be only around particular memories, events, or individuals.

For example, Joanna was molested by an elderly gentleman friend of her family when she was three years old. When we did the EMDR processing, she saw that she had stored the good memories of this man acting kind to her and small animals in one memory compartment and the bad memories of his painful abuse of her and frightening threats to kill her pet if she ever told in another. She was not able to comprehend in her child's mind that the same man could be kind and gentle *and* brutally abusive. It was as if the man was really two entirely different people. She also held disparate views of herself. The part of her that experienced any pleasure when he touched her private parts was considered "bad girl." The part of her that didn't remember the pleasure in the molestation was in the "good girl" compartment. With EMDR processing she experienced an integration of the good and bad self and the good and bad man and was able to see and hold all the different aspects together as she cleared the disturbance from her system. This "splitting" of her experience as a child did not seem to affect her ability as an adult to develop a cohesive sense of self and others. She had deeply loving intimate relationships in which this splitting was not evident. The abuse affected her life in many ways, but it did not lead to a pathologically fragmented sense of self and others.

When the child self has been accessed, the EMDR therapist must speak to the child using language and vocabulary he/she can understand. Simple terms and metaphors that a child can relate to should be used; otherwise the client in the child state may become confused. This is important in helping the client develop the negative cognition that most powerfully stimulates the memory network, aiding in effective processing of the memory.

The use of a child's language is also important in developing appropriate interweaves. Questions like "Who is bigger, the daddy or the little girl?" help elicit a response from the child self. If questions are asked using adult language and concepts, the client may be forced to leave completely the child state in an effort to answer the question from his or her adult self, which can disrupt processing.

Interweaves are often used by the therapist to help link the adult and child memory networks when they are not linking up automatically with the eye movements. As you may recall from Chapter 1, interweaves are employed when using the eye movements and following the client's process are not sufficient to keep the information flowing to a positive resolution. Clients sometimes enter into cognitive or emotional loops, repeating the same thoughts or feelings (or both) over and over. Interweaves are a proactive EMDR strategy that serves to jump-start blocked processing by introducing information from the therapist, rather than depending solely on what arises from the client. They create a bridge between parts of the client's mind that have been separated. It is appropriate to use more adult language and questioning in the interweave if the intention is to elicit the adult self. After the interweave has been introduced and accepted by the client, the processing begins to flow again. These interweaves may involve asking the adult self to explain something to the child self, asking the client a question that will elicit an answer from the adult self, and/or educating the child and adult selves about certain issues neither has knowledge of.

Rules, concepts, and negative beliefs about oneself get set in during childhood trauma and form the foundation upon which a negatively skewed or distorted personal identity and view of the world are built. These negative self-referencing beliefs can be internalized for a lifetime. EMDR is particularly powerful and effective at clearing these early core beliefs. Examples of core beliefs are "I am unlovable," "I am dirty," "there is something terribly wrong with me," and "I am a victim."

What gets locked into the memory network are the child's perceptions and subjective experience and can be based on misperception or misinterpretation of events. For example, a child who was molested by a neighborhood teenager never tells her parents about the abuse but withdraws from the family emotionally for a period of time because she perceives her parents as uncaring and not loving her. She may internalize the belief that she is unlovable and unprotected. It may have been that her parents had no idea that their daughter was being abused and believed her withdrawal had to do with a problem she was having at school. They may have loved their daughter very much and were later horrified to learn what had happened to her. It is important that the therapist refrain from judgments about events the client is describing from the child's perspective and keep an open mind to what might unfold as the client revisits old memories with EMDR and arrives at a new, more comprehensive understanding.

FOCUSING ON SYPTOM RELIEF RATHER THAN MEMORY RETRIEVAL

EMDR therapists are not concerned about memory retrieval even though it is common for previously forgotten material to arise spontaneously during EMDR sessions. With EMDR, healing from the past is not dependent on memory retrieval. What is emphasized is clearing the disturbing images, limiting beliefs, and dysfunctional behaviors that have become locked in the body-mind because of past experiences—real or imagined—so the client can live fully and freely in the present.

EMDR therapists take a client-centered approach to the therapy, attempting to follow rather than lead clients. It is important to refrain from interpreting content that comes up during EMDR sessions because any interpretation both interferes with clients' unfolding process of self-discovery and increases the possibility of creating false impressions. Clients should be supported in drawing their own conclusions about what arises during sessions. It may be impossible to know for certain whether a specific memory is true, especially if there is no external corroborating evidence.

The imagery and impressions that arise during EMDR sessions can have various origins. They may be symbolic representations, which can include dream imagery from childhood that can seem very real. The fact that the image of a woman's father having sex with her pops into her mind during EMDR processing does not necessarily mean it *actually* happened to her in the past. She could have been exposed to girlie magazines as a child, witnessed her parents making love, or just felt uncomfortable around her father because of suggestive language he used in her presence. There are a number of possible explanations, including that he *did* sexually abuse her. What we observe is that these feelings and impressions are locked in the body-mind because of *something* experienced in the past. What that something is is impossible to determine without outside corroborating evidence.

I have had a number of adult clients referred to me by other therapists because they believed the clients had been sexually abused as children. Their symptoms all seemed to point to this kind of history: difficulty with intimacy, lack of trust, aversion to sexual intimacy, and anger toward men. Interestingly, I have found that when I used EMDR targeting the beliefs and emotions, despite the strong suggestions from the referring therapists, no imagery or memories of sexual abuse emerged. In all of the cases, the origins of the problems were found to be other than sexual abuse, and the symptoms cleared without sexual trauma being an actual issue. In many cases, symptoms that appeared to be caused by sexual abuse had their origins in medical procedure trauma.

Laura, whose case is described in *Transforming Trauma: EMDR* (Parnell, 1997a), had been referred to me by her couples therapist because she had symptoms that looked like she had been sexually abused. This client hated sex with her husband, whom she loved, felt like a victim in her life, and had many psychosomatic problems. After EMDR processing, it turned out her problems all stemmed from dental traumas she had experienced as a girl. The feelings of aversion to men and sexuality, feelings of being a powerless victim, and her rage all originated from these very unpleasant experiences with an insensitive, rather sadistic dentist who caused her physical and emotional pain while she was in a vulnerable position.

Some clients with sexual abuse-like symptoms were traumatized by their experiences of receiving enemas as children. In these cases the enemas—similar to sexual abuse—caused the clients to feel humiliated, bad about themselves, dirty, helpless, and exposed. One woman's memory included being held down by her mother as the enema nozzle was painfully inserted into her rectum. This procedure was done to her frequently because her mother believed it was necessary for her health. The experience left the girl feeling helpless, humiliated, and victimized. She believed that she couldn't say no or she would be punished and that this procedure was necessary to keep her well. The use of enemas was a very common practice for a generation of parents who believed that they were doing this for their children's good.

Sometimes a client's problems are the result of something that did not actually happened to him or her directly. *Vicarious traumatization* occurs when one becomes traumatized by imagined participation in a traumatic experience. It seems that when one hears about a terrible event, especially if it has touched one in some way personally, an image of the event is created in the mind with accompanying emotions and beliefs. These images, emotions, and beliefs become stuck in the body-mind as if they actually occurred to oneself personally. Therefore, a child who heard about or saw another child abused may have experienced it internally as if it were happening to him or her and may have had images and emotions that were quite "real" and which affected the way in which the child perceived him or herself and the world. The stimulating event could even be something that they saw on television or in a movie or read in the newspaper.

Some children in the San Francisco area were traumatized by the kidnapping and murder of Polly Klaas. These children may have an image in their minds that is disturbing to them, having substituted themselves for Polly in their fantasy of what happened to her and how she might have felt at the time (Lovett, 1999). These images can feel quite real and become part of their memory networks. The images, emotions, and beliefs that arise when they think about the incident with Polly would be the targets for EMDR processing.

When clients feel uncertain whether the image they have of abuse is true or not, we tell them that factual reality doesn't matter. We are interested in processing what is subjectively held in the body-mind—not in discovering what is true or false objectively. What is important in EMDR is that we follow the emotional charge. The image we begin with has a charge to it and that makes it "real" to the client. If the image is laden with fear and anger, it holds information that is important to free. We follow this energy by asking the client to "go with" the most charged images and emotions as the processing unfolds.

Confrontation of Perpetrators

The confrontation of a perpetrator is a very controversial action. It should be done with much care and caution and only if there is corroborating evidence of the abuse. In my clinical experience using EMDR, I have found it unnecessary for clients to "confront" their perpetrators in order for them to get better. In the words of one client, to make her healing dependent upon her perpetrator's response continues to "give him the power." Clients who feel anger and a need to confront the perpetrator can do it safely in their EMDR therapy by imagining the confrontation along with the bilateral stimulation. I have found this very effective in helping to clear the disturbance. The emphasis is on helping clients free themselves from their fear and anger. Confrontation can unnecessarily disrupt a family, especially when the abuse occurred decades earlier and the perpetrator is elderly or infirm. The residual anger is justified, but healing can occur without a confrontation. Often, by the time the adult victim of abuse is ready to confront the perpetrator, so many years have passed that the perpetrator has changed significantly and the confrontation has lost its meaning. The client is angry at the person the perpetrator was when the client was a child. That is the person the client confronts in the imagery during EMDR.

EMDR and "False" Memory

There has been a great deal of controversy about so-called "false memory." This has developed partly out of a backlash against some therapists who have overdiagnosed child sexual abuse based on scanty evidence and partly out of the fury of perpetrators who are out to defend themselves by attacking therapists. I have seen clients who were certain they had been sexually abused because their therapists had told them so. In one case a client even confronted her father as an abuser without having *any* memories that implicated him. She felt he had done it because of her symptoms, which looked like *something* traumatic sexually had happened to her and because she felt an aversion to him physically. During our EMDR work, no memories emerged linking her father to abuse. Instead, images of being drugged and raped emerged, which then generalized to fear of all men. Books she had read and therapists she had seen all convinced her that her father was the perpetrator.

I want to emphasize again that it is *essential* that therapists be adequately trained before treating clients. Too often, poorly trained therapists or inadequately supervised interns cause harm to clients by leading them to believe that their symptoms mean that they must have been molested by a family member. Certainly, when someone has disturbing symptoms, something has happened to cause them, but it is important for therapists to withhold their judgment and allow the process to unfold, clearing the disturbing images and body sensations from the system.

TRANSFERENCE ISSUES

Herman (1992) called the transference that occurs with adults abused as children "traumatic transference." A primary issue with these clients is *trust,* which must be developed in the therapeutic relationship and continuously worked on. Can the client trust her therapist to not judge her as she reveals her most shameful secrets? Can she trust her therapist to be able to bring her back to an adult functioning self at the end of the session? Can he trust that his therapist won't victimize or exploit him as his abuser did? Can she trust that her therapist won't be overwhelmed by the horrors of her abuse memories and will be able to maintain a steady presence for her? The therapeutic relationship may be continuously tested throughout the course of treatment. Betrayal of the child's trust was one of the greatest harms done, and the therapist's compassionate, steadfast willingness to work on the trust issues—and be tested by the client over and over again—is an extremely important part of the healing. This feeling of trust is also installed into the client's new memory network as she reprocesses abuse memories. The experience of trusting the therapist goes into the client's system as part of a new schema that includes feelings of empowerment and safety.

Judy and I had been working together for about a year doing intensive EMDR processing of sexual abuse by a female babysitter. At this point in the therapy Judy was feeling a lot of anger toward the perpetrator. In Judy's family there was an unspoken family rule that it was not OK to express anger. During this EMDR processing session Judy began to express her anger and she talked about her projection of the perpetrator onto me.

JUDY: I felt like people were always fucking me . . . I feel lots of anger. ►◄►◄►◄ I wish this big strong ugly man would do to Mrs. Jones what she did to me so she'd know what she did to me and also tie her up. ►◄►◄►◄ I got really calm. ►◄►◄►◄ The anger is blocked. It won't come out. ►◄►◄►◄ *Sometimes I think you're Mrs. Jones. . . . Maybe it's not safe to be mad here.* ►◄►◄►◄ Years ago I would blow up at the wrong time and I'd get in trouble.

(At this time she told me that she felt angry with me but wasn't sure why. I suggested that she explore why and let her know that it was OK with

me and that I wasn't afraid or put off by her anger. Her anger at me did not threaten our relationship.)

JUDY: ►◄►◄►◄ You led me to believe that you were married when you weren't.

(She had felt betrayed by me. I had separated from my husband and hadn't told her because I kept my personal life out of the therapy. My answering machine message, which used to include my husband, also a therapist, no longer did, which caused her to feel I had misled her. I explained the situation to her satisfaction and then asked her to focus on her feelings with the eye movements.)

JUDY: ►◄►◄►◄ This isn't logical or rational. I'm mad at myself. ►◄►◄►◄ I'm telling myself not to worry and that you won't get mad at me and that it's OK that it doesn't make sense. I can see Mrs. Jones now. I liked and trusted her.

(Judy is making the connection. She had liked Mrs. Jones, who betrayed her. She and I had a close therapeutic relationship and she was concerned that I would also betray her. This insight was very important to her.)

During this session Judy was able to express her anger at the perpetrator and at me in a productive way. We were able to maintain our connection and explore the transference, enabling her to discover its meaning. She also learned that anger was not to be feared; rather, it provided important information that could be used for healing. This experience deepened our relationship.

Like any therapy, EMDR can elicit in some clients a feeling of having *something done to them,* of being victimized or objectified by the therapist. For that reason it is important that therapists not "push" EMDR too much on their clients even though they think it might benefit them. Sometimes clients have a strong or disturbing reaction and associations to the therapist's hand or fingers as the therapist directs the eye movements. If this happens, talk about it with the client and then find a way to continue the processing so that it isn't too upsetting. For instance, you might want to use your hand instead of your fingers or use tapping or auditory stimulation.

After talking with the client about transference issues it can be helpful to use the transference to develop an EMDR target for processing primary historical material. If the transference issue triggered by the therapist's hand as it moves in front of the client's eyes is fear of being hurt, the therapist might ask the client, "Who in your life has hurt you in this way?" The client might respond, "my father." The therapist might next ask the client to think of a time when he was hurt by his father in that way. The incident the client reports can be used as a target, along with the image, beliefs, and body sensations.

If the client has difficulty coming up with an answer to that question, the therapist might ask, "What do you feel in your body when you see my hand move in this way? . . . What do you believe about yourself? . . . As you bring your awareness to your body and the belief, let your mind go back in time to another time when you felt and believed this way. . . . Be aware of what comes up for you. . . . It can be memory, an image, or a picture. Let me know when you are aware of it." When the client comes up with the requested information, the therapist can begin the bilateral stimulation and the EMDR processing.

Flashback transference (Loewenstein, 1993) is a type of traumatic transference where the client perceives the therapist literally as the abuser. It could be that something the therapist said or did reminds the client of the abuser and triggers a flashback experience, during which time the client loses his or her present-time perception of the therapist. This can be a very frightening experience for the client and for the therapist.

Sometimes clients will not be able to tolerate certain intense emotions and will unconsciously cause the therapist to feel these feelings for them. I had a particularly intense experience of such projective identification (Ogden, 1996). A woman was processing a very traumatic incest experience with her father in her first EMDR session. Without affect, she described, the very disturbing scene during the breaks from the eye movements. As she was processing, I felt a sense of horror and terror in my body and was surprised that she reported so little affect. I directed her back to her body and feelings, but no feelings came up for her in the session. During the debriefing we talked about our experiences. She admitted that she had dissociated the feelings that I was feeling. When she came back the next week, she was ready to take in what she had split off the previous session. She acknowledged again that what I had been feeling were her split-off feelings. During her EMDR processing, she was able to experience her feelings fully and reprocess the abuse memory. I also felt relief when she completed her processing.

For another client, Gabrielle, trust was a significant transference issue, because as a child she had not been believed by authorities when she disclosed the sexual abuse. Gabrielle was referred for EMDR by her couples therapist because the marital therapy had reached an impasse. Her presenting symptom was extreme ambivalence about having children. After the EMDR therapist had spent the first two sessions taking her history, Gabrielle came in visibly shaken and distraught for her third session.

GABRIELLE: There is something I didn't tell you about last week. In fact I've never told my husband either, but I realize it might be important and we are spending all this money so I can't waste time. But, I'm afraid what will happen when I tell you. Even though you're nice. . . . I'm just afraid.

TH: What do you imagine will happen when you tell me?

GABRIELLE: That you will have to tell our couples therapist, my husband will be told, and he will leave me.

TH: I assure you that everything you say in here is confidential. By law I cannot disclose to anyone anything you say to me without your permission.

GABRIELLE: That's good. But I'm also afraid you won't believe me. That you'll think it's an excuse to avoid having children.

TH: I want to know you and if something is causing you confusion right now, I believe that it is important and valuable to our work.

GABRIELLE: I was abused as a child by my father. My mother didn't believe me. When I told the teacher at school, she told the psychologist, who told my parents that I was having sexual fantasies about my father. The psychologist said these fantasies were normal for a young child and that I was daydreaming to avoid doing my school work. Things with my father got worse and I never told anyone again.

TH: I appreciate your trusting me with this information. The incest is serious and how it affected your life is very important to explore further— as well as how it affects the relationship with your husband and your decision about children.

This is an example of how clients transfer to the therapist feelings and beliefs from the past. Also, it illustrates how some clients enter into therapy still keeping secrets for fear of reprisal. In Gabrielle's case, it was abandonment by her husband and betrayal by the therapist. The next week Gabrielle and her therapist agreed to do an EMDR session targeting the incident in the school psychologist's office when she was eight years old. In that session Gabrielle began to work on the historical origins of her transference.

The picture was of herself, her mother, and her father in the school psychologist's office. Her negative cognition was "I'm not valued," and her positive cognition was "I am a valuable person." She rated the VoC a 2. The image evoked fear and shame, which she rated a SUDS of 9, and she felt the sensations in the area of her stomach. Focusing on the target, she began a set of eye movements. After a few minutes of processing:

TH: Take a breath, what's coming up?

GABRIELLE: Fear, my stomach is hurting.

TH: Notice that. Put your hands on your stomach and press in lightly. (*The therapist is helping Gabrielle amplify the sensation with the applied pressure.*) ►◄►◄►◄

TH: What are you getting now?

GABRIELLE: It's tight. ►◄►◄►◄ I knew it was true but no one believed me. Why did I tell?

TH: Ask yourself that question and watch my fingers.►◄►◄►◄

GABRIELLE: Because I wanted it to stop. ►◄►◄►◄ I'm so angry. That psychologist. What a jerk. I hated him for telling. I wish I could blast him.

TH: Let yourself imagine that. ►◄►◄►◄

GABRIELLE: I told him he was a jerk and that I was mad at him for telling my parents. That I needed his help and instead I was hurt more. I told him it went on after that and he would have to live with that. I told him I hated him. That he was a horrible therapist, that he blew it and didn't deserve to work with children. Then I fired him! *(smiling)* ►◄►◄►◄ I feel relieved, the tightness in my stomach is gone.

TH: Let's go back to the original picture. What do you get now?

GABRIELLE: I feel sad. No one was there for her.

TH: *(Does an interweave bringing in Gabrielle's adult self.)* Can you see yourself telling the girl what you understand as an adult and what she needs to hear from a supportive adult?

GABRIELLE: Yes. ►◄►◄►◄

TH: What happened?

GABRIELLE: I told her I believed her. That I knew she was telling the truth. That she did the right thing by telling an adult but at that time therapists didn't have the knowledge about abuse that they have now. I told her I was sorry she was hurt and I'm sure that the psychologist was too. That adults don't have the right to ever hurt children and that she was a very brave girl. I hugged her and told her I loved her and that I would always support her. ►◄►◄►◄

TH: What do you get now?

GABRIELLE: My mother's face.

TH: And when you see her face how do you feel in your body?

GABRIELLE: A mixture of anger and sadness. ►◄►◄►◄ She didn't help me either. I was all alone.

At this point Gabrielle was going down another channel associated with her relationship with her mother, and she continued to work on the issue of betrayal by her mother until the end of the session. Gabrielle felt her mother had chosen her father over her. She realized that her mother was stressed from having so many children and working full-time. Further, Gabrielle saw that her mother had sacrificed Gabrielle to her father so that her father would leave her alone. During the session Gabrielle was very angry at her mother but realized that she wasn't capable of more. In later sessions Gabrielle continued to work on these early issues associated with the transference.

Chapter 4

Adjunctive Therapeutic Tools

Journal writing, guided imagery, artwork, and mindfulness practices are useful adjunctive therapeutic tools to augment EMDR therapy with adults abused as children. These methods provide access and expression to implicit memory, which is stored in the brain's right hemisphere and cannot be reached by left brain methods such as verbal therapies. The specific use of these tools and their integration in the EMDR work will be explained in the chapters that follow.

Adjunctive Tools

The adjunctive tools described below can be used as part of the therapy, during EMDR processing sessions, and between sessions. The therapist can introduce or teach clients these methods, or refer them to the appropriate classes. While they have great potential, they may not be suitable for every client.

JOURNAL WRITING

Many authors have written about the use of journals (Bass & Davis, 1988; Davis, 1990; Taylor, 1991). I recommend that clients find a quiet undisturbed time to write in a journal or notebook that is kept strictly confidential. In these journals clients can write their thoughts, feelings, insights, and dreams. Because the writing is for them, they should be instructed to write whatever comes to mind without censoring it and without worrying about proper grammar and sentence structure. For many, writing helps them to process material between sessions.

For example, one client created a nightly ritual during which she would light candles, sit in a quiet private space, silence her mind, tune into her inner experience, and begin to write. By doing so, she contacted an inner wisdom that helped her understand her irrational thoughts and feelings. From her pen would flow an understanding she did not know she had of her inner process. She could ask her inner child questions and answer through the writing. She also began to write poetry for the first time. Journal writing continued to be a valuable resource for her after therapy ended.

In the midst of intense EMDR therapy, many clients have active and very vivid dreams that are a continuation of the EMDR processing. Encourage clients to record their dreams and bring them into sessions because they make very good targets for EMDR.

Often adults who have been abused do not understand the connection between their symptoms and their early experiences. Distressing experiences, such as flashbacks, nightmares, anxiety, and fear triggered by TV or movies, can be experienced as assaults that are seemingly disconnected from and unrelated to their present-day life. These experiences can make them feel as though their lives are out of control. Encouraging clients to note these experiences helps them to target them and work on them systematically with EMDR. This helps to give the symptoms meaning by revealing the connection between the triggers and the early experiences.

Clients often feel like detectives collecting clues. Thoughts, feelings, dreams, and insights are collected and brought into sessions for processing. Distressing symptoms become meaningful and not only open doors to the past but also aid in healing. All of their experiences become grist for the EMDR mill.

In addition to giving clients a sense that they have some control, the journal also serves as a permanent record of the healing process. Because EMDR is typically intense and many changes can happen rapidly, it can be helpful to have this record for review. It can be quite encouraging from time to time to review the many changes that have taken place. Because of the length and intensity of the therapy, clients may forget how they were when they first came into treatment as they focus on the suffering they wish to alleviate in the future. One client inventoried all of her problems in many different areas of her life a few times a year. When she reviewed what she had written in the previous months, she felt encouraged, despite currently being in a difficult place in her treatment. For her and many other clients, once one disturbing memory was cleared with EMDR, it did not return. Things that were problems in the past were no longer problems and sometimes were forgotten as having been problematic unless recorded.

Many clients continue to use journal writing after therapy is over. It enables them to maintain an ongoing relationship with their deeper selves.

GUIDED IMAGERY

With guided imagery the therapist gently helps the client evoke imagery that is helpful and meaningful to him or her. Typically, the client is helped to relax, and then the therapist, in a soft, low voice, asks the client questions that bring up the desired imagery from his/her unconscious mind. The visualization can be deepened by asking for details that engage the senses and imagination. What do clients see, hear, feel, smell, or taste? It is important that the therapist stay out of the client's way as much as possible and not impose upon what he or she is experiencing. Guided imagery can be used in a number of ways with EMDR:

- *Relaxation and stress reduction.* Stress control techniques can be used after EMDR processing to close sessions and between sessions when anxiety and emotional distress arise. (Some of these techniques will be described in detail in Chapter 10.)
- *The development of a safe place.* Guided imagery is used to help the client find and develop a safe place. This is a real or imaginary place where the client feels totally safe and protected. (The safe place will be discussed in Chapter 5.)
- *Inner child work.* Because the child self is activated during EMDR, it can be helpful to meet the child self through imagery work prior to processing. In this way the therapist can assess the emotional state of child and the child self-adult self relationship. (This will be discussed at length in Chapter 5.)
- *The identification and development of inner and outer resources.* During imagery work the client may identify and develop resources that can be used for interweaves and for closing difficult sessions. Examples of resources include: inner advisors; protector figures, which can be animals, supernatural figures, or people from their lives or their imagination; loving/nurturing figures from their early life, current life, or imagination; wisdom figures; and their adult self. (This is discussed in Chapter 5.)
- *Imaginal interweaves.* Imagery in combination with cognitions can be more powerful and effective than cognitions alone. There are a number of ways imagery is used in the creation of interweaves. This use of imagery is an intuitive, creative process that engages the client and therapist in solving problems. I have found imagery to be very powerful and useful when clients are looping in stuck processing. (Chapter 9 discusses this in detail.)
- *Closing down incomplete sessions.* Many of the imagery techniques used for closing incomplete sessions have their origins in hypnotherapy and involve suggestions to place disturbing unprocessed material in containers. Imagery can also involve using the resources identified and developed earlier to bring a sense of safety and protection to the client. Meditation techniques that incorporate imagery help to evoke a feeling of peace and safety. (All of these techniques will be described in Chapter 10.)

THE USE OF ART WITH EMDR

Art can be employed during all three phases of EMDR therapy (Cohn, 1993a, 1993b; Parnell & Cohn, 1995; Thompson, Cohn, & Parnell, 1996), either in the session itself or between sessions as a continuation of the therapy. Clients work with a wide range of art materials, including crayons, pastels, watercolors, finger paints, marker pens, clay, and collage.

Beginning Phase of EMDR Therapy

In the beginning phase of treatment, art can be used to help the client get in touch with feelings and/or inner information through drawing. The act of drawing and creating reactivates the childlike/innocent part of a client's self, an authentic part that has often been disowned by the client. Through artwork, it can be reclaimed and the child's feelings experienced.

Artwork also provides a nonthreatening way for the client to tell her secrets without fear of reprisal from the perpetrator. To speak about the acts out loud may be much too threatening for severely abused clients. Because artwork is representational and distant, it allows information to be expressed in loosely disguised, metaphoric form, as in dreams (Cohen & Cox, 1995).

The artwork a client produces can facilitate diagnosis. Early pictures may shed light on ego strength, defenses, regression and progression, as well as fostering uncovering and insights (Cohn, 1993a, 1993b). In addition, development of the therapeutic relationship can be enhanced by the use of artwork, which allows the therapist to "see" the client's pain. Commonly shared artistic images help the therapist to concretely see what the client is imagining; this is important because sexual abuse survivors have lived a long time in their own world. This sharing of the client's inner world increases trust, empathy, and a sense of working together.

Art can also be used to help in the development of the safe place. (This will be explained in more detail in Chapter 5.)

Middle Phase of EMDR Therapy

In the middle phase of EMDR therapy artwork is especially useful for aiding in the development of EMDR targets. The client can "draw the feeling" or "draw the disturbing scene." The art object is a projection of the client's inner experience. Feelings, ideas, and images are externalized in the picture. The drawing helps clients to gain distance from overwhelming feelings and to clarify the feelings and/or incidents.

In one picture, the therapist and client can learn a wealth of information about the client's inner experience (e.g., closeness, distance, bonds, divisions, similarities, differences, energy investment, and context of family relationships). Unlike verbal processing, which tends to be linear, drawings provide a spatial matrix. In art, relationships occur in space. Line, form, color, texture, omissions, and page placement can magnify relationships. Because "a picture is worth a thousand words," a multitude of EMDR cognitions can come from one such picture.

As therapy progresses, artwork enables the therapist to pace and modulate intensity. It provides the therapist with a bridge between the slower pace of verbal therapy and the faster pace of EMDR. Art may be more comfortable at times, such as the beginning of a session, when the client needs to feel more in control, or occasions when the client needs time to integrate EMDR material between sessions. Doing artwork, along with journal writing, on one's own between sessions helps a client to integrate the information that comes up during EMDR processing sessions. It provides continuity to the therapeutic process and gives clients a sense of autonomy and self-reliance. They take charge of their healing process and bring to the session new insights and awareness, as well as targets for future processing.

The artwork clients create becomes a permanent record of their work in therapy. Unlike verbal images, the art object is a tangible, permanent record that is not subject to transformation in memory recall. The client/artist cannot *deny* ownership of the material; the client knows that he or she created it and the therapist has been a witness. Since sexual abuse survivors often use dissociation and repression as defense mechanisms, having concrete "evidence" of their inner experience is helpful for them in "believing" their own experience and helping to integrate it into a broader schema.

Art images (two- or three-dimensional) can be reviewed with clients at any time before and after EMDR and can be used to help them "see" an issue, refresh memory from past sessions, or view progress. The artwork provides these clients with something tangible to "hold onto." Art productions furnish abuse survivors with a map of the past that is connected to the present and this helps them differentiate and integrate these two realities, thus making implicit memory explicit.

In addition, drawings can be used after EMDR to aid in client closure. The physical act of drawing can ground a sexual abuse survivor and help him or her to feel more embodied. Clients can objectify the drawing as separate from who they are now, as just a drawing of something from the past, not something that is happening now.

End Phase of EMDR Therapy

Review of a series of drawings can aid in termination by providing documentation of significant issues throughout the entire therapeutic process. The client's self-esteem can be increased as both therapist (as witness) and client review the client's transformation from survivor to thriver.

MINDFULNESS PRACTICES

Mindfulness practices have their origins in ancient Buddhist meditative traditions. These practices have been taught in the West for many years. Detailed description of the practices have been presented by several authors, including psychologists who have integrated the practices into their clinical work (Goldstein, 1976; Kabat-Zinn, 1990; Kornfield, 1993; Linehan, 1993a, b; Parnell, 1996a, b, 1997b). Several meditation teachers have taken these practices out of the meditation hall and brought them to people's everyday life. Notably, Jon Kabat-Zinn, a long-time meditation practitioner, developed a pain reduction program at University of Massachusetts Medical Center that was featured on Bill Moyer's program "Healing and the Mind" and is now being taught in hospital settings across the country for pain and stress reduction (Kabat-Zinn, 1990). Linehan saw that this practice could help her borderline clients become more present in their daily lives and better able to cope and so made mindfulness skill development central to her dialectical behavior therapy (Linehan, 1993a, b).

Mindfulness practice helps people develop the ability to be more present for whatever arises. When practiced over time it can decrease dissociation and enable people to be more fully "grounded" and "embodied." Mindfulness practice develops a witness awareness or observing ego that helps people observe and describe their experience without judgment. Clients learn that they can be with whatever arises with less personal identification and reactivity. This practice cultivates the ability to be "mindful," a continuity of presence and awareness in daily life.

The ability to notice and be with ordinary life experiences is undeveloped in many people who have been traumatized as children (McFarlane et al., 1993). Thus, mindfulness training is very important for developing new neuropathways in the plastic brain. Mindfulness training also develops "bare attention"—the ability to be present, curious, and open to the body and mind in a balanced, nonjudgmental way. Mindfulness practitioners develop a compassionate attitude toward themselves, as the body and mind are no longer experienced as enemies. People also report increased equanimity—a more balanced experience of life, an understanding that phenomena arise and pass away in an open field of awareness, with lessened attachment to pleasant and unpleasant states of mind and body.

Both Vipassana meditation and EMDR use dual attention or awareness. For Vipassana meditators, the attention is on the breath or other predominant objects of awareness. The EMDR client focuses both on the therapist's fingers or other stimuli and an inner object like an image or body sensation. In each case, a detached, impartial witness awareness is cultivated and developed. An important part of the instructions given to EMDR clients is to "just let whatever happens, happen without discarding anything as unimportant" (Shapiro, 1995, p. 142). Clients are asked to notice any changes in thoughts, feelings, and body sensations and to simply report to the therapist what they are experiencing. Therapists ask clients after a set of eye movements, "What do you get now?" or "What's happening now?" (Shapiro, 1995, p. 143). A simple objective report is given of the latest phenomenon to arise. This simple reporting without interpretation or discussion seems to aid clients in disidentifying with the psychological material and, as with Vipassana meditation, developing a witness awareness. Clients experiencing strong abreactions are told in a calm, compassionate, reassuring manner that what they are experiencing is in the past, it is old stuff, it is like the scenery and they are safely in the present on a passing train (Shapiro, 1995).

Vipassana meditation enhances the development of "bare attention." According to Goldstein (1976), "bare attention means observing things as they are, without choosing, without comparing, without evaluating, without laying our projections and expectations onto what is happening; cultivating instead a choiceless and non-interfering awareness" (p. 20). The quality of bare attention allows one to be more fully grounded in the present; it allows one to be open to the here and now without adding anything else to it.

The practice of mindfulness cultivates a continuity of presence and awareness throughout one's daily life experience. This practice overlaps and complements EMDR treatment (Parnell, 1996a, 1997b) and can be helpful in several ways to clients were abused as children and are in EMDR therapy. The formal practice as taught in a retreat setting is divided into three parts, which are briefly described: sitting meditation (Vipassana meditation), walking meditation, and eating meditation.

Sitting or Vipassana Meditation

One begins sitting meditation by finding a quiet undisturbed place to meditate. The ringer should be turned off the phone, and the person should let others know that he or she is not to be interrupted for the time of the meditation. It is helpful to meditate at the same time each day for a set period of time. First thing in the morning or last thing before going to sleep are good times. For people who have been sexually abused and have quite a lot of trauma in the mind and body, beginning with short periods of meditation—5 to 10 minutes—is recommended; then the time can be increased as the individual feels more comfortable. One should sit in a comfortable upright position, on a cushion, on the floor, or on a chair with one's feet firmly planted on the floor. Vipassana meditators are instructed to simply observe the breath, thoughts, feelings, and body sensations without clinging, condemning, or identifying with them (Goldstein, 1976). Phenomena that arise are observed by a detached witness awareness.

The meditation begins with a focus on the sensation of the breath either at the nostrils or in the belly. The meditator notices the sensation of the in and out of the breath or the rising and falling of the belly. When the mind wanders from the breath, one is to notice it and then gently return the attention to the breath. Mental notes, such as "in and out" or "rising and falling," are used to keep the mind focused. This focus on the breath is the first instruction given in the practice. Gently returning to the present moment over and over again trains the mind to be more present.

After meditators have learned how to be somewhat present with the breath, they are taught to notice when thoughts arise that take their attention from the breath, to make the mental note "thinking, thinking," and then return to the breath. They are not to analyze the content of the thoughts, just to notice that thinking is occurring. Later instructions add the noticing of other mental and physical phenomena, such as emotions, body sensations, and judgments. These are noted, and then the meditator returns to the breath. For example, if a strong emotion like fear arises, the meditator feels it, notes "fear, fear," stays with the sensation until it no longer pulls his or her attention, and then returns to the breath. If the thought arises, "I'm never going to be able to concentrate," she notices that, notes "judging, judging," and returns to the breath. An entire meditation session can be spent finding the mind has wandered away and bringing it back, over and over again. Meditators over time increase their ability to be present with whatever should arise in their field of experience.

Walking Meditation

Walking meditation involves discrete periods of time from 10 minutes to 45 minutes or longer of slow walking, during which the meditator is instructed to pay attention to the sensation of the movement of lifting, moving, and placing the foot. The meditator chooses an unobstructed path of several feet to walk and focuses on the sensation of the movement in a moment-to-moment unfolding process. Upon reaching the end of the path, the meditator turns around and begins again. The goal is attained in each moment—there is nowhere to go except here. During the walking meditation, like the sitting meditation, one notices when the mind wanders off and gently returns to the walking after making a mental note, for instance, of "thinking, thinking." The walking can be extremely slow, almost microscopic in noticing every subtle sensation, or faster, focusing on grosser sensations like the large muscle groups of the foot and leg or the feeling of the foot's contact with the ground. What is most important is the development of a continuity of presence, "being here now." This practice can help abuse survivors to become more aware of their bodies in movement. It may feel very painful and difficult, but beginning with short periods of the meditation and increasing the time enables them gradually to become more grounded and present in their bodies.

Eating Meditation

Most of us tend to become unconscious during the eating of a meal. We finish our food before we have even tasted it. Mindful eating begins with the experience of eating a raisin. Meditators are given a handful of raisins and instructed to notice and to be present as fully as they can be for the experience of eating one raisin at a time. They are told to notice the sensation of lifting the arm, the feeling of the raisin in the fingers, the feeling of the raisin in the mouth, and the sensation and taste of the raisin as they bite down on it. Attention is paid to chewing, to swallowing, and then to the desire to repeat the process. Again, the aim is to be present to the full experience of eating. For many people, this is a remarkable experience, because such an ordinary act is experienced as something quite new. After several minutes of discovering a fresh relationship to raisins, meditators are instructed to bring this same attention to their regular meals, eating slowly and mindfully, noticing when the mind wanders away and bringing it back to the experience of eating.

One can see how this practice might help clients who have been sexually abused to become more conscious when they are eating. Many of our clients have eating disorders as a result of the abuse and their disconnection from their bodies. Bringing more awareness to the process of eating can also bring awareness of the triggers for overeating, bingeing, purging, and insights to the connections. If clients tend to dissociate during eating, that can be noted and worked on during sessions. Triggers for problematic eating behavior may also be targeted with EMDR.

Meditation Group for Sexual Abuse Survivors

For two years I led a weekly meditation group composed of six sexual abuse survivors who, as it turned out, were all ritual abuse survivors with DID. We spent one hour doing guided lovingkindness meditation, grounded breathing, and a variant of Vipassana meditation, followed by a check-in period during which each woman would talk about what came up in her meditation. Over a period of two years, the women in the group reported feeling safer in their bodies and better able both to be present to physical sensations, body memories, and disturbing thoughts and images, and to notice when the desire to "switch" or dissociate would arise. The sitting meditation was about 30 minutes, and I provided verbal guidance every few minutes to help them come back to their breath or bodies if they had become lost. In addition to the basic Vipassana meditation, I also added, at their request, a lovingkindness meditation (Levine, 1987; Salzberg, 1996; Salzberg & Kabat-Zinn, 1997), which I adapted to their needs. The meditation was followed by sharing, which was quite meaningful and moving to everyone and helped to ground the meditation experiences, answer any questions, and develop a group bond.

This meditation group became a safe haven for these women, who had been terribly abused, and they felt safe enough to let their feelings emerge during the meditation. Such revelation would have been uncomfortable at best in a different, more formal group setting. I kept adapting the meditation length and the focus, according to their needs and feedback. One woman, for example, needed to know how much time remained during the meditation, because it felt like forever to her child self. A time reminder was comforting to her. At formal retreats the sitting periods are usually 45 minutes to one hour or longer; for abuse survivors this can feel like an eternity because of the intensity of the feelings that arise when they sit still. Shorter sitting periods that are increased as they come to tolerate the meditative silence give them a sense of control.

. . . .

Part II

The Phases and Organization of EMDR Sessions and Treatment

Chapter 5

The Beginning Phase:
Assessment, Preparation, and
Ego Strengthening

The beginning phase of treatment consists of laying the groundwork and preparing the client for the EMDR trauma processing, which occurs in the middle phase of treatment. Depending on the needs of the client, this phase lasts anywhere from a few weeks to years.

In the beginning phase the therapeutic relationship develops and a strong therapeutic container evolves within which the difficult and painful reprocessing of traumatic material can take place. The therapist takes a *thorough* history and assesses the client's ego strengths and coping skills. EMDR processing is used during this phase primarily to strengthen ego resources and to clear minor disturbances. It is important to remember that EMDR processing is *integrated* into a comprehensive treatment plan that includes many other essential parts and adjunctive tools.

For instance, I had been seeing Dorothy for more than a year before she was ready to do EMDR on the sexual abuse that had spanned several years of her childhood. Her elderly uncle and an emotionally disturbed cousin were the perpetrators. Dorothy had a very difficult time trusting anyone, and it was many months before she trusted me enough to express her feelings.

Dorothy grew up on a farm in the rural midwest in a family whose members did not communicate very much and never talked about feelings. Children were to be seen and not heard. Her mother was a cold, hard woman who did not want children and resented her fate. When Dorothy finally spoke to me about the abuse, she felt quite awkward and foolish. She feared I would not believe her, that I would think she was making a big deal out of nothing and would humiliate her as her mother had, or that I would blame her as her mother did. We spent a long time in the preparation phase before starting EMDR processing.

Presenting Problems

Sometimes clients come into treatment because they remember that they were abused as children, understand the connection between the past abuse and their current problems, and want to clear the past using EMDR. In these cases treatment planning is apt to be straightforward and systematic. The therapist takes the client's history, a therapeutic relationship develops, the therapist identifies and develops the client's inner and outer resources, and, when the therapist determines that the client is emotionally stabilized and his or her life is not in crisis, the therapist and client define the targets for EMDR processing and begin.

Some clients come to treatment knowing that they were abused as children but do not tell their EMDR therapists until they feel sufficient trust. These clients may have been betrayed or disappointed by previous therapists or feel so much shame and humiliation around the abuse that they need to feel secure in the therapeutic relationship before sharing this information.

Many clients, however, do not come to therapy with clear visual and narrative memory of abuse incidents. Some clients have no clear memories of incidents—only "a feeling" something happened to them—but they manifest symptoms of possible abuse. Other clients report no clear memories of abuse. However, *something* triggered their flashbacks and nightmares, which they may or may not believe relate to early abuse.

For example, a client who has needed dental work and avoided it because of her anxiety finally sees the dentist for emergency treatment and experiences an overwhelming panic attack when he begins to work on her mouth. She reports no remembered abuse by a dentist but feels rage, panic, powerlessness, and an unbearable tingling in her genital area. She does not relate this to sexual abuse but feels like she is crazy. She seeks treatment because of her fear of dentists, not because of sexual abuse memories.

As therapists we must not assume that these symptoms mean that there has been sexual abuse. However, we may suspect it and thus must take the necessary precautions in the preparation phase of treatment. We want a thorough history, and we need to look for triggers for the symptoms.

Many of us who have used EMDR in our practices for several years have encountered clients who had no memory of sexual abuse and came to therapy for another reason but who uncovered apparent sexual abuse memories during EMDR processing. Sometimes clients who are in treatment for a phobia discover during the EMDR processing that the phobia is linked to early childhood abuse. Such sessions can be quite intense and disturbing for the client and for the therapist. The abreactions may be very strong and upsetting, and the information that is revealed may disorient the client. The therapist may need to spend time in subsequent sessions helping the client to integrate this new information and developing a workable treatment plan that takes into account the possibilty of early childhood abuse.

It is important in the beginning of treatment to find out the client's *current symptoms*. What are the most problematic behaviors, limiting beliefs, and somatic complaints? What are the current triggers? What, when, where, and how often does your client feel triggered and experience symptoms of distress? Perhaps a movie, a passage from a book, or driving in a certain part of town is a catalyst. How long has your client been suffering from these symptoms? What has she done in the past to try to remedy her problems? What has been helpful and what hasn't? Do your clients see a connection between the emergence or shift in their current symptoms and trauma-related triggers? These triggers could include events like the a parent's death or one of their children's approaching the age at which the client was abused. How is the client currently coping with her problems? How is the client's current life being affected by his symptoms and emotional difficulties? How is she being held back from fully expressing her potential in her relationships and in her career?

History-Taking and Evaluation

ASSESSMENT

Clients who have been physically and/or sexually abused as children run the gamut from highly disturbed individuals with severe character pathology and few coping skills to people with intact ego structures who have some life-limiting symptoms and good coping skills. In general, the severity of symptomatology depends on the severity, frequency, and duration of abuse; the age of the victim at the time of the abuse; the victim's relationship to the perpetrator(s); the victimizer's treatment of the victim; the family's and/or system's response to the abuse; and "host" factors such as temperament, ego strength, general resiliency, quality of early attachment, and family history of mental illness.

As noted earlier, the EMDR therapist does not always know if the client sitting before him or her at the initial session experienced sexual abuse in early childhood. Because of that, it is important to *always* take a history before beginning EMDR processing. One never knows what might come out during the processing sessions (e.g., dissociative disorder), and so it is best to be prepared. I advise viewing the gathering of historical information as part of the rapport building process, so that clients do not feel like they are being interrogated and objectified (a potential trigger for sexual abuse survivors who were treated as objects by the perpetrators). The therapist attempts to know the client, and at the same time the client gets to know the therapist.

Pacing is important. Clients may feel overexposed if they reveal too much about themselves too quickly. Therapists should be sensitive to this and refrain from asking questions that may be too evocative. History-taking can be as simple as a conversation during which the client tells the therapist what she thinks is most important about her childhood and how that may be affecting her now. The therapist fills out this narrative by asking questions that lead to hypotheses about the etiology of the presenting problems. As clients tell their stories, the therapist listens for events, themes, limiting self beliefs, and negative beliefs about the world—any of these may be good targets for EMDR processing.

It is helpful to ask for information about clients' birth and early infancy and for a narrative account of their childhood, particularly their relationship with their parents or other caregivers. You want to evaluate the nature of their early attachment. Was it consistent or chaotic? Was their mother borderline or simply anxious? Clients who had chaotic, borderline early attachment figures are more prone to PTSD and will require more time to build a secure relationship with the therapist (Schore, 1994). Prior to EMDR processing of traumatic memories, they may require more work to develop resources that can aid in interweaves and session closure. Clients who were neglected in early childhood may have a more difficult time developing a trusting relationship with the therapist. Also, they may have large gaps in their childhood memories, which may be the result not of abuse, but rather of neglect (Schore, 1994). Who were the primary caregivers? Were there disruptions of attachment due to death, divorce, substance abuse, hospitalizations, or other causes?

It is important to know about a client's *current health and history of medical problems,* including physical illnesses, accidents, hospitalizations, or past medical procedures. What happened and how did the family respond? Many people who have suffered from early trauma develop somatic problems. Are they taking any medications? If they haven't had a physical examination recently, you might suggest that they schedule one. Because adults who have been sexually abused as children were betrayed by adults who were in positions of power and authority, the idea of visiting a doctor or dentist may arouse anxiety and so be avoided. This avoidance can jeopardize their health if this issue isn't addressed.

During history-taking note how the client relates to you. Does he or she seem comfortable and able to talk easily to you? Or, does she or he seem detached, anxious, or hostile? Does the client have a character disorder? Many people who were sexually abused as children have borderline personality disorders (Herman, 1992), a factor that affects the use of EMDR in treatment. How good is his or her ego functioning? How does the client handle anxiety? What are his/her primary defenses? Does this person dissociate when talking about disturbing memories? You may want to evaluate for *dissociative disorder* by using a screening device such as the Dissociative Experiences Scale (DES; Bernstein & Putnam, 1986b; Carlson & Putnam, 1993) or the Dissociative Disorders Interview Schedule (DDIS;

Ross, Herber, Norton, Anderson, & Garchet, 1989). Putnam (1989) and Ross (1989) have written helpful books on DID. You also want to know about any history of mental health treatment. What worked and what didn't—and why? Clients who report a long history of unsuccessful therapy may have DID. There are some assessment tools available in addition to the DES for assessing trauma symptoms, most notably Briere's (1995) Trauma Symptom Inventory. (See Table 5.1 for Puk's summary of symptoms.)

Does the client have a history of *self-destructive behavior,* such as sexual acting out, self-mutilation, drug or alcohol abuse, gambling, or abusive relationships? Information about drug and alcohol use is important. Who in the family used, what, how much, and with what consequences? Is the client currently using substances? Is she/he in recovery?

It is important to inquire about *social and sexual development.* Did they have close friends growing up, or were they isolated and alone? Did they form childhood and adolescent friendships? Did the family move frequently, causing disruptions in the development of lasting friendships? How did the client do in school? Oftentimes children who have been traumatized have a difficult time concentrating in school and have learning difficulties, which then contribute to low self-esteem.

How did they relate to the opposite sex? What was their experience with dating? What was the quality of their relationships? What is their history of intimate relationships? How did they feel about their own sexual development? How did they feel about their bodies? Did they avoid all sexual contact or were they promiscuous during their adolescence?

It is important to find out about their *current functioning and social supports,* and about their employment status. Are they currently employed? Do they have close friends and family, or are they alone and alienated? How do they get along with others? Are they part of a support group like AA, ALANON, NA, or a survivor group?

ABUSE HISTORY

An important part of the history-taking involves gathering information about the client's abuse history. Who was the perpetrator(s)? When did the abuse begin? How old was the client at the time? When did it end? Was the abuse a one-time occurrence or did it occur over a period of time? What was the frequency? Did the client tell anyone about the abuse? Did others know about the abuse? If it was reported, what was the response from the adults and/or system? Was the client ignored? Punished? Rescued? Blamed? Disbelieved? What kind of abuse took place? What was the severity? Were there threats involved? Was there physical violence involved? Did your client always remember the abuse or did memories of the abuse emerge at some time later in her or his life? What beliefs about

Table 5.1

. . . .

Clinical Signs of Dissociative Disorders

1. *History of years of psychotherapy with little progress*
   (Kluft, 1985; Putnam et al., 1986).
   Client has varying diagnoses over the years.
   Client may have a history of multiple psychiatric hospitalizations with different diagnoses.
2. *Symptoms of depersonalization and/or derealization*
   (Putnam et al., 1986).
   For example, the client:
   a. doesn't feel like her/himself (e.g., bigger or smaller),
   b. reports that her/his surroundings do not look the same,
   c. looks in the mirror and sees something other than his/her typical reflection,
   d. experiences floating alongside or above his/her body,
   e. reports that the daily environment seems dream-like or as if she/he were walking in a fog.
3. *Memory lapses* (Putnam et al., 1986).
   For example, the client:
   a. does not recall how she/he got to the shopping mall,
   b. finds unfamiliar items at home and does not recall buying them or how they were acquired.
   She/he cannot offer a coherent narrative history. However, this also may occur because of substance abuse, illness, depression, dementia. Note that a highly organized DID patient may confabulate and fill in the amnestic gaps.
4. *Flashback and intrusive thoughts*
   The client has flashbacks and intrusive thoughts of childhood traumatic events or recent traumas.
   DID can be conceptualized as resulting from chronic, serial PTSD (Spiegel, 1993).
5. *Schneiderian symptoms* (Kluft, 1987; Ross et al., 1990).
   Of the 11 first-rank Schneiderian symptoms, the client may endorse several of them. The most frequently reported include:
   a. hearing "audible thoughts" or "voices arguing." However, DID clients usually say that they hear voices in the head, not externally (as in schizophrenia),
   b. experiencing "made" feelings, i.e., feelings that come out of the "blue" with no logical basis,
   c. having "made" thoughts and behavior.
   DID patients report more frequent first-rank symptoms than patients having schizophrenia (Ross et al., 1990).

The DID patient will show a full range of affect, whereas the schizo-phrenic patient usually will demonstrate blunted affect.

6. *Somatic symptoms* (Putnam, 1989, pp. 65–67)

The client may:

a. report chronic headaches that are intractable to over-the-counter analgesics,

b. Have physical complaints and pain that physicians cannot account for and which may be "somatic memories."

7. *Sleep disturbance* (Loewenstein, 1991)

The client may report frequent nightmares or night terrors. Note that sleepwalking is usually associated with a dissociative disorder.

8. *Depression*

One of the primary complaints of the DID patient is a affective dis-order. Frequently, there is a history of suicide attempts or suicidal ideation (Putnam et al., 1986).

All new clients should complete the Dissociative Experience Scale (DES; Carlson & Putnam, 1992). On the DES, a cut-off score of 20 is recom-mended (Ross, 1995). For clients scoring greater than that and/or respond-ing positively to these clinical signs, the clinician should suspect the pres-ence of an underlying dissociative disorder. Administration of the Dissociative Disorders Interview Schedule (Ross, 1989, pp. 313–334) or the Structured Clinical Interview for *DSM-IV*–Dissociation Revised (SCID-D Revised; see Steinberg, 1995) will help to confirm the actual diagnosis.

Reprinted with permission from Puk, G. (1999).

. . . .

himself or herself and the world did the client develop as a result of the abuse? Does the client see herself as bad because she enjoyed the attention of the abuser or experienced sexual arousal? Does he feel ashamed or worthless for his failure to protect himself or others? Did he or she as a child or teen perpetrate abuse on others? Has the client engaged in abusive behaviors as an adult?

This information may be gathered over time in a way that is comfort-able for clients. It is important that they not feel like they are being inter-rogated and that they feel safe enough to reveal the information to the therapist. Information about triggers, dreams, body memories, and flash-back images should be noted for use as potential EMDR targets. As men-tioned earlier, many adults who have been sexually abused don't have clear visual memories of abuse but have symptoms indicating that abuse may have occurred.

IDENTIFICATION OF CLIENT RESOURCES

The identification of resources from the client's earlier and current life is very important in this work. These resources, which may include positive memories, can be used throughout the EMDR therapy to add wholeness, ego strength, empowerment, and a sense of integration to the client. They can be memories of trust, pride, safety, comfort, support, nurturance, and achievement. They may include memories of being mentored, images of positive role models, and experiences of social recognition.

As part of the history-taking, the therapist also helps the client to identify those people in the client's life who were important loving, nurturers, or protectors, such as relatives, friends, friends' parents, teachers, counselors, clergy people, etc. Some clients cannot name anyone from their immediate family who was kind, but when questioned might be able to find a teacher who "saw" them, "recognized" their specialness, and cared about them.

Along with the important support people in the client's early life, you want to find out *what did they do to survive? What did they do to cope then, and what do they do* now *to cope with difficult circumstances?* Did they go for walks in nature or to a special place? Did they have an imaginary friend or an angelic presence for solace? As a child, one client would go up to the top of a grassy hill a mile from her farmhouse, a place no one else visited, and commune with nature there. The image of this place became her safe place during our EMDR work

SPIRITUALITY

It is helpful to know what spiritual resources the client has. What religion did he have as a child, and what are his spiritual beliefs now? What brings her a sense of peace and well-being? Are there religious figures who comfort her? Does she believe in God? If so, is there an image that represents the Divine Being? Some people connect to something bigger than themselves when they are in nature. What images evoke spiritual feelings for them? Have they had what they would consider spiritual experiences? Experiences of awe and beauty can be summoned to bring inspiration and a broader perspective.

Establishing a Strong, Safe Therapeutic Container

Many clients who have been abused as children require help with ego strengthening in the beginning phase of EMDR, as well as during the middle phase of treatment when EMDR processing of traumatic memories is occurring. Ego strengthening can be likened to the development of a container that will be strong enough to hold the emotional turmoil the processing of traumatic memories may evoke. Ego strengthening is also like increasing the capacity of a cable to carry a strong electric current. If the cable is not strong enough, there will be resistance that will impede the flow of energy. Because of the intensity of abreactions that EMDR frequently evokes during the processing of childhood abuse memories, it is essential that clients develop sufficient ego resources prior to EMDR processing. Clients who have been abused require ego strengthening so that they can develop a greater capacity for self-soothing, clarity of thinking, and the ability to experience and process strong emotions.

Resource development refers to strategies therapists employ to support the clients' development of positive resources. Hypnotherapists have worked with resource development for years and have developed many effective techniques (Phillips & Frederick, 1995). Milton Erickson believed that the unconscious mind of the individual contained all the resources needed to resolve the person's problems and that it was the therapist's task to help the patient activate her own natural inner resources (Erickson & Rossi, 1976).

The development of client resources can take weeks, months, or years, depending upon the needs of the client. For some chronically depressed clients who were severely neglected as children, resource development and ego strengthening may be the focus of their therapy and the trauma processing a less important aspect (Wildwind, 1993).

THE THERAPEUTIC RELATIONSHIP

A sense of safety is an important issue for clients who have been abused as children. Because their trust was violated and they were physically and emotionally harmed, it is essential before any trauma reprocessing begins that they feel secure in their relationship with the therapist. This development can take weeks, months, or years, depending on the needs of the client. Clients must feel safe enough to trust the therapist to tell him or her *truthfully* what they are experiencing during the reprocessing of a traumatic incident. They don't have to tell you all of the details, but they do need to tell you enough to let you know that the traumatic material is moving through the system and is not stuck.

The client's ability to trust the therapist is also important during the reprocessing of the traumatic memories, because when a client accesses his child self during the reprocessing of traumas that occurred during childhood he may lose all contact with his adult self. As with any therapy, "flashback transference"(Loewenstein, 1993)—when the client perceives the therapist as the "historical" antagonist—can occur during EMDR processing. The following dramatic example illustrates this.

Melanie was in the middle of reprocessing a horrific memory of being tied to a bed and molested by two aunts when she was three years old.

Suddenly, she looked at me with terror in her eyes, as if I was about to hurt her. She left her chair and cowered in a corner of my office with her back to the wall and continued to look with wild distrust and fear at me. Her child self had forgotten who I was and now saw me as the perpetrator who was harming her. My adult client had *totally* lost her sense of who I was. In such a moment, the therapist may have to act as the adult awareness and guide the client out of frightening memories. So I got up and, talking to her all the while in a calm, caring voice reminding her of who I was and what we were doing together, walked over to her. I repeated, "I am here to help you clear these old memories. What is frightening you is from the past." I tried to connect with her adult self, who knew that these memories were from the past, even though they *felt* so real in the present.

After talking to her calmly for a while, I was finally able to reassure her. She agreed to return to her chair and to resume the eye movements. Because of her trust in me, Melanie told me what she was seeing—a new horrific scene that seemed very real—and was then able to complete the reprocessing. She ended the session feeling clear and at peace and with a strengthened trust in our relationship.

The therapist and therapeutic relationship are also important ego resources for the client. The client incorporates the therapist as a positive self-object, who then becomes a source of caring and support during times of difficulty. Some clients report hearing my voice giving them advice or consolation during difficult times.

The therapist and therapeutic relationship can be used as resources when the client is stuck during EMDR processing sessions. For example, the therapist can come in and rescue and comfort the client's child self, if necessary, when the client is looping in distress. Eventually, the client's internal voice replaces that of the therapist. I believe that during EMDR processing and resolution of trauma, the therapist's kind presence is installed along with the positive cognition and new image. I have not purposely installed myself as a positive resource for my clients, and I do not suggest doing that. But I cannot stress too much the importance of the therapeutic relationship as an essential resource for the client prior to middle phase processing work.

COMMITMENT TO SAFETY AND TREATMENT

Along with the development of a strong therapeutic relationship, it is important that there be a commitment to safety and treatment and that the client address issues and behaviors that interfere with treatment. Ideally, these issues should be dealt with and the client sufficiently stabilized before beginning EMDR processing of traumatic memories.

These issues and behaviors include alcohol and substance abuse problems, eating disorders, suicidal and parasuicidal behavior such as self-mutilation, and serious relationship difficulties such as sexual acting out and abusive relationships. Clients may need adjunctive treatments for such issues as drug and alcohol abuse, compulsive behaviors, and eating disorders. Some may need to be stabilized on psychotropic medication. Make sure that their lives are sufficiently stable, that they have a good support system, and that they are not undergoing any major crises such as impending loss of home or employment.

THE DEVELOPMENT OF COPING SKILLS

During this beginning phase of preparation, the therapist can help the client develop a number of coping skills.

Relaxation/stress reduction skills are very important for clients who have been sexually abused. For many of them life is full of stressful triggers; consequently, these relaxation techniques can be very useful between EMDR sessions to calm clients. There are many forms of stress reduction, including systematic relaxation and guided imagery techniques. The light stream visualization technique (Shapiro, 1995) is useful, and there are many commercial tapes available (e.g., Emmett Miller's "Letting Go of Stress," 1996). Also, therapists can make relaxation tapes for their clients in the office for use between sessions. As clients learn to relax, they gain a newfound sense of control over their bodies.

Grounding skills are also important to teach clients who have been sexually abused. These clients commonly dissociate and go "out of their bodies" when stressed or triggered. Teaching clients to feel their bodies, to be aware of sensation, and to be present during sessions is helpful. Engaging in regular physical exercise helps clients to become more embodied, and walking outdoors in a beautiful setting can be physically and spiritually rewarding. Yoga practice, especially slow-moving, mindful yoga that stresses presence rather than physical prowess, is recommended. Mindfulness training, which was described in Chapter 4, is also a useful grounding practice.

Identification, Development, and Installation of Inner and Outer Resources

Many clients who have been abused and neglected as children lack the necessary internal resources for successful EMDR processing of traumatic memories. Some have difficulty connecting with positive inner resources. For others, the positive resolution of the image at the end of a session does not hold and they experience distress later during the week, with their SUDS elevating. Their stored negative life experiences overwhelm their internal reservoir of positive experiences, self-esteem, and resilience. Often these clients, instead of processing these memories to an adaptive resolution, get caught in a gigantic negative memory network, from which they can't extricate themselves. Unable to connect to positive internal resources, they loop and become stuck. In particular, clients who were neglected in early childhood don't naturally access nurturing or protective ego states or memories. Because of these diffculties, I spend quite a long time developing and installing positive internal resources in the preparation phase of EMDR with clients with severe early childhood histories of abuse and neglect. Spending more time in the development and installation of inner resources increases the success rate with traumatized clients and decreases the chances of retraumatizing them.

EMDR can be used to strengthen positive internal resources. We have found that eye movements or other bilateral stimulation increase or further develop positive feelings or experiences (Shapiro, 1995). As mentioned earlier, people who have been subjected to early trauma or neglect experience what Schore (1994, 1998) calls synaptic pruning, which makes them more vulnerable to PTSD, overly attentive to adverse stimuli, and hypersensitive to their environments. They tend to interpret experiences negatively. These people also don't notice benign everyday experiences; rather, they scan the environment for what might be dangerous (McFarlane et al., 1993).

It may be that by developing and installing positive resources with EMDR, we are helping to make changes in the brain's circuitry. It is as if the adult who was traumatized as a child has a brain where the circuitry is "lit up" around negative life experiences; positive, or benign, life experiences are stored in the dark. What we may be doing with the development and installation of positive resources is lighting the dark part of the brain and adding new pathways between memory networks that heretofore were separate.

The use of resource development and installation with EMDR has been developed and elaborated by Foster and Lendl (1996; Lendl & Foster, 1997) for performance enhancement. It was applied to the treatment of addictions with EMDR by Popky (1997), and to childhood trauma by Wildwind (1993), Parnell (1995–1998, 1997a, 1998a, b; Parnell & Cohn, 1995a; Thompson, Cohn, & Parnell 1996) and Leeds and colleagues (Leeds, 1997, 1998; Leeds & Korn, 1998; Leeds & Shapiro, in press). I have collected a number of suggestions for resource development and installation from these colleagues and others, many of which have been borrowed from guided imagery. Use your clinical judgment and attunement with your clients to determine which ones might be most helpful.

I suggest that therapists spend time in the beginning phase of treatment identifying the needed resources with the client and then installing them during the sessions. By "installation" of resources I mean the use of bilateral stimulation paired with the positive resource to increase and strengthen it. In theory, EMDR clears what is dysfunctional from the system, allowing what is adaptive to come to the fore in awareness. We have also found that when bilateral stimulation is used with memories or experiences that were positive, neutral, or adaptive, they get stronger. Therefore, to increase a client's positive resources, have him or her bring up memories that were positive or adaptive; evoke the image, body sensations, emotions, sounds, and other sensory associations; and then add the bilateral stimulation for a *short* set. It is important to use short sets because often clients will flip to the polar opposite and associate to negative memories. After one short set of bilateral stimulation (10 to 14 passes) ask, "What do you get now?" If it is strengthened, do another short set. You may continue with a few sets if it remains positive.

Following are suggestions for the development and installation of resources. Let me remind you that in my view the use of EMDR is an art—not a science or a technique—and it is important that the therapist remain attuned to the client and the needs of the moment. While I offer suggestions that may stir your imagination and creativity and help you to find a way of working with clients with complex problems, feel free to improvise on the theme.

ESTABLISHING A SAFE PLACE

Before beginning reprocessing we need to help the client establish a place where she can go in her imagination and feel totally safe and protected. Therapists may begin sessions with the safe place, use it as a place the client can go to during difficult processing to take a break and regain a sense of control, and use it to close down incomplete sessions. For clients who need to develop more of a sense of self-constancy, each EMDR session can begin and end with the safe place. This increases the sense that they are the same person in different situations and can hold onto the safe place at home between sessions. Clients can practice going to their safe place before going to sleep at night. The safe place can also be a place where the client's allies gather to add extra safety and support. (This will be described in more detail later in this chapter.)

The therapist and client work together to develop the safe place, and the therapist adapts the safe place instructions for each client's unique needs. What is important to achieve? Do you want to create a place of peace and calm where the person can turn off the outside world and the triggers to emotional upset? Do you want this to be a place where the person can access his or her inner resources? The safe place can be a known place or an imaginary one. It can also be symbolic, such as a place in the soft white clouds floating above the earth. Together the therapist and client create a place of safety, comfort, and self-nourishment, a place where they can be creative; this is especially useful for depressed clients. A protective barrier around the place provides extra safety.

It is best to avoid a place from childhood that might be associated with pain from the past. If no other place can be found, the therapeutic relationship and therapist's office can be used as the safe place. For those clients who find it is too dangerous to imagine a safe place, try substituting "comfortable place."

By elaborating the safe place with drawings or sculpture, clients form a stable connection with it. They can also write about it in their journals. One client had a difficult time finding a safe place because the perpetrator was a very powerful man. Together we explored what she needed to feel safe, and she came up with the image of a circle of giant redwood trees with deep roots and branches that went high into the sky. To make this place even more secure, she imagined a powerful force field around the circle of trees with fierce protector deities outside.

Once the client feels secure inside the safe place, the therapist installs the feeling of safety with eye movements or other bilateral stimulation. For many clients, eye movements work quite well to install the feeling and imagery. For some clients, however, eye movements open up processing of traumatic material instead of installing the safe place. If this happens, stop the eye movements and explore with the client what he or she is experiencing. The therapist and client may need to develop another safe place using imagery only. Therapists should use their clinical judgment. I have done it both ways and have had different experiences with different clients.

Before beginning the safe place experience, the therapist should help the client enter a state of general relaxation by using a variety of known relaxation exercises. Or, the client may have his/her own way to relax. Since this is very individual, the time necessary for relaxation depends on the emotional/body state of the client.

Following is a very common method of guiding a client into a relaxed state.

Guided Relaxation to Safe Place

Have the client sit in a comfortable, relaxed manner, with the legs uncrossed and the hands gently resting on her knees. Ask her to close her eyes and take a deep breath. Tell her that she is going to go down a flight of ten steps, and at the bottom she will find a place where she feels totally safe and protected. With each step she takes down she will feel more and more relaxed, letting go of all tension. The therapist counts down one step at a time, with suggestions about the client getting more relaxed, tension melting away, etc. When she reaches the bottom of the stairway, instruct her to go and find her safe place, a place where she feels totally safe and protected. It can be a real or imagined place. Help her increase the intensity of the experience, making it more vivid for her by asking her to notice what she sees, hears, feels, smells, tastes, etc. Make sure that she is feeling totally relaxed, safe, and comfortable in this place. For some clients, you might suggest that they secure this place even more by imaging a protective circle or shield around them which keeps out anything that is harmful.

Safe Place Script*

This is a script for helping the client develop a safe place after becoming relaxed:

With your eyes closed, imagine yourself now in a beautiful, peaceful place.... This might be somewhere you've visited before or somewhere you just make up in your imagination. . . . just let the image of the place come to you. . . . It really doesn't matter what kind of place you imagine as long as it's beautiful, quiet, peaceful, and serene. . . . Let this be a special inner place for you. . . somewhere that you feel particularly at ease . . . a place where you feel safe and secure . . . at one with your surroundings. . . . Maybe you've had a place like this in your life . . . somewhere to go to be quiet and reflective . . . somewhere special and healing for you. . . . Or it could be a place you've seen in a movie . . . read about . . . or just dreamed of. . . . It could be a real place . . . a place you know. . . or an imaginary place . . . .

Let yourself explore and experience whatever quiet imaginary place you go to as if you were there now. . . . Notice what you see there . . . what sounds you hear . . . even the smells and aroma you sense there. . . . Notice especially what it feels like to be there, and immerse yourself in the beauty, the feelings of peacefulness . . . of being secure and at ease. . . .

As you explore this special inner place, find a spot that feels particularly good to be in . . . a spot where you feel especially calm . . . centered . . . safe and at ease. . . . Let yourself become comfortable in this spot. . . . Let this be your safe place. . . . Let this be your power spot . . . a place in which you draw from the deep sense of peacefulness and safety you feel here. . . . Now just let yourself experience what it is like to be in this place. . . . (Wait a few moments before beginning again, continue to keep your voice lower than usual because the client is in a deeper relaxed state.) Keeping your eyes closed . . . would you describe this place.

At this point begin tapping on the client's hands or knees (make sure you ask permission first). Explain this procedure to the client before you begin the imagery. Touch and surprise can be very difficult for abused clients. Depending on the response, ask a few questions to help strengthen the imagery.

What season of the year is it? . . . What time of day is it? . . . What aromas can you smell? . . . What sounds can you hear? . . . Where are you?. . . How are you dressed? . . . How are you experiencing your safe place? . . .

---

* Adapted from Interactive Guided Imagery™ techniques developed by Martin L. Rossman, M.D., and David Bresler, Ph.D., from the Academy for Guided Imagery, POB 2070, Mill Valley, CA 94942.

As you relax and are aware of how it feels to be here ... tell yourself you can return any time you wish. ... This is your special place ... a place where safety, rest, and peace are always available at your own choosing. ...

When you are ready, slowly open your eyes and come back to your waking state. ...

SUGGESTIONS FOR CLIENTS WHO CANNOT DEVELOP A SAFE PLACE

Some clients who have been severely traumatized as children cannot seem to develop a safe place. Attempts are met with negative or scary imagery and more feelings of unsafety. In such cases I offer suggestions.

1. Suggest to the client that he or she bring a *safe object* into the session. This object can be something like a teddy bear, blanket, or an object associated with a safe person in their lives. One man had a strong connection with his grandmother, whose image we used in the work. She smoked a corn-cob pipe when he was a boy, which gave this object special significance to him. He would bring the pipe with him into sessions, carry it with him between sessions, and call it up in imagery when he needed to as a way to evoke feelings of safety and comfort.

2. Bring up an *image or metaphor of stability, resilience, and triumph* (Korn, 1997). For example, the client might bring up an image of a large mountain. Ask the client to notice what he feels in his body when he brings up that image. The therapist reinforces the image and feeling by adding bilateral stimulation. If the feeling of stability, resilience, and triumph increases, add the positive cognition "I am safe" with the feeling and image. Ask the client to press his palm with his fingers to further anchor the experience and do another set of eye movements or tapping to further install it. At a future time the client can invoke this feeling of safety by pressing on the palm and bringing to mind the image of the tree. In this way the client is taking more control of his life and emotions and reinforcing a feeling of safety.

3. Develop and install a *positive, conflict-free image* (Phillips, 1997a, b; in press). Many people who have experienced early traumatization develop nervous systems that are attuned only to potentially dangerous stimuli. Thus, they totally miss, or do not register in their memories ordinary, nontraumatic daily life experiences that would counter their perception of the world as an entirely dangerous place (McFarlane et al., 1993). The development of positive, conflict-free images, along with mindfulness practices, serves to develop new neuropathways in the brain and to strengthen the ego.

   The positive conflict-free image derives from an experience in the client's life when he felt present and whole. It should be a real experience from the person's daily life such as standing in the shower, walking the dog, or cooking a meal. The image is strengthened by asking for sensory details and then installed by using eye movements or other bilateral stimulation. The conflict-free image helps to create a sense of wholeness and increased feeling in the client that his life is not all terrible. It helps with self-soothing and affect control.

Table 5.2 shows a protocol for development and use of a positive, conflict-free image.

Table 5.2

. . . .

Protocol for Development of the Positive, Conflict-Free Image

1. Help the client identify the conflict-free image by asking questions such as "Where in your life do you feel wholly yourself? What is an activity that all of you feels free to engage in? When is a time when you do not have any of the difficulties you came here to resolve?"
2. Select an image that represents a conflict-free area of functioning and evokes completely positive feelings. Install this image with bilateral stimulation.
3. The client must be able to hold this image in a consistently positive manner and actually strengthen the image through the sets. If this does not happen, return to step #2.
4. Listen for and identify positive cognitions that emerge.
5. Have the client practice using this technique between sessions to manage distressing affect related to her symptoms. For example she may want to bring up the image before going to sleep, public speaking, etc.
6. Use the conflict-free image as an interweave during processing of negative material in the standard EMDR protocol. [This will be described in Chapter 9]

Reprinted with permission from Phillips, M. (1997a, b, in press)

. . . .

Positive Internal Resource Images for Further Ego Strengthening

CHILD SELF AND ADULT SELF RELATIONSHIP ASSESSMENT AND DEVELOPMENT

As described in Chapter 3, very often during EMDR processing with an adult sexually abused as a child, the client suddenly accesses the child self in its separate memory compartment and begins to process the past from the child's perspective. Commonly clients become caught in looping or stuck processing and need help from the therapist in the way of interweaves. I have found it useful to have the client access the child self *before* EMDR processing and evaluate the state of the child self and adult self relationship. Sometimes I find that the child does not like or trust the adult or that the adult does not like or trust the child. This is important information, because during the processing of a traumatic event with EMDR the therapist may find that the adult has turned on the child self or that the child cannot depend on the adult self to act as a protector resource. It is better to know this ahead of time. Having a good, strong, loving relationship between the client's adult and child selves is useful for interweaves and aids tremendously in the healing process.

The following is a description of how the adult self–child self relationship can be accessed and evaluated:

The therapist begins by guiding the client in finding his safe place. After the safe place has been established, ask the client to invite his child self into the protective circle. Begin a dialogue between the adult and child selves to evaluate the nature of their relationship. Generally the client keeps his eyes closed and the therapist asks the client questions directed either to the adult self or to the child self. For example, the therapist might ask the child how old she is, how she is feeling, what she needs, how she feels about the adult, and what is happening in her life. The client might respond "I am three years old. I feel scared, I know my daddy's in the house somewhere and my mommy's not home." The answer to any of the questions can lead to more questions as the therapist gathers information. At some point the attention can shift to the adult self to get her opinions and impressions of the child self, asking "How do you feel about her? Do you think you can meet her needs?" The therapist is attempting to find out what the child is like, her current emotional state, and the quality of the relationship between the adult and the child. If there are problems between the two (for instance the child may feel betrayed by the adult), the therapist must seek a way to remedy the situation. It is like doing inner family therapy. One or more sessions may be taken up with trying to heal hurts from the past and developing a caring bond between the adult and child selves.

When a caring relationship has been established, ask the client to imagine holding her child self on her lap, playing with her, or engaging the child in some positive, nurturing way. This feeling can also be installed with the bilateral stimulation. Once the relationship has been established, the adult can serve as a resource for the child self during times of blocked processing and help create an increased sense of safety for closing sessions.

SYMBOLS OR IMAGES THAT EMERGE DURING GUIDED IMAGERY, DREAMS, DAYDREAMS, OR ACTIVE IMAGINATION

For some clients, positive symbols or images that emerge can be used as resources. Many of these images arise during EMDR processing and between sessions in the form of dreams or day dreams. Christina, whose case is presented in Chapter 12, began to receive inner support and guidance from an "inner shaman" who appeared during EMDR processing of abuse memories. Another client used her "inner guide" as a regular resource. For another woman, the sense of a spirit mother appeared during EMDR processing and was then used as a resource.

INNER ADVISOR

The "inner advisor" is an aspect of the ego that represents wisdom and offers a balanced perspective (Rossman, 1987). After the client is in his safe place, the therapist can tell him that he is going to meet his inner advisor, an aspect of himself that is wise and can offer him guidance when he asks for it. When the inner advisor appears, the therapist asks the client what the advisor looks like and if he or she has any advice to give him at this time. The therapist may choose to install the feeling of the inner advisor with bilateral stimulation. The therapist tells the client that the inner advisor is available when he needs him or her and that he can call on him or her when necessary. The inner advisor, a very valuable ally during EMDR processing and between sessions, can be called on in times of difficulty or if the processing becomes stuck. Clients derive a greater sense of connection to their own inner resources as they develop the inner advisor. Inner advisors appear spontaneously to clients during the guided imagery and take a variety of forms. They have included fairies, wise women, grandfathers, trees, waterfalls, elves, etc. It is important that the client not judge what comes up for her and that she accept the advice that is given, as long as it is compassionate.

Inner Advisor Script*

The most critical and important aspect of the inner advisor is to empower the client. The advisor can also be present as a source of support and comfort. When finding the inner advisor for abused clients have them frequent their safe place first. Here is the script:

As you relax in your safe place, invite your inner advisor to join you in this special place. . . . Just allow an image to form that represents your inner advisor, a wise, kind, loving figure who knows you well. . . . Let it appear in

---

* Adapted from Interactive Guided Imagery™ techniques developed by Martin L. Rossman, M.D., and David Bresler, Ph.D., from the Academy for Guided Imagery, POB 2070, Mill Valley, CA 94942.

any way that comes and accept it as it is. . . . It may come in many forms—man, woman, animal, friend, someone you know, or a character from a movie or book.

Accept your advisor as it appears, as long as it seems wise, kind, loving and compassionate. . . .You will be able to sense its caring for you and its wisdom. . . . Invite it to be comfortable there with you, and ask it its name. . . . Accept what comes. . . .

Keeping your eyes closed, ...would you describe your inner advisor and tell me its name. *At this point begin tapping on the client's hands or knees (make sure you ask permission first). Explain this procedure before you begin the imagery, since touch and surprise can be very difficult for sexually abused clients.*

When you are ready, tell it about your problem. . . . Ask any questions you have concerning this situation. . . . Now listen carefully to the response from (name of advisor/advisors). . . . You may imagine (name of advisor/advisors) talking with you or you may simply have a direct sense of its message in some other way. . . . Allow it to communicate in whatever way seems natural. . . . If you are uncertain about the meaning of the advice or if there are other questions you want to ask, continue the conversation until you feel you have learned all you can at this time. . .

After a long pause, ask the client what is happening. Continue to tap.

As you consider what your advisor told you, imagine what your life would be like if you took the advice you have received. . . . If you have more questions, continue the conversation.

If the client resumes the conversation with the advisor, pause, then ask what is happening. Continue to tap the entire time.

When it seems right, thank your advisor for meeting with you and ask it to tell you the easiest, surest method for getting back in touch with it. . . . realize that you can call another meeting whenever you feel the need for some advice or support. . . . Say good-bye for now in whatever way seems appropriate, and allow yourself to come back to the room. . . .

NURTURING FIGURES

For clients who have been abused it is very helpful to identify caring figures to use as inner resources during EMDR therapy. These inner allies can include real or imaginary figures from the present or past, inner guides, and animals. During the history-taking the therapist looks for those people from the client's past who were loving, safe, and nurturing figures. A parent or stepparent, grandparent, aunt or uncle, teacher, doctor, counselor, friend's parent, clergy person, or even a pet may have provided caring or protection. People currently in the client's life, such as a current spouse, friend, or lover, are important resources as well. Images or memories of interactions with these nurturing figures can be strengthened with bilateral stimulation.

PROTECTORS

Protector figures are people or animals, real or imagined, from the client's early or current life who the client feels can provide protection. The client's adult self can be a protector figure for his or her child self. The therapist and the client's spouse or partner can also be protectors. For instance, a client who had no one in her childhood who protected or defended her but was currently in a loving marriage with a man who would defend her ferociously if necessary was able to bring him up in imagery when her child self felt threatened by the perpetrator during EMDR processing. Memories of positive interactions with these protector figures can be installed with bilateral stimulation.

ANIMALS

Animals may be valuable resources. These include pets from the client's present or past (e.g., a protective dog) or animal images that the client feels a strong affinity for or resonance with (for example, wolf, bear, lion, panther, coyote, eagle) and that may carry the numen of a power animal (Harner, 1980). Sometimes an affectionate dog was the only friend an abused child had. Therapists can identify and install these resources and use them to begin or close EMDR sessions. They can also call upon them and use them as part of interweaves during times in the processing when the client is stuck or overwhelmed by too much emotion.

Thirty-four-year-old Melanie had been severely molested as a child between the ages of three and nine. We had been working together for about a year reprocessing horrific abuse memories involving sexual abuse and torture. During the course of our work together she suddenly began to have night-time dreams and day-time images of a lion. Together we explored these dreams and discovered that the lion was an important ally to her. Whenever she would become overwhelmed and/or stuck during the processing, we called on him to protect the little girl from the perpetrators. Her level of distress would rapidly drop from a 10 to a 0 when she imagined him scaring away the perpetrators. Along with his fierce protectiveness, he was also compassionate and nurturing of the little girl, who would snuggle on his soft strong back feeling safe and comforted. Melanie would say to herself "I am safe now" as she did the eye movements with the imagery. She found summoning his presence before going to sleep at night gave her more peaceful sleep.

Using Guided Imagery and Developing Resources: A Case Example
In this case guided imagery was used to assess the client's adult self-child self relationship and to develop nurturing and protective resources in the client's safe place. Joe had been severely physically and sexually abused by

both of his parents for several years beginning when he was around two years old. When he came in to see me he was quite fragile and extremely distraught over a betrayal by his girlfriend and the subsequent break-up of their relationship. Before beginning EMDR, I needed to develop his inner and outer resources, beginning with an assessment of his child self to adult self relationship. The following is a transcript of a dialogue I had with Joe's inner child after I had guided him to his safe place and had him imagine a protective circle around the adult Joe and another one around the child Joe.

LP: How old are you?

JOE: I'm four—or maybe two.

LP: What does little Joe need?

JOE: He needs love. . . . He needs people around him to love him and appreciate him. . . . He needs to be fed—he was hungry sometimes.

LP: How does he feel?

JOE: He doesn't feel too good. *(Joe switches to first person, speaking from the child's perspective, and the emotional charge increases.)* I'm tired of them hitting and yelling at me. Leave me alone in the genitals. Someone has been touching me there. I have been overstimulated, messed with.

LP: Who are you close to? *(I am inquiring about other resources.)*

JOE: My grandmother. She lets me eat when I want to eat and doesn't put me on a schedule or program my head. I feel safe with her. She wouldn't let anything happen to me—she'd be absolutely fierce.

LP: How do you like big Joe? *(I'm gathering information about the adult self-child self relationship to find out if big Joe can be a resource for little Joe.)*

JOE: I like big Joe.

LP: What do you like about him?

JOE: He's big and strong and protective of me and his friends. He knows how to do things. . . . He's generally nice and gracious to people, he's basically honest. He's more of a poet and lover than a warrior, inside he's happy-go-lucky. He's got a big heart, he could love the world, he's adventurous. . . . He tries new things.

(It is obvious from little Joe's response that he can connect with his adult self, but now I need to find out if the adult Joe can connect with the child Joe.)

LP: How does big Joe feel about little Joe?

JOE: Big Joe likes little Joe. He's a sweet, happy, bubbly boy. He rattles around, tries to talk and understand things. He's very caring and affectionate, nice little being to be around. He tries to be independent. He has a calm nature. He wants to live. He's hoping things will change. His parents call him a hopeless case.

(At this time, after seeing that there was a good adult self-child self connection, I wanted to further reinforce this sense of safety and the feeling that Joe's adult self could be a protector figure for his child self. I begin by talking to little Joe, who is in a protective circle separate from big Joe's space.)

LP: Go inside big Joe's circle and sit on his lap. Feel his arms around you giving you a feeling of protection and safety.

JOE: *(After a few minutes Joe reported the following.)* Surrounding our circle are big huge cats like cheetahs and leopards—about six feet tall at their haunches. They won't let anything hurt us. They are like my real family. The circle is composed of giant cats and inside nothing can happen to me. They are fiercely protective. Also inside the circle is my grandma, who is nurturing and protective of me. There is love and protection in the circle. The cats are outside protecting us.

From this inner dialogue I was able to determine that there was a strong positive adult self-child self relationship. I also found out that Joe had his grandmother as a nurturing and protective ally as well as a fierce circle of giant cats. I felt very encouraged by Joe's feeling a strong connection to all of his allies. Despite the years of abuse, Joe was able to love and nurture himself through the imagery and was able to summon other resources for help when needed. Joe and I used these resources throughout our work together; we used them to begin sessions, as interweaves, to reinforce his safe place when the processing became too intense and he wanted a break, and to close sessions. He was very comfortable using imagery, which would evoke in him the desired feelings of safety and nurturing.

SPIRITUAL RESOURCES

Clients may also identify important spiritual resources. These may include figures such as Jesus, Mary, Kwan Yin, the Buddha, angelic beings, spirit guides, or images from nature. These figures are imbued with a power that feels numinous and suprahuman. After the client identifies the spiritual figure, the therapist asks for more sensory detail to fully evoke the experience. As the client holds in her mind the image and feeling of the figure, the therapist employs the bilateral stimulation to install the resource.

If the spiritual figure has appeared in a dream or has been called on in the past for support, memories of these times can be targeted and the positive image and feeling further strengthened with bilateral stimulation.

Molly felt a strong affinity with Kwan Yin, the female Buddha of compassion. She brought up the image of Kwan Yin, which felt strong and compassionate. As she held the image and feeling in her mind, I tapped on her knees. She felt the image strengthen and experienced a more intimate relationship with Kwan Yin. Afterwards, when Molly felt overwhelmed by the terrible abuse memories she was processing and the excruciating physical pain she felt in her child's body, she would take a break and imagine being held in Kwan Yin's loving arms. I would tap on Molly's knees to install this feeling of warmth and safety from a power that felt infinitely compassionate. After feeling renewed energy from the experience, she would return again to the disturbing memory and process it to the end. Her ability to shift from a traumatic memory to the experience of love and safety gave her a sense of increased control and confidence in the therapeutic process.

Another client contacted what she called her childhood "spirit guide," and we spent time bringing up memories of help she had gotten from her inner guide. I knew that her spirit guide could be a resource when and if she needed it.

Clients can also process and strengthen experiences they felt were spiritual, e.g., meditation or prayer, sitting on the top of a mountain, or a peak experience during an athletic feat. After they are installed, these experiences can be recalled to bring strength and comfort.

INNER STRENGTH

Inner strength is the ego capacity that enables our clients to make it to our office and engage in the difficult and painful healing work. Somehow, they have been able to cope with unbearable circumstances and keep going. Phillips and Frederick (1995) focus specifically on the development of inner strength as a powerful ego-strengthening strategy. The following is their script for the development of inner strength, which I have adapted for use with EMDR and resource installation.

Script for Meeting Inner Strength*

I would like to invite you to take a journey within yourself to a place that feels like the very center of your being, that place where it is very quiet . . . and peaceful . . . and still. And when you're in that place . . . it's possible for you to have a sense of finding a part of yourself . . . a part that I will refer to as your *inner strength*.

This is a part of yourself that has always been there since the moment of birth . . . even though at times it may be difficult for you to feel . . . and it is with you now. It's that part of yourself that has allowed you to survive . . . and to overcome obstacles wherever you face them. Maybe you'd like to take a few moments of time to get in touch with that part of yourself . . . and you can notice what images . . . or feelings . . . what thoughts . . . what

* Adapted with permission from Phillips, M., and Frederick, C. (1995). *Healing the divided self* (p. 88). New York: Norton; originally from McNeal and Frederick, 1993, pp. 172–173.

bodily sensations are associated with being in touch with your inner strength. And when those images or thoughts or feelings or bodily sensations or however it is coming to you are clear to you in your inner mind, and when you have a sense that the experience is completed for you . . . then let me know. *(When the client indicates "yes," begin bilateral stimulation—tapping or auditory stimulation. Clients can be instructed to tap on their own knees if touch from the therapist is not OK. Continue tapping.)*

In the future, when you wish to get in touch with inner strength, . . . you will find that you can do so by calling forth these images, thoughts, feelings, bodily sensations, and that by so doing you will be in touch with inner strength again. *(Continue tapping.)*

And when you're in touch with this part of yourself, you will be able to feel more confident . . . confident with the knowledge that you have, within yourself, all the resources you really need to take steps in the direction that you wish to go . . . to be able to set goals and to be able to achieve them . . . and this part of yourself, it's possible to feel more calm, more optimistic, to look forward to the future. *(At this point particular goals that the client has shared with the therapist may be stated.)*

And in the next days and weeks to come, you may find yourself becoming calmer and more optimistic about your life . . . and you will find that at any time during the day it will be possible for you to get in touch with your own inner strength by simply closing your eyes for a moment, bringing your hand to your forehead, evoking the image of your inner strength, and reminding yourself that you have within you . . . all the resources you really need. The more you use these methods to be in touch with your inner strength, the more you will be able to trust your inner self, your intuition, your feelings, and the more you will be able to use them as your guide.

You can make a tape of your voice guiding your client in this exercise, which he or she can play between sessions to take an active role in the development of inner strength.

IMAGE OF A WISE BEING

The image or feeling (if no image arises) of a man or woman of wisdom can be used as a resource. This image represents an integrated whole being who is wise and powerful, for example, a Greek goddess or an Indian medicine man. These images can come from client dreams, active imagination, or guided imagery, or they may arise during EMDR processing.

FIGURES FROM BOOKS, STORIES, MOVIES, TV, HISTORICAL FIGURES, OR CARTOON CHARACTERS

Figures from books, stories, movies, TV, history, or cartoon characters can also be used as positive resources. If the client has been inspired by a particular figure and finds it strengthening, it can be used as a resource—even if the figure is fictional.

One of my African-American clients used Frederick Douglass as a resource. Douglass was born a slave and was severely abused but had the internal strength to escape slavery and become a great abolitionist and leader. One chapter in Douglass's autobiography, *The Life and Times of Frederick Douglass,* was particularly important to my client. It was entitled "Resisting the Slave Breaker" and was Douglass's account of his inner conviction that he could never be beaten again by the slave breaker. In a scene Douglass struggles for hours with the man, who is trying to break his spirit, and finally Douglass succeeds in defeating him. Together, we often referred to Frederick Douglass and used him as a role model and resource for inner strength.

Some clients may want to draw on imaginary superheros like Wonder Woman or Superman for inner strength, power, and courage. Others use historical figures like Eleanor Roosevelt, Martin Luther King, or Mahatma Ghandi.

One man lacked courage to ask a woman out for a date. When asked what image represented the courage he needed, he came up with Humphrey Bogart, because he always liked the way Bogart was able to approach women. During the resource installation he imagined Humphrey Bogart over his shoulder telling him (with his Humphrey Bogart voice and cool confidence), "just ask the lady for a date." Holding that image he did a short set of eye movements, which increased his sense of confidence and courage.

POSITIVE MEMORIES AS RESOURCES

It can be helpful to draw upon a client's history and focus sessions on memories of when he or she felt loved, nurtured, powerful, in control, and/or safe. These can include memories of receiving support, nurturance, or guidance from parents, siblings, grandparents, aunts and uncles, other relatives, teachers, clergy, friends, and lovers or partners. For example, if the client had been listened to and cared for by a certain teacher in grade school, have the client bring up the memory, with the emotions, body sensations, and other senses if possible. Then add the bilateral stimulation. This processing of positive memories breaks up the old story the client has of never being listened to or cared for, and new associations may arise of other times the client was listened to. Suddenly, she may see that she had created an erroneous assumption about herself and her life. EMDR processing of the positive life experiences can dissolve the solidity of the negative self-concept, as it strengthens what is positive and adaptive.

Sally, a client with an early history of physical and sexual abuse and the traumatic loss of her mother as a young child, struggled with chronic depression. We focused several EMDR sessions on fragments of memories of being loved by her mother. Part of Sally's trauma was the loss of the memories of her mother; this loss resulted in difficulty in providing nurturing and comforting to herself. We began the bilateral knee tapping while she focused on body memories (she had no visual memories) of her mother holding her in her lap, and she could feel the comforting of her mother's embrace as I tapped on her knees. Visual memories emerged during the sets of tapping; these strengthened the feeling. Prior to the resource installation, she believed she had not been loved and was unlovable. After the strengthening of the positive memory of her mother's loving her, she felt that her mother did love her and could assert that she was lovable. Later, during the processing of traumatic memories, we used the memory of her mother to help with interweaves and session closure.

Memories of positive or neutral experiences and adaptive coping efforts can also be targeted. One man I worked with had a terrible history of emotional neglect. He suffered from chronic low-grade depression and diminished self-esteem. His early childhood was quite bleak and included sexual abuse. We began our EMDR work by focusing on any positive memories he had of his childhood. We targeted these positive memories and processed them; as his depression and the global feeling that his whole life was miserable lifted, he felt lighter and more hopeful.

MUSIC AS A RESOURCE

Some music evokes a sense of strength, courage, peace, beauty, and joy. Music that strengthens positive feelings and has meaning to the client can be installed with bilateral stimulation. The client can bring in pieces that she deems particularly inspiring. As she listens to the music, the therapist adds bilateral stimulation to strengthen the positive feelings. The therapist may also choose music with lyrics that he or she feels would be beneficial to the client. Another variation would be to have the client sing a soothing lullaby to his or her child self during the installation.

MOVEMENT

Movement is another valuable resource. The client can be asked to remember a time when he or she did something physically empowering. "Remember when you were running and you felt strong and in your body!" "Remember doing Tai Chi!" "Remember how it felt during your model mugging course to be able to protect yourself!"

Clients can also move their bodies during the session and install the movement with bilateral stimulation. One man I worked with felt empowered when he stood up. As he stood up and felt himself large and physically grounded, I tapped on his back to install the feeling. Other clients may want to move their hands and arms and bodies more fully. The use of bilateral auditory tones can make it possible to install the movements.

IMAGES FROM NATURE AS RESOURCES

Nature provides a wealth of positive images. The image of a clear mountain lake can bring a feeling of peace and calm. A towering mountain can evoke a sense of enduring strength and power. The vastness of the ocean, in which one's problems are seen as mere waves, is another resource image from nature. One client used the image of the weeping willow tree providing shelter, refuge from summer heat, and a swing from its supple branches as a positive resource.

Resource Installation

A SAMPLE PROTOCOL

Leeds has developed a protocol for the identification and installation of resources that focuses on current life difficulties, blocking beliefs, and maladaptive schemas. The following is a modification of his protocol. (Leeds, 1997, 1998; Leeds & Korn, 1998; Leeds & Shapiro, in press). A more complete presentation of this protocol can be found in Leeds and Shapiro (in press).

1. The therapist can begin the identification of the needed resource by asking the client to focus on a current life situation that is difficult for her, a blocking belief, or a life issue.
   For example, one woman was having difficulty feeling her own power and standing up for herself in her work situation.

2. Next the therapist asks the client what quality or qualities she would need to better deal with the situation, belief, or issue.
   In this case the client said she would need to feel a sense of self-esteem and empowerment.
   Explore with the client times when she felt some self-esteem and empowerment. If she cannot think of even one time, she can think of someone else dealing effectively with this type of situation. The person could be someone she knows personally, someone from a movie, TV, or book, a historical or religious figure—anyone at all. It could even be a symbolic representation of this resource.
   In the above case the client chose Maya Angelou as an example of someone who had strong self-esteem and was powerful.

3. Next ask the client to describe the image or memory she has chosen in more detail. Have the client provide sensory detail; what does she see, hear, feel, smell, or taste? What emotions does she feel and what does she feel in her body?

   In the above example the client said that when she thought about Maya Angelou she could feel strength in her body. She began to give animated descriptions of how Maya had been able to speak calmly in public after some difficult situations.

4. The therapist asks the client to say a cue word or phrase with the resource he or she wants to amplify.

   In this case the client chose the cue word "Maya."

   The installation of the positive resource may or may not be done, depending on the client. Some clients will flip to the polar opposite when the bilateral stimulation is used or may begin processing traumatic memories. For others, the addition of the bilateral stimulation will enhance the felt sense of the resource.

5. The installation of the positive resource is done much as with the standard protocol for traumatic memories: The client is asked to focus on the image, feelings, the cue word or phrase (if one is used), and the therapist adds the bilateral stimulation. A short set of bilateral stimulation is used (10 to 14 passes or taps). Watch the client for changes. If she looks distressed, stop immediately. Otherwise, after the set ask her what comes up for her. If she reports that the positive feelings have gotten stronger, continue for two to three sets of bilateral stimulation. Stop the bilateral stimulation when you feel that the resource has been strengthened. If the processing has become negative, stop immediately and consider choosing another resource.

   As the client focused on Maya and how competently she handled a difficult situation, she moved her eyes back and forth. The sensation of strength increased and the client remembered times when she had felt strong and competent.

6. You can repeat this process for many different qualities that the client wants to develop and strengthen. A future template can be added by having the client imagine using the resource in different situations. After the resource installation, the client felt *herself* more powerful and capable of handling difficult situations. Adding the eye movements, she then was able to take her new sense of empowerment into an imagined scene at her workplace

CASE EXAMPLE

Marguerite, a bright, competent middle-aged woman who was seeking employment in another state, found resource installation work valuable. One week, she came to her regular session and complained of extreme anxiety. She was dreading the phone call she had to make later that day to the CEO of the firm that was considering her for a position. All of her prior contact with that company had been by letter and e-mail.

Her fear was that the man would yell at her. She knew her fear was irrational, but she was unable to get past it. When asked if she'd ever had an experience like that, she described a former male boss who yelled at all of her co-workers. Always afraid he would yell at her, she went to great lengths to keep him happy. Describing this, her neck and shoulders became tense and her head ached.

Her therapist asked her if she could recall a time when she felt strong and confident. She remembered a scene and time when she felt full of self-confidence and was comporting herself in a way in which she would like to deal with the CEO later that day. When she did, she focused on her body sensation and the positive cognition, "I am intelligent and competent and a good person for the job." She did three short sets of eye movements and then imagined the presence of three support figures whom she wished to be with her when she made the call. Visualizing them and herself as she would like to be on the phone with the CEO, she did a couple more short sets. She left the office feeling enthusiastic about making the call!

After making the call, she was *amazed* at her success and how powerful the EMDR had been! She had not experienced *any* dread whatsoever after the session that morning—only a few flutters of excitement. She said, "I sailed through the call! It was really easy, and I couldn't believe I was doing it."

Reinforcing Skill Development and Sense of Mastery

Korn (1997) recommends using EMDR in the first phase of treatment to develop a sense of mastery and to increase ego strength. Bilateral stimulation can install positive coping thoughts and images the client reports to the therapist. These can include success at handling triggers, tolerating distress, and being assertive. As the client thinks about these positive incidents, ask her to attend to how that feels in her body. What positive belief does she have about herself when she thinks about the experience? Have her hold the positive image, body sensation, emotion, and positive cognition together and do some sets of bilateral stimulation.

Popky (1997) suggests asking the client to imagine a positive goal state or future self. When the client can bring up the image, bilateral stimulation is employed to strengthen it.

During this beginning phase of treatment, as is standard in EMDR preparation, the therapist informs clients about EMDR—the procedure, what to expect, theories about how it works, and when they might begin to use EMDR in the reprocessing of traumatic memories. Together therapist and client determine the best time to begin the reprocessing work.

Chapter 6

The Middle Phase: Processing and Integration

The middle phase is the often intense and painful targeting and reprocessing period. It begins when the client and therapist feel prepared to begin the reprocessing of traumatic memories. This chapter provides an overview of this phase of treatment, which is then detailed in Chapters 8–10.

Treatment does not move in a linear fashion but in stages, because it is individualized for each client and follows the process of reexperiencing and integrating the trauma. Sometimes this stage of therapy feels like two steps forward and one step back.

For a period of time clients may process one incident or a set of memories related to a particular theme intensively, which may affect functioning in their relationships and work life. They may feel worse for a while, as their inner life is consumed with memories and their significance. But, after the memories have cleared, and clients have integrated the new information, they may feel better and function at a *higher* level. Then, while uncovering and reprocessing new memories, they may feel worse again until those new memories are cleared. Clients might need to let members of their family know that they are working on these issues. As I explained in Chapter 3, this work is usually not short-term treatment or a quick fix with severely abused clients. Consequently, clients should be adequately prepared for extended treatment that may be intense and disrupt their lives for a while.

EMDR processing sessions should be scheduled in a way that takes into account that the client will most likely feel open, raw, and vulnerable afterwards. Clients should be encouraged to make whatever personal arrangements are needed for post-session care. The client may want to be picked up by a loved one after the session and should not have pressing personal or professional responsibilities. EMDR processing sessions should not be done right before the therapist or client goes out of town.

Safety, Responsibility, and Choices

There are three main issues with corresponding beliefs, that most abuse survivors share: *safety, responsibility,* and *choice* (see pp. 20–23; Parnell, 1997a; Shapiro, 1995). These issues come up repeatedly during the work with adults who have been sexually abused as children. It is important to listen for these issues when they arise and intervene appropriately. They arise in all three phases of the treatment, affect the transference and therapeutic relationship, and are important themes in the EMDR processing sessions. Beliefs associated with these three issues may cause processing to become blocked and looping to occur. (In Chapter 9, I provide many examples of how interweaves can be used to release blocked processing.)

Treatment Planning

EMDR use varies according to client needs and presenting problems. Treatment planning is done collaboratively, with the therapist and client discussing and revising the plan as the treatment goes along. Sometimes clients come into treatment desiring EMDR and wanting to work very intensely on their disturbing memories; they don't want to "waste time" with the history-taking or relationship development. I have been pressured by clients in this way and have at times accommodated clients against my clinical judgment, only to have problems develop later when the transference became very strong and the relationship wasn't strong enough to work it through. This is particularly true with borderline or narcissistic clients who have had prior therapy and dismiss the importance of the therapeutic relationship. It is essential that the therapist have enough historical information and a strong feeling of connection with the client before engaging in the EMDR processing. Even if the client feels ready, the therapist must feel ready also. Remember, it is a relationship. You want to be attuned to the client's needs, have a good intuitive sense of the client, and understand his/her ego structure and primary beliefs.

There are many ways to go about developing a plan of action in the middle phase of treatment. Some clients want to focus on their presenting problems, like an aversion to sex with their partners, low self-esteem, phobias and fears, eating disorders, and/or limiting beliefs about themselves they believe are associated with childhood abuse. In these cases, one might develop a treatment plan that focuses on these issues and the associated memories.

For example, Carole felt strong aversion to sex with her husband, whom she loved. She believed that the sexual aversion was related to sexual abuse she was subjected to by her babysitter's husband when Carole was a little girl. Memories of the sexual abuse were targeted and processed. Some sessions were also spent processing related issues, such as feeling betrayed and abandoned by her mother, who left her with the babysitter and her husband for long periods of time. The effects of the processing sessions were checked from time to time, and she was asked how she felt about making love with her husband. Different aspects of the problem were identified, such as difficulty stating her needs in the relationship, and they were then targeted and processed. The focus of the therapy remained the improvement of her marital relationship through reprocessing the past. When this had been completed to her satisfaction, she terminated treatment, with the understanding that she could return if she so desired.

Pete, a middle-aged man from the Midwest with no prior experience in therapy, wanted to work on relationship issues. He thought he may have been molested as a child by his grandfather. He had a drinking problem, for which he was receiving treatment elsewhere, and was attending AA meetings. His presenting problem was compulsive exhibitionism: masturbating in public places with the risk of discovery creating sexual arousal. This long-term problem was becoming more and more out of control, and he was in increasing danger of being discovered.

He was seen nine times over three months and did talk therapy, inner child work, and EMDR. He focused primarily on relationship issues and on some fears and phobias. His treatment included four 90-minute EMDR sessions; only one session focused on the acting out behavior.

The EMDR target for that session was a vague memory that had a sexual feeling and involved his grandfather. During the processing, what he believed was the full memory of what had happened was revealed to him in bits and pieces. These pieces came together and formed a cohesive picture that made sense to him. He realized that his bizarre sexual acting out behavior was a repetition of what his grandfather had done to him. He had a strong "ah ha!" feeling and a sense of relief and clarity at the end of the session.

The following session Pete reported that his desire to act out sexually was gone. Soon after, he ended therapy and continued with his recovery treatment. In a phone call two years later he reported that he felt the EMDR had helped him a lot and that important "puzzle pieces" had fallen into place and continued to do so. He felt that more work was still needed to clear it all out, but it was not a major concern for him, and he no longer felt that the behavior was out of control.

Sometimes clients want to work on disturbing memories and flashbacks or dreams that have plagued them for years. These memories can be systematically organized in a way that makes sense to the client. The therapy then focuses on clearing the memories. Memories can be organized in several different ways. They can be grouped around *perpetrator* (father, mother, sibling, neighbor, etc.), *location of abuse* (all incidents that took place in the bedroom, bathroom, basement, etc.), *age of the victim* (work on all of the memories of abuse in preschool age, latency, teen years), *type of trauma* (intercourse, oral sex, fondling, etc.), *schema* (themes of fears of abandonment, negative body image, etc.), *issues,* or *somatic complaints.*

For example, the client may want to clear all the memories of abuse with her brother. EMDR processing can begin by working on the worst, earliest, or most representative memory. Each EMDR session targets these memories until the client feels free of their emotional charge. When the problem has been alleviated, the client may wish to end treatment, take a break from treatment, or work on another issue or group of memories.

EMDR treatment of abuse survivors is not usually straightforward or systematic. Often, work begins with one set of memories or presenting problems, but new issues, memories, or concerns open up during the course of treatment. After an EMDR session focusing on a particular memory, new information may arise between sessions in the form of memories, flashbacks, dreams, or body sensations. These may be chosen as targets for the next session, as they feel the most compelling to the client and therapist. The therapist and client discuss whether they want to diverge from the original issue and work on the new one for a while or continue to focus on the original issue until it has been satisfactorily resolved, and then turn to the new issue. The treatment plan is changed and adapted as the therapy goes along. Therapy is a co-creative process in which the therapist and client work together, conferring and discussing the best ways to do the healing work.

Sometimes clients bring new issues into therapy, diverting focus from the more intense early material. This may be an attempt to more comfortably pace the treatment, or it may be resistance. Again, it is important to discuss this with the client and together decide the best course of action.

Working with Abreactions

Clients who have been abused as children commonly have strong emotional responses while processing traumatic material from the past. I have a number of recommendations for working with abreactions, some from Shapiro's book (1995) and others from my clinical experience.

Abreactions are a common experience, *but they are not necessary for client healing.* Some therapists and clients mistakenly think that the EMDR processing isn't going well if the client isn't having a strong emotional release. There is no right or wrong way to process, and everyone processes differently. Some people process the past in a much more subtle way than others. Some have enormous emotional releases, during which they emit blood-curdling screams and cry uncontrollably. Therapists should be prepared for either experience. It is helpful for therapists to remember that EMDR is not causing the client's distress but rather is releasing it from the client's system (Shapiro, 1995). Abreactions usually occur as information is being processed. When the client has passed through the abreaction, she usually feels some relief that the past painful information has been cleared from her body-mind.

Abreactions can continue for several minutes at a time and can appear like waves. There is a build-up—a crescendo—and then the intensity diminishes. Sometimes a client will experience one wave after another in close succession as associated memories link. In these cases the therapist can continue with the bilateral stimulation until it appears that the client either has completed the processing or wants a break. A client may have several abreactions in a session. The therapist watches the client's body signals to know when to stop the bilateral stimulation. The client may take a deep breath, stop crying, stop twisting her hands, and/or appear more relaxed.

Throughout the abreaction the therapist provides gentle encouragement to follow his or her fingers (or the light if using a light bar). If the client is having difficulty following the fingers (or light bar), the therapist might suggest that he or she "push my fingers (or the light) with your eyes." If the client is crying hard and the therapist is using eye movements, the therapist may want to change to tapping on the client's hands or knees—*after* asking the client's permission. It is important to have spoken with the client ahead of time to prepare him or her for this possibility and to get his or her permission.

Therapists should prepare clients for abreactions ahead of time and teach them that it is important to continue with the eye movements or other bilateral stimulation until the disturbance has subsided. The eye movements have been likened to keeping one's foot on the accelerator of a car as one moves through a tunnel. One doesn't take one's foot off until one is out of the tunnel. Taking one's foot off of the accelerator will mean that it will take longer to get out of the tunnel. One might even become stuck in the tunnel. The therapist tells clients at the beginning of EMDR processing that they can stop at any time if they so wish. Therapist and client agree upon a stop signal. This gives clients a sense of control over the process. As the client moves his or her eyes back and forth, the therapist gently encourages him/her to keep going, that it is "old stuff," like scenery seen from a train. The therapist reinforces the client's dual awareness that he or she is safe in the present while processing the past.

The therapist should be compassionately *present* for the client, providing emotional stability and a sense of safety during the abreactions. It is important that the therapist maintain a position of "detached compassion" (Shapiro, 1995), supporting the client without becoming overwhelmed by the client's process. It is as if a life rope connects the two; the client has gone deep below the water and depends on the therapist to guide him or her up to the surface if needed. The therapist's occasional gentle reminders, "It's in the past" and "I am with you now," reassure the client while he is immersed in the early traumatic memories.

It is important that the therapist not give the client the message that the therapist can't handle the intensity of the feelings expressed. This can feel very shaming to the client who already believes that she is bad or crazy. It can also frighten or alarm the client and give her the impression that something is wrong. Therapists should not try to shut down abreactions too soon or attempt interweaves before the client is allowed to fully feel her feelings and move through them on her own. Intervening prematurely is a common error made by newly-trained EMDR therapists, because they don't understand or trust the client's ability to process trauma with the bilateral stimulation. I strongly recommend that EMDR therapists experience EMDR as clients, so that they know what it feels like to process an abreaction to the end. Clients in the throes of a strong emotional release may frighten the therapist; however, it feels much worse to the client to be stopped by the therapist in the middle of an abreaction because the therapist is afraid. Clients can feel the information moving and clearing, even though this may not be apparent to the therapist. The therapist's countertransference can interfere with the client's healing and trust in the EMDR therapy.

Some clients abreact so loudly that it can present a problem to therapists who don't have sound-proof offices and are concerned about disturbing or alarming their neighbors. Some of the screams sound like someone is being murdered! These strong responses may come unexpectedly and surprise the client and therapist. If a client regularly has strong abreactions, it might be best to schedule him/her at a time when the work will not disturb others in the building and to warn neighbors that this might occur.

There are a number of ways to prepare a client for abreactive work. It is important that the client feel safe in the present as he is processing trauma from the past. Some clients who are following the lights on the light bar feel safer having the therapist sitting next to them holding their hand as they process. Clients may wish to have their partner, a close friend, or a concurrent therapist with them as they process. These present-day caring figures can give survivors support and encouragement to process their past traumas. It is important that these support people be adequately prepared for the processing sessions and that the therapist feel comfortable that they won't interfere or be traumatized by the experience. Some clients derive comfort from having with them an object that represents safety, e.g., a stuffed animal, a blanket, or a photograph of a loved one.

Some clients have difficulty expressing strong emotions in front of the therapist and inhibit their emotional releasing. They might correlate the expression of emotion with losing control. They might believe that if they were to let go of emotional control, they would fall apart completely and go crazy. They might also have difficulty trusting the therapist as they become vulnerable and regressed in the session. It is important to work with the client's beliefs about having feelings, expressing feelings, and letting his or her feelings be seen. Some of these beliefs may stem from childhood experiences of punishment for expressing feelings. "I'll give you something to cry about," one angry father said before severely whipping his son. On the other hand, some children control their emotional expression as a way to retain a sense of dignity and control. "I decided I would never give him the satisfaction of seeing me cry." These experiences and beliefs might be important targets for EMDR processing sessions.

There are a number of other techniques therapists can use to decrease the client's level of disturbance by manipulating the disturbing imagery (Shapiro, 1995). The therapist can suggest to the client that he or she:

- Change the memory into a photograph
- Change the memory into a black-and-white videotape
- Imagine the child self holding the hand of her adult self
- Imagine the child self being held by other nurturing or protective figures
- Imagine placing a protective glass wall between the self and the perpetrator, who is placed at a distance
- Imagine placing a protective glass wall between the self and the event

Varieties of Client Experience during EMDR Processing

DISSOCIATION

Clients who have been severely abused as children may dissociate during EMDR processing of traumatic memories. This normal response to overwhelming trauma can take many different forms. The client may feel disconnected from her body, report no emotion in the middle of processing a terribly traumatic experience, report feeling like she is floating above her body, feel spaced-out or dizzy, become sleepy, or go numb. She might also suddenly speak in a completely different voice and have no idea what she is doing in the therapist's office! The client's experience of dissociating during the processing may be a *memory* of dissociating during the traumatic incident being processed, or it may be that the client is actually dissociating in the session as a defense against the intensity of the affect. Possibly the client has a dissociative disorder.

Before deciding what to do when dissociation is suspected, the therapist should stop the bilateral stimulation and talk about what is happening with the client. If the dissociation observed is a memory of dissociating in the past, this memory can continue to be processed with EMDR in the session.

Help the client attend to her body sensations and maintain her dual awareness of being safe in the present as she processes old memories. You might want to make the client aware of the arms of the chair and the sensation of her feet on the floor. Clients might even be directed to pound on the arms of the chair in rhythm with the eye movements (Shapiro, 1995) to increase awareness of their body sensations. If the client has her eyes closed and the therapist is using tapping or auditory stimulation, the therapist can ask the client to open her eyes and "look at me directly." This brings her back to the present and reminds her of her connection to the therapist.

Clients can be asked to tap on the *therapist's* hands—left right, left right—as a means of creating the bilateral stimulation and keeping the client present in her body. The therapist can gently squeeze the client's hands, left right, to bring her back to her body awareness as she continues to move through the processing. In one case the therapist began by tapping the client's palms, then moved to squeezing the client's hands as the client began to dissociate. Then at one point in the processing, as the client became more "embodied," she began to squeeze the therapist's hands, continuing the bilateral stimulation.

I have heard of a client who brought ice in a small ice chest to sessions as a means of quickly restoring body awareness. When the client began to dissociate, she picked up an ice cube and held it in her hand, feeling herself present in her body and in the therapist's office.

Clients should be encouraged to talk about what they are experiencing during the processing if they are dissociating. Talking during the processing can increase the feeling of safety and connection between the therapist and client. It can decrease the sense of isolation so many abuse survivors felt both during and subsequent to the abuse. The information clients provide during their narrative can also be used to develop interweaves if the client becomes stuck. Finally, talking during the processing can help clients be more aware of being in the present moment. The therapist can also remind the client that she is safely in the therapist's office and that it is a safe place.

The therapist should pay close attention to the client and notice when the client begins to dissociate. The therapist can then gently remind the client to "keep your eyes moving. You are here with me now in my office, you are safe now, stay with me, feel your body, good . . . good."

The therapist's voice can be used to keep the client connected and present during the processing. It reassures the client that she isn't lost in the ozone. "That's it," "good," and "it's in the past," "I'm here with you now" calm the client and let her know that you are with her in the present.

If the client is dissociating because the incident is very upsetting to her, the client and therapist may decide to close down the session, return to the safe place for a break, or debrief for a while and then return to the EMDR processing with attention paid to the body, safety, and dual awareness. The therapist and client may want to talk about what caused the dissociation, which can provide valuable information about triggers. If the client decides she wants to continue with the processing, the above mentioned techniques can be used to keep the client in her body and aware of her presence in the therapist's office as she processes with EMDR.

If it is suspected that the client has a previously undiagnosed dissociative disorder, it is recommended that the therapist close the session, debrief the client, and seek appropriate consultation or referral for the client. Working with clients with dissociative disorders requires special training and expertise and is beyond the scope of this book.

CLIENT SLEEPINESS

Some clients become sleepy during EMDR processing, which may mean many different things. The therapist should talk with the client about it and determine what is causing it to occur. Perhaps the client is tired because of lack of sleep and the processing work is relaxing her and making her sleepy. The client's eyes may be tired. If this is the case, she may want to stop EMDR for the session or change to tapping or auditory stimulation.

Sleepiness may also be the client's resistance to the processing of emotionally charged information. If that is the case, talk with the client about what he or she is avoiding by falling asleep. The resistance itself can be targeted with EMDR and processed. "Where do you feel the resistance in your body?" "What belief about yourself is associated with the resistance?" "Is there a memory or image that goes with the resistance?"

As discussed earlier, sleepiness can also be a form of dissociation. Eve was a client who would immediately close her eyes and nod off when processing an abuse memory with her brother. As soon as she would begin to close her eyes I would remind her to "stay awake, keep your eyes open, it's old stuff," and she would open her eyes and continue to process the memory to completion. During the processing, Eve remembered that throughout her life she had used sleep as a means of escaping unpleasantness; her bed became a safe place or refuge. She realized that in her relatively happy present life she no longer needed to do that. She saw that she hadn't been fully awake to her life and that she had been repeating the old pattern out of habit.

Sleepiness during EMDR processing can also be a stimulated memory of being in that state of consciousness. Many clients who were sexually abused as children were molested while they were asleep in their beds. During EMDR processing they may never feel fully awake, and the abuse memory may have a dream-like quality that coincides with the state they were in at the time of the abuse. Some clients were also drugged or given alcohol as children before or after the abuse. One client felt very sleepy, nodded, and noticed the smell of alcohol during EMDR processing of an abuse memory. As the memory unfolded, she remembered that the abusers would force her to drink alcohol before they abused her. Another client recalled being raped while she was stoned. In these cases the therapist should keep the client awake and continue to process the memory to completion with EMDR. It is helpful to have the client talk, describing her experience, in order to keep the mind alert so she can complete the processing of the memory. Usually, after the memory has been processed, the client who a few minutes earlier could hardly keep her eyes open returns to a state of normal wakeful consciousness.

Some clients become sleepy during EMDR because they have been hypnotized by the eye movements. One woman was processing a horrendous rape with eye movements without any affect. After the first set of eye movements she reported no disturbance at all, a 0 SUDS. When she was asked to bring to her mind the original image of the rape scene to check if anything had been processed, she reported a SUDS of 10. She told the therapist that she had been informed in the past by a hypnotherapist that she was highly hypnotizable. For the next set of eye movements, she was asked to give a narrative account of her experience. As she spoke, she became aware of her emotions, which she was able to process. At the end of the session, when she returned to the original image, it had lowered to a SUDS of 0.

CLIENT NUMBNESS

Sometimes clients report feeling "numb" during EMDR processing. This is not necessarily an indication that they are not processing or that they have dissociated. Like sleepiness, it may be a memory that has been stimulated by the EMDR processing. I recommend that the therapist treat the numbness just like any other body sensation or experience. The therapist can ask the client, "Where do you feel the numbness in your body?" and take a SUDS reading. "On a scale from 0 to 10 how numb do you feel?" The therapist instructs the client to pay attention to the numbness in the body and begins eye movements. In my experience, the numbness usually changes with the bilateral stimulation, and memories or associations emerge. If the numbness does not change, the therapist can ask the client what he believes about himself. It could be that a belief such as "It's not safe to feel" is blocking the processing. Any beliefs can be explored with the client and then targeted with EMDR. The therapist can also ask, "What image goes with the numbness?" For example, Gillian reported an image of an enormous wad of cotton that represented the numbness and targeted that along with the feeling of numbness. Clients can also draw the feeling using art supplies the therapist has in the office. With the image or drawing, the sensation of numbness, and any belief that goes with it, the therapist can then incorporate the bilateral stimulation and process the target.

CLIENTS WITH BODY MEMORIES WITHOUT VISUAL MEMORIES

Many clients come into treatment with body memories that feel to them like they are related to some kind of early sexual abuse; however, they lack visual or narrative memory of what might have occurred. For instance, a woman sexually abused as a child who lacks a visual memory of the incident may not know why she is afraid of men, avoids intimacy, can't seem to trust anybody, is sexually inhibited, and wants to scream with rage and terror when her husband touches her in a loving, sexual way. Her *body* remembers (van der Kolk, 1994), but the body memory is not consciously linked with a visual memory of the abuse incident. To herself and others her reactions seem "irrational." For some of these clients, the processing of the body memory opens the door to the separate visual memory and brings about an integration of the disparate information. In these cases, EMDR seems to dissolve the barriers to information locked away in separate memory compartments; as a result, clients experience an integration of the images, body sensations, and behaviors that didn't make sense when experienced separately. These experiences are often described by clients as "puzzle pieces falling into place."

Many clients process body memories, but associated visual memories never arise during the sessions. While they experience many different physical sensations, they do not *see* anything. There are different reasons for this phenomenon. For some clients it may be that the body memory is in a separate compartment from the visual and narrative memory, which has been *completely* disassociated. Both whole memories and memory fragments often seem to be locked in separate "compartments" in the body-mind. The images may be stored in one compartment; the body's memory may reside in another. In some of these cases the visual memory never links with the body memory. For some reason the linkage might be broken, or the neural pathways linking the different compartments are not stimulated during EMDR processing. In my experience, clients have still benefited from the EMDR treatment despite the lack of visual memories. The following is an example of such a case.

Anya, whom I describe in Chapter 11, came into treatment because she was having difficulty in her relationship with her partner and believed the difficulty was linked to something traumatic she *felt* had happened to her as a child. Despite many years of therapy, she had no visual or narrative memory of what she believed had been sexual abuse but continued to have symptoms of abuse and a *feeling* something had happened. We targeted her body sensations and associated beliefs and very intense somatic processing resulted. During one EMDR session her body jerked, and she writhed in agony. Despite the intensity of her body's response, no visual memories arose. When I asked her what she believed was happening, she replied that she believed that she was reprocessing an experience of labor and child-birth. She could not recall this ever happening to her, and no clear images emerged—just vague dream-like imagery. I kept her moving through the intense body abreactions by continuing the eye movements until she reached a plateau and seemed calm. She had several of these intense body abreactions, which lasted several minutes, during the session and experienced a sense of relief after each one. At the end of the session she felt calm and cleared of the disturbance in her body. Following the sessions she reported an improvement in her symptoms and a change in the previously held negative beliefs about herself. Her sessions typically involved this intense body processing without a clear sense of the historical origins. After several months' work, her symptoms and relationship with her partner had improved significantly and she decided to end her treatment.

One woman began to cry in panic during EMDR processing and slipped off of the couch onto the floor. She was then overtaken by spasmodic jerk-ing simulating an orgasm. In her case, the therapist got down on the floor near her and gently encouraged her to continue with the eye movements, following the therapist's fingers, until the body reaction had subsided. The therapist and client were exhausted by the experience. In the week that followed her symptoms improved.

Many clients do not have visual memories of abuse because for some reason they couldn't see during the abuse. It could be that their eyes were closed or that the abuse occurred in the dark. Many children are molest-ed at night in bed. In one case the client had no visual memory because the perpetrator put something over her head. Clients often worry that they aren't doing EMDR correctly or it isn't working for them because visual memories aren't appearing. Clients should be reassured that it isn't a problem and encouraged to continue to process what is coming up for them.

MEMORY CHAINING

Clients who have multiple early traumas often have a difficult time com-pletely reprocessing a single memory because the memory they begin with links to another memory, which then links to another and another, with none of them resolved during a session. These associated memories are like links in a long chain. Clients can become overwhelmed by the memories unlocked during EMDR processing and can feel like multiple doors have been opened and all the horrible skeletons in the closet are emerging at once. There are a number of suggestions for preventing this from occurring.

As the session begins, the therapist can use guided imagery to help the client go to his safe place. When the client is there, surrounded by his nur-turing or protector figures, the therapist can suggest that he bring up the memory he wants to work on and imagine it on a movie or video screen.

The therapist states that they will work on one memory only. It will have a beginning, a middle, and an end. If the client wants to take a break, he can do so at any time and return to the safe place. A signal for stopping is agreed upon. When the client is ready, the memory can be brought to mind and the EMDR processing begun. This technique has been very helpful for clients who have a tendency to chain. It comforts them to know that they have control and will only work on one memory at a time. This process can be done with the client in the safe place, projecting the memory on a screen, or leaving the safe place, knowing he or she can return there as needed and bring up the memory to be worked on.

Another technique I use when a client seems to be chaining is to return frequently to the target image and check it. In this way the therapist keeps the client on a short tether, so that he or she doesn't go very far from the target memory. The motto is "When in doubt, return to the original picture and check it." Let's say the client has been working on a memory of having been abused at age three by her father in the bedroom and after several sets begins to process memories at age five and six at the family farm. Ask the client to "please return to mind the image we started with, the one of you and your father in the bedroom. What do you get *now* when you bring up the image?" The therapist is looking for change in the image, emotions, beliefs, or body sensations. If the client says, "I now feel angry, not afraid," the therapist instructs the client to "go with that" and again begins the bilateral stimulation. Clients don't seem to mind returning to the target memory when they have chained onto other disturbing memories. It doesn't seem to interfere with their processing and in fact seems to increase their trust in the therapist who is paying attention to their process and not allowing them to wander off too far and open too many of those memory closets. The therapist should take note of the memories that have been opened up and use them as potential future targets.

Pacing of Treatment

Depending on the needs of the client, EMDR can be used every session or interspersed between integrative talk sessions. I have seen clients on many different schedules, according to their needs. For example, I saw one woman twice a week for two years—one 90-minute EMDR session followed three days later by a 50-minute integrative session. She later decreased the frequency of her sessions to a weekly 90-minute session and then to a weekly, 50-minute session with occasional 90-minute EMDR sessions. Finally, she decreased to one 50-minute session every other week until she ended treatment. Some people have worked every session with 90-minute EMDR sessions, while others will do intensive EMDR work for several weeks and then want several shorter integrative sessions. I believe it is important for therapists to be flexible and accommodate their clients' needs.

In EMDR clients have to learn to process their memories at a pace they can tolerate so they will not feel overwhelmed and revictimized. This can be a problem because many sexual abuse clients have difficulty asking for what they want or are not in touch with themselves enough to recognize their needs. Therapists should pay attention to the pacing because some clients, believing EMDR will immediately erase years of abuse, may try to push their therapist into doing EMDR processing every session. They may come into treatment wanting an EMDR session every week or twice a week. For many sexual abuse clients this is contraindicated.

After intense EMDR processing of an abuse memory, the client may want to spend several sessions talking about and integrating the information that came up during the EMDR work. At the end of an EMDR session, it is helpful to discuss with the client what he feels he needs the following session. Some clients, even if they think they want to do another 90-minute EMDR session the following week, may change their minds when they return and, with the therapist's guidance, assess how they feel. Postponement of EMDR processing should not necessarily be interpreted as resistance. The work can be so intense that some clients need to spread the EMDR sessions out. That enables them to integrate the information that comes up and feel sufficiently grounded and stabilized before further processing.

As discussed in Chapter 4, art is useful in pacing treatment. It helps the client integrate the information that has come up and gives the client more of a sense of control over the process. Art can be done in the session or between sessions.

Chapter 7

The End Phase:
Creativity, Spirituality, and Integration

The end phase of treatment begins after most of the traumatic memories have been cleared with EMDR, the flashbacks and nightmares have ceased, and the client feels like he or she is free from his or her disturbing past. During this phase the therapist and client review the work that has been done—rejoicing in and celebrating the changes, noting any places where there is still work to be done, clearing any hot spots or triggers, working on identity exploration and development, focusing on the future, and filling developmental holes when possible with new life experiences.

In this phase clients typically experience an opening of creativity and spirituality. Free from the burden of past traumas, clients experience life as they never experienced it before: full of potential and endless possibilities for creative expression, exploration, and self development. As one client put it, "Now I have a life. Before EMDR I just existed; I went through my day-to-day routines on automatic pilot. My existence was very isolated, lonely, painful, and joyless. Now, however, I AM ALIVE, I AM FREE, I AM INDEPENDENT, AND I AM HAPPY!!"

This phase may last from a few sessions to several months, depending on the needs of the client and the situation. There is no fixed way this is supposed to be. Ideally, time is taken in this phase to complete and integrate the healing work that was done during EMDR processing, but for various reasons, including financial ones, not all clients desire to spend much time doing this. In my experience, many EMDR clients arrive at a place where they feel like they have cleared all of the trauma and simply don't have anything more to work on. They feel complete with the work and desire to move on and try their own wings.

This may feel sudden to the therapist. For example, Christina, who prior to her EMDR therapy had spent several years in long-term talk therapy, completed what she felt was a "piece of work" in a few months' time and wanted to live her life for a while without therapy. She spent only a couple of sessions in the termination phase and then left, knowing she could return. She knew she still had work to do but did not feel anything pressing at the time she left treatment.

Some come to EMDR therapy to work on a specific issue or memory and after reaching their goal wish to take a break to test what they have completed. Others describe the therapeutic work as occurring in layers. They complete all they can at one layer and perhaps return later, if necessary, if another layer of memories or symptoms reveals itself.

At the other end of the spectrum are clients like Melanie, who had been severely abused over several years at a young age by multiple perpetrators. Her EMDR treatment lasted three years, and she required about a year in this end phase of treatment. Afterwards she came back at different times for "tune-ups" when she found herself triggered by things in her life or felt stuck in some way.

Who Am I Now?

Once the pressure of the traumatic memories has been lifted and no longer keeps clients from living fully in the present, they may spontaneously begin to ask broader existential questions, such as, "Now that I am free from the limiting beliefs and terrifying images from the past, who am I?" The identification as survivor or victim of any kind has vanished and no longer defines who they are in the present. As one client put it, "The abuse happened in the past and so did a lot of other things. None of these things is who I am." This is a time for identity exploration and development. Melanie, whom I mention in *Transforming Trauma: EMDR*, expressed this well.

During my recovery, I started questioning "Who am I?" This was very frightening for quite some time, because the question was new to me. Other questions followed: Who am I in relation to myself? to my family? to nature? to the world in which I live? What am I doing with my life? Where am I headed? What is my purpose in being alive?

Time passed and I experienced small bursts of wisdom and insight. I realized that discovering the answers to my questions was the beginning of my inner journey, my quest to wholeness. I realized, too, that as in any journey there will be times when I am frightened, but there will also be times of pure joy and peace and that I couldn't let fear control and immobilize me. (Parnell, 1997a, p. 271)

Some clients, after fully expressing and processing their anger with EMDR, feel empowered in a new way, which may manifest in shifts in behavior. Clients may look for new careers, new relationships, new educational opportunities, and new creative ventures. Clients may feel that they are able to play for the first time. They do the things they could not do as a child. One woman who felt her child self enjoying the new freedom said, "I can do whatever I want now. I have a choice now."

EMDR therapists can further the process by sharing their clients' enthusiasm for their new selves and their joy in discovering the world. In many ways the therapist is like a parent who reflects the child's wondrous view of the world. This helps to increase the client's self-esteem and self-respect. It is good for clients to be able to share good times as well as bad, successes as well as failures, with the therapist.

During this time, the therapist may choose to encourage the client to work on issues of intimacy and healthy connections with others. This may require that the client actively engage with the world and develop friendships. It is important for clients to go out in the world and test the inner changes. Socialization skills may need to be taught. How do you talk to people? How do you make friends? Any fears or stuck places can be targeted and processed with EMDR. There may be old memories related to rejection that may be impeding connections with others.

Many clients need to reclaim their sexuality. Sexual issues can be targets for EMDR processing. A sex therapist who can sensitively work with a couple to find a safe, intimate, and pleasurable way of relating can be very helpful. Education about sexuality may be needed. Basic sex information that was never learned can often help clients who are confused about their own bodily responses (Maltz, 1991).

With some clients, the EMDR therapist may want to work to establish goals in the areas of work, education, or relationships. Clients may initiate new projects and begin to take reasonable risks with the support of the therapist. The client ventures out more and more into the world, gathering new life experiences and skills to replace the old. A new positive identity develops that is more powerful and secure because it comes from a connection with themselves. Melanie described this connection and self-assurance:

I feel connected to myself and to the world in a way that few people are. I'm one with myself on all levels: physically, emotionally, spiritually, and intuitively. I can contact my intuition and use it to guide my decisions, knowing that what I am doing is right and true to me. Because I can wait patiently for my wisdom surface, I can remain calm. I experience little stress for I know that the answers will come. . . .

My new connection with the world amazes me. I am discovering many facets of it through all of my senses. It's so exciting! I hear birds singing and children laughing. When I commute to work, I see beautiful rainbows to which other drivers seem oblivious. I purposely stand out in the rain so I can feel the drops touch my body. . . .

Whereas my life prior to EMDR work lacked direction, now I am constantly headed forward. I am not worried about tomorrow because I know that the actions and decisions that I make today will shape my future. I truly believe that I can handle whatever comes my way. My newfound confidence assures me that I can deal with the good and bad, happiness and pain, easy and difficult times. (Parnell, 1997a, pp. 272–273)

For many clients, spiritual questions arise, along with a desire to explore them more deeply. They experience a profound connection to their true selves and a trust in the world. One woman found after EMDR therapy that she was clairsentient—she had the intuitive gift of being able to sense in her body what other people were feeling. She went on to explore and develop this gift through formal intuition training, which brought a deep sense of purpose and meaning to her life. She envisioned a completely new career for herself, quite different from her previous stressful one. This new career involved healing work that felt *right* to her and was much more in harmony with who she was.

As a result of EMDR work another woman became very interested in women's spirituality and meditation. In particular, she felt a very strong affinity for goddesses. She immersed herself in fluid, expressive dance and art, which brought much joy to her life and led to newfound freedom in the expression of her femininity and sensuality.

Uses for EMDR in the End Phase

TARGETING CURRENT TRIGGERS

From time to time clients will report upsets in their lives that may be caused by people and situations. These may be as simple as anxiety at work because the client feels uncomfortable around the boss. EMDR should be used to clear remnants of shame, fear, anger, and anxiety. The present triggering situation can be traced to an early related event. The earlier event is targeted and reprocessed, after which the old is linked with the current situation, which is also cleared. If the client has difficulty connecting a past event with the current trigger, the EMDR therapist can begin with the current situation and process that. Clients who have been sober can become triggered and feel a desire to drink emerge. The EMDR therapist can target the triggering situation and the urge to drink. During this phase mostly mid- to low-level SUDS memories arise, although more disturbing ones sometimes do come up.

FILLING DEVELOPMENTAL GAPS

Adults who suffered from physical and/or sexual abuse as children often have gaps in different areas of their social, psychological, and educational development. These gaps may manifest in problems such as social inhibition, sexual problems, difficulty trusting others and making friends, dysfunctional interpersonal relationships, and difficulties with their employment. In this phase the therapist may need to provide education and guidance to help clients begin to fill some of these gaps. Referrals to special interest groups, assertiveness training, adult psychotherapy groups (not with a sexual abuse focus) for the development of socialization skills, classes at the local community college, or volunteer work may be helpful to clients as an entry into social relationships. Clients may need education and role-playing to develop social skills. Difficulties can be targeted and processed with EMDR, installing positive images and cognitions.

Clients may also need encouragement to learn how to play and then support to go out and do it. Therapists support their clients in doing the things the clients would have loved to do as children if they'd had the chance. Clients might even be encouraged to ask their child selves "What would you like to do?" and listen for an answer. Art classes, theater classes, dancing, river rafting, nature hikes, creative writing, and photography are some ways they might play as adults.

As they become healthier and more aware of themselves and the outside world and come to enjoy being active participants in their lives, clients also become painfully aware of what they never got in childhood. They may need to grieve for the childhood they never had. This can be a very poignant time, because the child's lost innocence can never be replaced, even by EMDR. The truth is that there are things they never got in childhood, like feeling safe in the company of adults, developing a healthy relationship with their bodies, and building the foundation for intimate relationships. EMDR cannot restore lost innocence, but it can increase the feeling of self-worth and of meaning in life. The therapist must be able to tolerate and hold these sad feelings, which may not necessarily go away with EMDR, since the client is regularly reminded of what he or she missed in childhood because of the abuse.

PROCESSING CURRENT FEARS RELATED TO MOVING OUT INTO THE WORLD

As the therapist and client focus on moving out into the world more, EMDR can be used to reprocess any fears that arise, such as fears of failure or of success, concerns about a new job, dating and relationships issues, and limiting beliefs or imagined uncomfortable situations. For example, if a client is going to interview for a new job and feels very nervous and insecure, the situation as the client imagines it can be targeted and reprocessed, and a positive cognition and image that will help the client feel more secure and prepared installed. Fear of the unknown can also be processed. One client imagined a black void as the picture that went with the fear. The image and fear were processed until the client felt relief. Any number of imagined difficulties can be reprocessed before they ever occur. This preemptive processing can be quite empowering.

A Case Example

Darleen had not worked in several months because of debilitating depression and anxiety. After several months of EMDR processing of the sexual abuse that contributed to her emotional instability, she felt ready to go back to work as a secretary. Darleen had gotten a job in an insurance office but felt anxious about her ability to perform her job. We decided to target her fears about working in this session.

The target image was the new office where she was going to work. The negative belief was "Change is stressful, and I can't adapt." The positive cognition was "I can change, and it will be good for me." Her SUDS was an 8. She felt anxiety and fear located in her stomach and chest.

DARLEEN: ►◄►◄►◄ I get stressed out answering the phones. I don't know why. . . . I do OK. Sometimes my mind goes totally blank. . . . People will think I'm an idiot . . . . I'm new here. ►◄►◄►◄

> *(Darleen then remembered her last job, where answering the phone was stressful because her employer was always late and was stressed. She reminded herself that in her new job there were more employees to help out and the job itself was less stressful.*

DARLEEN: It shouldn't be that stressful. ►◄►◄►◄ I do have a lot more support here and can ask John if Karen isn't there to help me . . . . he's another person if there's a problem. . . and I love that I have my own space and can be alone. . . . *(She then had a strong realization, with a positive cognition.) I can handle this...and I like it.* ►◄►◄►◄ I feel a lot calmer. . . . I didn't realize I had a lot of support there. We each have our own computer and space ... I can set things up the way I want. *(She had a sense of having control over her surroundings, an important issue for her.)* ►◄►◄►◄ I do have my own space and it makes me feel secure . . . my corner of the room.

LP: How do you feel now?

DARLEEN: It all feels right.

LP: Does anything not feel right? *(I want to check for any triggers or anxiety.)*

DARLEEN: I don't like the file room . . . it's too small. . . . *(She begins to become agitated.)*

LP: What would make you feel better about being in there?

DARLEEN: There's a door so I can get out . . . . and windows so I can see outside . . . and I don't feel the people to be threatening. *(She is realizing that the current situation is different from the past situation in which she was small, trapped, and unsafe.)*

LP: Imagine filing things in that room with all of those things you are aware of now: the windows, door, nonthreatening people.

DARLEEN: ►◄►◄►◄ I flashed back to the times when I was locked in the closet and was trapped before my father abused me. *I'm big now. I have control.*

LP: Think about that. ►◄►◄►◄ *(Installing the positive cognition.)*

DARLEEN: *(The positive cognition and imagery increase.)* I have my own space . . . there's a door. . . a lot of sunshine and fresh air . . . a lot of support I never had before. . . . I'm big and I'm in control . . . and after this I can relax a bit.

LP: Let's go back to the original picture. How disturbing is it to you now on the scale from 0 to 10?

DARLEEN: It's a 5.

LP: What keeps it from being a 0? *(I was surprised; I thought it would be much lower.)*

DARLEEN: ►◄►◄►◄ I'm being judged for two weeks to see if they want me. I don't like that. That makes me anxious. *(She had to pass a probationary period before she became a permanent employee of the company.)*

LP: Go with the feeling of being judged in your job for the next two weeks.

DARLEEN: ►◄►◄►◄ I am perfectly qualified and suited to the job. . . I know Microsoft Word and I can learn the other computer system. I'm not worried about learning it. . . . I like it. ►◄►◄►◄ I'm a lot calmer and patient. . . . I'm clearer now. I'm bringing a whole new person to the job.

INSTALLING A POSITIVE FUTURE TEMPLATE

EMDR can also be used to incorporate a positive future template (Shapiro, 1995). As Korn (1997) describes it, the therapist begins by providing the client with the necessary education. For example, the therapist might educate the client about how to say "no" and set appropriate boundaries when someone crosses the line and she feels uncomfortable. This can be a kind of assertiveness training. The therapist and client may role play the interaction to increase mastery of the learned behaviors. The therapist next asks the client to imagine the optimal behavioral responses along with the positive cognitions that enhance the feeling of self-efficacy. Bilateral stimulation is used to install this positive template. In this example the client might imagine herself in a situation with a date pressuring her for sex when she is not comfortable. She imagines herself saying "no" and walking away from him and saying to herself, "I can take care of myself" as she feels herself fully in her power. When she has the image, the positive belief, and the empowerment feeling all together strongly in her mind, she installs this with the bilateral stimulation. EMDR can also be used to reinforce positive resources, strengths, and new skills.

REVIEWING THE THERAPY

It is also important during this phase to review the work that has been done and look for any areas of disturbance that have not been cleared. It is as if the client and therapist have just put out a major forest fire and are now looking for any hot spots that could flare up and cause more damage. This review can be done by going back over the client's journals and artwork and the therapist's notes. Old memories that were worked on in past sessions can be brought up and checked for emotional charge. Any areas of charge can be targeted and reprocessed. The therapist should be alert to limiting beliefs and target any that emerge. This review can be very moving and empowering for clients, as they see how far they have come and how much they have changed.

Tune-ups

Sometimes during the end phase or after they have left treatment, clients become triggered by something, including recurring issues associated with milestones or developmental stages. A marriage, divorce, birth or death in the family, assuming a caretaking role with an ailing perpetrator, death of a perpetrator, a child's reaching an age at which the client's abuse occurred, etc., may cause the resurfacing of symptoms. For instance, Emily, who had been seriously abused by her older brothers as a child and had a psychotic mother, returned to treatment after the birth of her son. She was suddenly seized by anxiety and fear that her new baby seemed to trigger. The EMDR therapy went to a new layer, in which issues around her mother and memories of her early childhood were processed.

Other triggers to symptoms include new relationships, movies or TV shows depicting abuse or violence, or a medical or dental procedure, seeing someone from their past—or someone who reminds them of someone from their past. They may experience panic and anxiety seemingly out of the blue and want to work on clearing the source of the problem. This is normal and not a problem. It may not be possible to clear every trigger point with the initial treatment. It does not indicate that the therapy failed. There may be some area that was not apparent at the time of treatment but comes up later. Clients should be advised that this may happen and that they can come in and clear the disturbance with EMDR sessions. When clients end treatment, I always tell them that they can come back for a "tune-up" if they should ever feel the need or if something new should come up for them. Knowing the door is always open is very reassuring.

Gail had successfully completed a two-year EMDR therapy that involved the reprocessing of severe early childhood abuse. After six months in the end phase she felt she had completed the work and was no longer being triggered. A year later she returned to therapy because she was experiencing anxiety and nightmares as a result of a medical procedure. We targeted the experience with the medical procedure during an EMDR session and found it linked to a childhood trauma that we had not previously processed. At the completion of the session she experienced an alleviation of her symptoms. We met for a few sessions focused on the medical procedures and then she left therapy, knowing that she could return again at any time.

Medical procedures in particular can be triggers, because the client is again in a vulnerable, sometimes helpless situation dependent on others who could harm him or her. Many medical procedures are quite invasive and stimulate memories of earlier invasions. It can help to remind clients that the procedures, even though invasive or painful, are done for their good—not to harm them, as in the past. Emphasizing the control they *do* have is also important.

Clients may also return to therapy because new issues have come up for them. A new relationship or a new job may require some support and guidance and additional EMDR. New layers of traumatic memories or previously unprocessed issues may arise. Clients who have taken breaks from treatment may return because they have found areas in their lives where they are not living fully. For many people treatment of severe childhood abuse seems to happen in layers, like the layers of an onion, with work on one layer leading to a deeper one and then a deeper one. The therapy may plateau until it is time to work on the next layer. Clients may want settle in one layer for a while, taking a break from treatment, before peeling back the next one. Each person has his or her own rhythm and pacing.

Part III

. . . .

Tools and Techniques for Individual EMDR Processing Sessions

Chapter 8

Beginning EMDR Processing Sessions

This chapter explains how the therapist prepares the client for EMDR processing at the beginning of the session. Information is provided about how to modify the standard EMDR procedural steps if necessary and on how to select and develop EMDR targets.

Check-in and Reevaluation

When clients come in for an EMDR session, the therapist checks in with them, asking them how they are doing, how their week went, and if they noticed anything come up for them during the week. Clients who keep journals, write poetry, or do artwork as part of their between-session work may bring in some production and talk about it. Some clients bring in very vivid dreams after sessions. For example, Jan regularly had intense, distressing dreams of being chased by "bad guys." The feeling of danger from the dreams would spill over into her waking life and alarm her, because, although the dream's origins were unknown, her fear was quite real. She would regularly report the dreams and associations when she came into sessions, and these dreams often became the targets for EMDR processing sessions.

Clients may notice flashback images or new body sensations. Often new memories come up after sessions, which clients note and report. Adults severely abused as children often do not attain a 0 SUDS at the end of the session, especially if there have been multiple traumas over a long period of time. For that reason the processing of a target can bring up associated memories that become more intense during the week. For instance, a woman working on the memory of being sexually abused by her neighbor may get the SUDS down to a 2 or 3 but feel something else connected to it—just a *feeling*. During the week fragments of the associated memory may come up for her, fleeting images appearing and disappearing in the corner of her eyes and leaving her feeling sick in the pit of her stomach. She may feel that these image fragments relate to the work that was done the previous week.

Triggers should also be reported, as well as any area of reactivity or difficulty. As the client is talking, the therapist takes notes and listens for possible targets. Is there a theme emerging that should be explored more fully? If the client is reporting persecutory dreams, feeling fearful at home and at work, and seems removed and cautious with the therapist, then fear is the theme that should be explored with the client.

The target from the previous EMDR session should also be checked to see if it has changed. The therapist asks the client to "bring up the image we worked on last week and tell me what comes up for you." As the client refers back to the image, he or she reports what is perceived. If the target was not reduced to a 0 SUDS in the prior session, it is likely that it is still charged and may reveal new information. For instance, the primary emotion with the target may have been fear; now it has changed to anger. This signifies that processing has occurred and a new "anger" channel has opened. Checking the target can also reveal an associated memory that was not apparent the previous session. By checking the target, therapists gain feedback about how the EMDR therapy is progressing (is the target image at a higher, lower, or unchanged SUDS from the previous session?) and additional information for target formulation.

Modifications of the Standard Procedural Steps

Therapists may want to make several modifications of the standard EMDR procedure reviewed in Chapter 1 when working with some adults abused as children.

SAFE PLACE AND RESOURCE INVOCATION

The first modification is the use of the safe place and resources before starting the processing. When a client is going to process what she knows to be something highly charged, it is best to guide her to her safe place after identifying the salient issue or memory. In the safe place the client can call on the resources developed in prior sessions to be with her as she processes the memory. Some clients may want a large contingent of protectors, and nurturing figures.

SOME HELPFUL INSTRUCTIONS FOR THE CLIENT

The instructions given to clients in their safe place are meant to increase their sense of safety and control. For clients who have the tendency to chain one memory to another, it can be helpful to tell them that they will process one memory and that it will have a beginning, a middle, and an end. They can also be reminded that they can stop at any time and return to the safe place. They are in control.

Clients who need to put the memories at a distance as they process can be told *"when you are ready you can bring up the incident and see it projected on a movie screen. As you watch the movie you can remind yourself it is just a movie."* Likewise, they can imagine that they are watching the memory on a video monitor. This gives them a sense of control and of distance from the memories. They can be told that they hold the remote control to the video player in their hands and can fast-forward, stop, rewind, or edit whenever they wish. *"Remember, you are safe in the present processing old memories from the past."* The desired wording can be established ahead of time with the client, who can tell the therapist which instructions work best for him or her.

MODIFICATIONS IN THE EMDR SET-UP

Therapists may encounter several problems using the standard EMDR protocol with abused clients, particularly severely sexually abused clients. Many do not have visual memories. They may have body memories, negative beliefs about themselves and the world, and strong emotional reactions—without a picture. Coming up with an initial picture can be frustrating or impossible.

Some clients abused as children have difficulty coming up with a positive cognition. With a traumatic memory activated, they feel so utterly terrible that trying to think of something positive feels preposterous and frustrating. In these cases, the therapist can try to help the client to a "process" positive cognition (such as, "I can learn to trust myself"). For instance, it may be very difficult for a client who has activated a memory of being orally raped and threatened with death to rate the positive cognition "I am safe" above a VoC of 1. However, the words, "I am safe in this office" can serve as a useful stabilizer and a light at the end of the tunnel. For others, because of the difficulties, the positive cognition may have to be omitted in the beginning, but a positive belief that emerges for the client at the end of the processing session should be installed. The therapist should be extremely sensitive to the needs of those clients who have great difficulty with the positive aspects of the standard protocol. The difficulty is itself diagnostic of those clients who need ego-strengthening procedures, such as establishing a safe place and using nurturer or protector figures, before beginning the processing. Struggling to achieve any outcome can derail the therapy process and harm a fragile therapeutic relationship.

Some clients require a modification of the numeric rating scales (VoC and SUDS). In theory the ratings are important to provide a baseline to help the client and therapist observe the changes that occur during the processing. I sometimes deviate from following this part of the protocol if I feel it will be disruptive to the client. For some clients, the use of number ratings is experienced as too clinical and unrelated. The measurements may cause them to feel objectified and dehumanized by the therapist, just as they were by the perpetrators. Some clients have performance anxiety and are sensitive to failure. The intention of the scales is not to elicit these other issues, which can be confusing and hinder processing the target trauma memory.

For some clients the memory is so obviously distressing that asking for a SUDS reading can break the empathic connection and disrupt the therapeutic alliance, particularly if they are obviously abreacting when the therapist asks for a reading. If taking measurements at that time would, in the therapist's judgment, disrupt the process and feel unempathic to the client, the therapist should omit the measurements in the beginning and start the bilateral stimulation with the elicited memory. In cases like this, it is important to establish the safe place and resource figures before the memory is elicited to provide a safe stable base from which to begin and to which the client can return. The SUDS reading can be taken later in the processing session to enable the therapist and client to determine the level of disturbance.

Some clients have a difficult time eliciting the memory at all. They have worked hard all of their lives to contain and control their painful memories. This is also the case for some dream material that might have been very distressing during the dream, but has since faded so that the client has difficulty evoking it. The client and therapist may both believe that the targeted memory has a high SUDS because of the content of the memory (for example, a childhood rape), but the client has a difficult time feeling the feelings associated with it. For these clients, if the therapist follows the standard set-up, directing the client to shift her focus from the image and negative cognition to the positive cognition and VoC (right brain, left brain), the client may lose any affect and connection to the memory that she felt at the beginning. In these cases, the emphasis in the set-up should be on eliciting the memory network as strongly as possible with the image, negative cognition, emotions, and body sensations activated, so that the client can successfully process the targeted memory to completion.

For example, Cindy, who had been abused by her father as a child and was suffering from low self-esteem, recounted a memory of being yelled at and threatened by her father. She knew this was an upsetting memory but didn't feel much emotion when she told the story. The negative cognition was "I'm bad." The positive cognition she struggled with, seeming to go up into her head to find "I'm OK as I am." She got further into her head with the VoC, which she again had difficulty with. When she tried to bring up the target picture after the VoC she almost couldn't find it. I could see that leaving the experience of the memory to get a positive cognition and VoC made it hard for her to reaccess the memory. Because of her difficulty with the VoC, I skipped the SUDS rating and began the eye movements after the emotions and body sensations. Later during the processing I got a SUDS rating to determine her level of distress. In future sessions I omitted the ratings at the beginning because of her difficulty evoking memories.

If the use of the measurements is experienced by the client as an impediment to the therapeutice relationship, then the measurements are not serving their intended purpose. A verbal description of the SUDS can be used instead, or the client can use his or her hands to indicate a large or small disturbance, as is done with children (Shapiro, 1995; Tinker & Wilson, 1999). While the therapist should try to get some form of positive cognition and VoC when possible, use your clinical judgment, as well as your knowledge of your client and how EMDR works, and do not force the client to try to make him or her fit into the protocol. This is particularly the case since at the end of the session an entirely new belief may emerge that is a perfect fit for where the client has arrived.

Table 8.1
. . . .

Typical Negative Cognitions for Sexual Abuse Survirors

Safety
I am not safe.
It isn't safe to be in my body.
I'll die if I tell.

Responsibility
It was my fault.
I have done something wrong to deserve this treatment.

Choice Control
I am a victim.
I am a child.
I am helpless.
I have no control.
I'm trapped.
I'll lose myself.
I have no choice.

Interpersonal Relationships
I have to take care of others before myself.
I don't deserve to have a healthy relationship.

I am invisible.
I have no voice.
I can't express my thoughts.
I don't deserve to want.
Self-esteem
I am bad.
I am dirty.
I am damaged goods.
I am unlovable.
There is something terribly wrong with me.
I am unworthy.
I'm not good enough.
I'm not valuable.
I'm evil.
I am a burden.

Trust
I cannot trust anyone.
My rage will destroy.
I'm disloyal if I tell.

Sexuality
I don't have any sexuality.
Love and sex don't go together.
Sex is gross.
Sex is bad.
I can't have sexual pleasure.
My body and its feelings of pleasure are bad.
Sex is only used to hurt people.
Sex is selfish.
I am bad for feeling sexual.

. . . .

Targets do not have to have all of the components in order for EMDR processing to be successful. Modifications can be made in the target by eliminating components that you either cannot find or that are not clinically appropriate or necessary for the client. Keep in mind that the modified protocol has not been validated by research. While therapists may choose to use modifications at various times, make sure that you have an experiential baseline with standard EMDR protocols as described in Shapiro's 1995 book and understand the reasons for the EMDR procedures and components before deciding to eliminate any of them in a given case.

EMDR sessions can be quite successful with a simplified protocol that uses only the most essential elements. Elements that can be eliminated when therapeutically necessary are the SUDS, positive cognition (in the initial set-up), and the VoC. This is similar to the protocol modifications used for EMDR with children (Tinker & Wilson, 1999), except that Tinker recommends taking a SUDS reading with children. (Adults show their emotions more visibly than young children and can tell the therapist how distressed they feel.) In rare instances the image and negative cognition can also be eliminated if clients cannot come up with them without becoming frustrated. This clinical decision relies on the therapist's empathic judgment. *The most important elements are body sensations and/or emotions, along with some kind of cognitive component combined with the bilateral stimulation.* It is possible to begin processing with only body sensations, but the processing is more likely to be diffuse and go into many different channels. *Well-developed targets, which include the image, negative cognition, positive cognition, VoC, emotions, SUDS, and body sensations, set the stage for thorough and complete processing and increase the likelihood of successfully resolving the target. The idea is to activate as much of the negative memory network as possible and then process it with the bilateral stimulation.*

According to Shapiro (1995), "The purpose of identifying a desired positive cognition is to set a direction for treatment, to stimulate the appropriate alternative neuro networks, and to offer the therapist and client a baseline (the VoC rating) from which to assess progress" (p. 59). "The ability to define an alternative view of the trauma in reasonable language offers hope of escape from the pain of self-denigration" (p. 60). Shapiro (personal communication, 1999) believes that the use of the positive cognition, SUDS, and VoC fosters in many clients both clinical containment and ease of processing. Many experienced EMDR therapists working with multiply traumatized abuse clients employ all of the components most of the time and validate its efficacy, while other seasoned EMDR therapists modify the protocol more frequently with their multiply traumatized clients and also report positive treatment results. The differences reported may have to do with therapists' theoretical orientations, varied treatment setting (inpatient, private practice, outpatient clinic), and the kinds of clients they see in treatment. However, keep in mind that the standard protocols are the ones that have been validated by research—the modified protocols have not been tested. Therefore, while clinical exigencies may necessitate a deviation, it is best to employ all of the components with any given client when possible.

It is advisable to develop the target in a fluid, easy way that is attuned to the client. Do your best to help your clients come up with each target component, but move on if too much difficulty arises. Do not struggle with the components. You don't want the set-up to traumatize you or your clients. You can guide them, offer suggestions, and do your best to come up with the parts. You might want to use the list of common negative cognitions for sexual abuse survivors (Table 8.1) for ideas.

Table 8.2
. . . .

Modified EMDR Protocol For Adults Abused as Children

1. *Check-in and reevaluation*
2. *Identification of the problem, issue, or memory*
   "What would you like to work on today?"
3. *Safe place and resources invocation for support (optional for adults abused as children. Make sure the safe place or other resources are strong and available.)*
4. *Picture*
   Identify the image or picture that is associated with the worst part of the memory.
   "What picture represents the worst part of the incident?"
   An abstract mental image or a drawing can be used.
   The picture can be skipped if the client cannot come up with one without difficulty. The therapist might say, "Just think of an incident."
5. *Negative cognition*
   "When you bring up the image what do you believe about yourself?"
   Have the client make the statement using "I" in the present tense. It should be a presently held negative self-referencing belief. It is useful when the child self is activated to use simple child's language. Look for language that intensifies the memory network like, "I am a bad girl" or "I am a bad boy."
6. *Positive cognition*
   "When you bring up the image what would you like to believe about yourself now?" A modified positive cognition can be used, such as "I can begin to heal," or "I can learn to love myself." (Skip only if disruptive to the process or therapeutically contraindicated.)
7. *VoC*
   "On a scale from 1 to 7, where 1 is completely false and 7 is completely true, how true does 'I can learn to love myself' feel to you now?" (Skip only if disruptive to the process or therapeutically contraindicated.)
8. *Emotions/feelings*
   "When you bring up that incident and those words (negative cognition, e.g., "I am a bad girl"), what emotion(s) do you feel now?"
9. *SUDS (skip only if it seems disruptive to the client's process)*
   "On a scale of 0 to 10, where 0 is no disturbance and 10 is the highest disturbance that you can imagine, how disturbing does it feel to you now?"
10. *Location of body sensation*
    "What sensations do you notice in your body as you think about the incident?"

11. *Desensitize*

"I'd like you to bring up the image, along with the emotions and body sensations and say to yourself [the negative cognition, e.g., 'I'm a bad girl') and follow my fingers."

. . . .

How to Develop and Use Specific Targets for EMDR Processing

The development of targets, a very important step in EMDR, causes many therapists difficulty. When clients report what came up after the previous session, the client and therapist talk about what the focus of the EMDR session might be. The client might want to continue working on the issue from the previous week, or something else might have come up that he or she wants to focus on.

Targets are like doorways or entryways into the memory complex. *If you do not find the doorway you will not be able to enter into the processing. Targets that are too vague or not emotionally charged will often lead to surface processing that does not feel engaged or productive.*

TIPS FOR TARGET DEVELOPMENT

1. *Light up the memory network as clearly and completely as possible, engaging the different components (image, negative cognition, emotion, and body sensations) so the train can move unimpeded down the track to completion.*

2. *Get some kind of image if possible.* Even if the image is vague, it stimulates the visual memory track. The image can be abstract, such as a red blob that represents the client's anger or a drawing that represents what he or she is experiencing. The image can be metaphorical, symbolic, or dream-like. For example, with a person who has no visual memory but has strong body sensations, you might ask, "What image goes with the feelings in your body?" The client might say, "I get the image of someone stepping on me." That image then can be used as the target image. If the client has difficulty visualizing, it is not a problem. Clients can go with a vague sense of a scene. However, *make the image as clear as possible.* Bring in details. Have clients *see* what is around them as fully as possible.

3. *Don't worry about the order of the set-up.* Try to elicit the information in the order designated by the standard protocol; however, allow clients to provide you with the necessary information as it unfolds for them. If a client tells you about her emotions and body sensations before the negative cognition, don't worry. Note them and move on.

4. *Skip the SUDS, PC, and VoC if the client begins to abreact, if it interferes with the client's process by stimulating performance issues, or if it compromises the therapeutic alliance.*

5. *Have clients who have difficulty finding and eliciting a memory network stay in the memory as strongly as possible while the different target components are identified and stimulated.* For some clients coming in and out of the childhood memory disrupts the flow and causes them to leave the experience to intellectualize. Therefore, get the image, negative cognition, emotion, and body sensations while the client is in the memory experience. *Having clients close their eyes as they bring up the memory can help them to stay with it without interruption.* The whole set-up can move smoothly and rapidly this way; however, be attuned to any tendency to dissociate. Optimal processing occurs when clients have one foot in the present and one in the past.

Some clients provide you with all or most of the target components as they are describing the memory they want to work on. You can ask clients for the information that wasn't provided in their narration and then begin the bilateral stimulation when you feel the memory network is well stimulated.

Case Example

The following session began with such a set-up. Monica was very fearful of EMDR and of exposing herself to criticism. As a child, she had been beaten mercilessly and humiliated by her mother. Our relationship was strong, but I wanted to move her into the processing as effortlessly as possible after getting the memory network stimulated. I chose not to use the scales, which I believed would stimulate her fears of failure and humiliation.

Monica had been molested by an uncle repeatedly over several years when she was a little girl. She targeted the first abusive incident because it was most representative of all of the others. She was full of fear, anxiety, sadness, and despair. "I'll never be OK and you will think I'm foolish and that it's not such a big deal." We began the session with her going to her safe place, which was a hill near her family home that had lovely views, a place where she felt very safe and protected.

As Monica began to describe the memory, feelings and vivid imagery immediately arose. I did not feel it was necessary to get a SUDS, positive cognition, or VoC before the eye movements were begun because I knew it would be disruptive and would interfere with her accessing and engaging the memory network, since she was particularly sensitive to criticism.

She described going with her mother, little sister, and uncle to the hospital to visit an elderly relative. Monica and her sister were waiting in the car with their uncle. "He would run his hand up my legs under my skirt, and his fingers were under my panties feeling around. I didn't like that and wriggled away but he kept doing it. . . I scooted away. He did it to my sister, too. I made Lynnette back away in the corner. I had to take care of her and he started grumbling about what was wrong? I wasn't being a nice girl, . . . and kept doing it. . . . . I tried to wiggle away...I couldn't get far enough away. He kept trying to put his fingers inside of me. He told me behave myself and sit still. He didn't want to have to tell my Mom. I was confused—I didn't like it, he kept telling me to be a good girl, that everything was all right. I wanted him to go away. . . . It was so hot in the car."

At this point I felt I had all of the target components except the negative self belief. She was very much in the memory.

LP: What do you believe about yourself?
MONICA: *There is something wrong with me.* Someone so nice and so wonderful wouldn't do something like that to a good person. ►◄►◄►◄ His face, how nice he was. ►◄►◄►◄ An image of an old well somewhere. ►◄►◄►◄ Thinking about Aunt Beatrice, Mom's middle sister. She was going to marry him one time. Her husband died . . . . He drank a lot. Uncle Jim started coming around. I remember Mom being upset. Aunt Beatrice changed her mind and didn't marry him and she met a really wonderful man and they're both happy now. . . . I thought maybe he'll be old enough and die. ►◄►◄►◄ I'm glad I wished him dead while he was alive. *(She is laughing and crying at the same time.)* ►◄►◄►◄ I'm glad I didn't have to go to his funeral. ►◄►◄►◄ *It's over. (She says this with a lot of feeling, realizing that he is dead and she is now safe from him. This was a spontaneous positive cognition, which I then installed with eye movements.)* ►◄►◄►◄

She continued to process for several more minutes. We closed the 90-minute session with her returning to her safe place.

6. *Use the negative cognition that best stimulates a strong emotional response.* The negative cognition is an irrational belief that was developed in the past and that the client still feels now when he brings up the memory. In some cases, for those clients who cannot otherwise access their feelings, you may need to guide them in experiencing the memory more fully to elicit the negative belief. To help develop the negative cognition, have clients fully bring up the memory and feel themselves small. Elicit the memory as strongly as you can. Bring in other senses if necessary. What was the child thinking at the time? When the child state is activated, ask what he believes about himself now. You can help the client find the best negative cognition, offering suggestions if he is having difficulty coming up with something. The list of negative cognitions on page 117 can give you some ideas. Use simple language and short sentences that the child in the memory would

use. I can tell we have found the right negative cognition when, as I repeat it to the client, he responds with a reflexive "ouch," a response that is clearly noticeable and recognizable like when someone touches a wound. You are looking for a negative emotional resonance that activates the memory network. The therapist or client may repeat the negative cognition aloud to help facilitate the activation. Note that in most cases you can simply say, "In your worst moments, what negative belief do you have about yourself?" in order to elicit a negative cognition.

7. *Emotions should also be emphasized.* Several different emotions may be felt, including seemingly contradictory feelings like love and rage. Some clients won't be able to identify an emotion. Don't worry about it! It may be in a compartment that is not as yet accessible. Sometimes clients are aware of an emotion that is not yet felt. They have a "sense" terror is there but cannot feel it. The SUDS may be low, but they have a "feeling" the memory is very charged.

If they cannot identify emotions, focus on the body sensations. Often clients don't have names for what they are feeling. They feel something but don't know what to call it. Don't push for a label. Ask them to pay attention to the feeling itself in the body. Again, what is important is that the emotional/somatic component is stimulated by the client's awareness.

8. *As the client focuses on the memory, have her scan her body for any sensations.* "What do you feel in your body when you bring up the image?" For many clients, attention to their bodies makes them aware of the location of emotions and sensations that may be body memories. These sensations can be important pieces of the memory that is being stimulated. Clients are often surprised by them.

Many people who were sexually abused as children have difficulty sensing their bodies. They left their bodies as a defense against the feelings, and they believe their bodies are not safe places. It is necessary to teach or guide them to experience the sensations in their bodies. They may dismiss or not attend to certain body sensations, since some sensations are subtle but very significant. Attending to a constriction in the throat or a tingling in the hands during the set-up may yield important information during the processing. If clients respond to the question about body sensations with "nothing," ask them to look more closely. Tell them that even subtle sensation is important information. The process of locating the body sensations is helpful training for these clients.

An area of sensation may be amplified by asking clients to use their hands to press on that area as the bilateral stimulation begins. This is helpful for clients who have a difficult time feeling their bodies and stimulates the sensation channel during the processing.

TYPES OF TARGETS

Visual Memories, Including Flashbacks

Visual memories are the most straightforward targets for EMDR processing. After the client has described the memory she wants to work on, the therapist asks her for the image of the *most disturbing part* of the memory. Some clients who have several memories of assaults might want to begin with the *first one, the most distressing one, or the most representative one.* Clients who do not have a very clear memory can begin with a vague memory. The image may get clearer with the processing. What is important is that there is a visual representation of the incident.

Some of my clients have created a composite of several different incidents. For example, a client might develop a composite image that represents all of the incidents that took place in the bedroom. Some clients have blurred many incidents in their minds and can't clearly distinguish one from the other. It is fine just to have them bring up the composite image. We are not looking for accuracy; rather, we are trying to stimulate the memory network with what the client can access now.

Many clients have memory fragments rather than full memories. For example, the image of a client's childhood bedroom may elicit a feeling of fear and stimulation in the genital area. In such a case, the therapist would target the image of the bedroom with the client's associated emotions and body sensations.

Many clients become triggered by things in their daily lives, and these triggers make good EMDR targets. What triggered them? What image represents that? If, for example, in exploring the trigger you find that it was a man's mustache that triggered a client, target the image of the mustache.

TH: What do you believe about yourself when you see the image of the man's mustache?

CL: I'm not safe.

TH: How would you like to feel?

CL: I am safe.

TH: How true does "I am safe" feel to you now on a scale of 1 to 7 where 1 is not true at all and 7 is completely true?

CL: A 2.

TH: What emotions come up for you when you bring up the image of the man's mustache?

CL: Fear, anger.

TH: How disturbing to you is that feeling on a 0 to 10 scale, with 0 not distressing and 10 the most distressing you can imagine?

CL: A 10.

TH: Where do you feel that in your body?

CL: In my chest, arms, genital area.

Many clients experience visual flashbacks, which can also be targeted with EMDR, just like other visual memories. Often, clients do not know what these flashbacks refer to and have very intense emotional responses. Reassure them that they don't have to know what the flashback is about and tell them whatever information that is needed will unfold during the EMDR processing. The following case illustrates using a flashback as an EMDR target.

Case Example

During her check-in, Zena reported that during the week following our last EMDR session she had had flashbacks. "I'm around five years old and I'm at someone else's house. I feel scared and it feels like someone is in the bedroom." That was all the information she had. She had no idea what the flashback was referring to, and it was very disturbing to her. She told me that it seemed to have been precipitated by an overnight stay at a friend's house when her friend's husband came home while Zena was sleeping and thus triggered Zena's anxiety.

We began the EMDR processing with the flashback image of the five-year-old on top of a bed at someone's house. The feeling was fear. The negative cognition was "I'm not safe." The positive cognition was "I am safe," VoC a 2, SUDS a 10.

ZENA: ►◄►◄►◄ I can see all the houses on the block. I feel scared. ►◄►◄►◄ I'm outside in front of the house. *(A memory is beginning to materialize.)* It's right next door to Johnny's house. ►◄►◄►◄ I'm still outside the house, there's a girl who lived there and I don't like her—she said she had better clothes than me. She had three brothers.

LP: What are you feeling?

ZENA: I'm feeling more scared and anxious. ►◄►◄►◄ I'm inside the house now.

LP: Do you recognize where you are? *(I am asking her, because if she recognizes it more of the pieces will come together faster for her. It will then leave the dream-like quality. I thought she had recognized where she was already.)*

ZENA: I don't know where this is.

LP: Go with that. ►◄►◄►◄

ZENA: I see the bedroom. There are posters and stuff on the walls .... boy's stuff.►◄►◄►◄ I'm still in the bedroom .... and somebody else is too. ►◄►◄►◄ I can see who's there.... It's her big brother. He's bigger than me but I like him and the way that he looks. *(She has now recognized who the people are and where she is. The pieces are coming together.)* ►◄►◄►◄ We're laying down on his bed and watching TV. He used to rub my back while we watched TV . . . I liked that, it felt good. ►◄►◄►◄ We did stuff. *(She becomes quiet. She is now into the disturbing part of the memory, which we continue to process to completion.)*

Dreams as Targets

Dreams make excellent targets for EMDR processing because they are doorways into the unconscious and provide a wealth of material. Often, clear and vivid dreams arise between EMDR sessions as a continuation of the work that was done in session.

Some dreams lead clients to believe that they were molested as children. Perhaps these are repetitive dreams beginning in childhood that have sexual content, or there may have been a single disturbing dream that was so strong that the client carries the memory of the dream for a lifetime. One woman had a very vivid childhood dream of a lady fox cartoon character engaging in sexual acts before the child "knew" anything about sex.

There are a number of different ways to work with dreams. Two suggested protocols are shown in Tables 8.3 and 8.4. Some clients choose to work with the most disturbing image (Table 8.3), while some prefer to start at the beginning of the dream, because all of it feels very significant to them and it does not make sense to them to begin in the middle. With dreams I typically do not use the positive cognition, VoC, or SUDS, because it is often difficult to evoke the dream that has faded and the ratings tend to take the client away from the dream experience.

For many clients, the dream immediately links into a memory. This memory then becomes the target that you refer back to during the processing. At the end of the session you can install a positive cognition that fits with the memory and then check the dream if time allows. If it seems useful, install a positive cognition that goes with the dream.

Some dreams have many different parts. Note them as the client recounts the dream. You can break the dream into the different parts, starting with the beginning of the dream. After completing the processing of that part, move on, and check the next part. If it is charged, process that part. In this way, continue processing each part to completion, until the entire dream has been processed and is no longer disturbing.

Case Example: EMDR Session Using a Nightmare as a Target

A session with Marge began with her reporting disturbing dreams of being chased, night after night. She felt "freaked out," anxious, and very depressed. She was also having difficulty concentrating. She believed the dreams had to do with the memories emerging around molestation by an elderly male neighbor, "John," when she was about ten. We began with her *image of being chased* and *feelings of fear and anxiety.* Her negative cognition was *"I'm not safe."* Her *body became quite agitated* as she thought about the dream, and she wrung her hands and squeezed a Kleenex.

Table 8.3

· · · · · · · · · · · · · · · ·

Protocol for Using Dreams as Targets

1. The client tells the therapist the dream. It can be helpful to have the client close his/her eyes and bring the dream to mind as vividly as possible.
2. Ask him/her to scan the dream and identify the most disturbing part. "What image best represents the most disturbing part of the dream?"
3. After the image is chosen, ask for the negative cognition. "What do you believe about yourself in this image?" If he/she cannot come up with anything, or the question does not make sense given the dream, skip the negative cognition and omit the positive cognition.
4. Identify the emotions and body sensations that go with the image— these should be readily available.
5. Then, as with the standard protocol, bring up the image, negative cognition, emotions, and body sensations and begin the bilateral stimulation.
6. Process until the dream is no longer charged—a SUDS of 1 or 0.
7. Ask the client what he/she believes about him/herself when the dream image is brought up and install the positive cognition.

· · · · · · · · · · · · · · · ·

MARGE: ►◄►◄►◄ Nothing yet.

LP: What do you feel? *(I ask this because I want to know what "nothing" means.)*

MARGE: Afraid. *("Nothing" meant the image had not changed.)* ►◄►◄►◄ I can see his house . . . the back of the house. *(She is referring to John's house. A memory related to John is emerging.)* ►◄►◄►◄ *(She is increasingly agitated as she processes, squirming in the chair, wringing her hands. Her breathing is rapid and shallow.)* I can still see the house.

LP: What are you feeling?

MARGE: Still freaked out. ►◄►◄►◄ I can see him. . . . He doesn't have a mean face. . . he looks nice at his house. ►◄►◄►◄ I can see the inside of the house . . . it's dark. . . . I don't like being in his house. . . . I feel strange. ►◄►◄►◄ He's gone . . . . It feels like an elephant is sitting on my chest. ►◄►◄►◄

We continued to process this memory of molestation by John until completion. When she came up with a positive cognition that went with the memory, we installed it. By the end of the session she felt safe in the present and relieved that the reason for her nightmares had been identified and processed.

Table 8.4

. . . .

Targeting the Beginning of a Dream

1. Begin with the first image in the dream and get as many of the target components as possible associated with that image (i.e., negative cognition, emotions, body sensations; get the positive cognition, VoC, and SUDS if you can do so without detracting from the dream experience).
2. The dream may unfold in symbolic form like a lucid dream, it may immediately link to a memory, or it may go back and forth between memory and dream symbolism.
3. From time to time go back and check the beginning of the dream for charge.
4. If there is no longer charge in the beginning of the dream, scan the rest of the dream for charge.
5. Target any charged places and process them.
6. Target and reprocess any "hot spots" until the client scans the entire dream from beginning to end without any charge.
7. When the client rates the dream a SUDS of 1 or 0, ask for a positive cognition that goes with the dream.
8. Install the positive cognition with the dream.

. . . .

Artwork as Targets

Sometimes during or between sessions clients produce artwork that is loaded with meaningful symbolism, and this art makes excellent targets. Clients can draw the feeling, which then creates a visual representation that can be referred back to during the processing. For instance, one client was very upset, feeling a kind of inner chaos, but didn't know why. When I asked her to draw what she was experiencing, she drew dark red swirls in a tight ball. "Anger and fear" went with that image. I asked her what she felt in her body, and she said, "A swirling energy in the front of my body." Finally, I asked her what she believed about herself, and she said "I'm out of control." She then began the eye movements. During the processing we would refer back to the picture she had drawn to check it, and by the end of the session her SUDS was down to a 0 and she felt in control and calm. She drew another picture that represented the new feeling, which we installed with eye movements.

Emotions, Physical Sensations, and Body Memories as Targets

Many clients do not have clear visual memories of the abuse they believe that were subjected to as children. Some have strong aversive emotional responses to sexual intimacy and do not know why, some have physical

129

sensations or symptoms that they believe are associated with early childhood abuse, while others experience what they believe to be body memories from early childhood abuse. In these cases, the somatic experience may or may not be related to early abusive experiences, as in the case I mentioned earlier of dental trauma that produced symptoms that looked like sexual abuse. In my experience, a strong somatic reaction is an indication that *something* happened. We may never know what that is, but we can go in and process the disturbance and attempt to clear it from the body with EMDR.

When a client has a somatic experience that is distressing to her in some way, I use the body's experience as the entryway into the processing. This is like the somatic bridge used in hypnotherapy for regression (Watkins, 1971, 1990). I ask her to close her eyes and bring her attention to the sensation in her body. I ask her to feel the sensations fully and describe them to me in detail. I then ask her, "What do you believe about yourself now as you feel the sensations?" If she is able to come up with a negative cognition associated with the sensations, I ask her to repeat the negative cognition to herself and trace the feeling back in time noticing any images or memories that come up for her. Often clients are silent for a few moments and then indicate they are startled by something that has arisen. Frequently, clients think that what has arisen is not associated with the sensations, but, trusting that the unconscious mind has its own logic, I nearly always explore the scene or image that has arisen with the client. Then, I use this image as the target image, even if it seems irrational. In every case in my experience, the new image has been a significant target that led to important new insights and information.

The Case of Claire

Claire told me that she was suffering from the emotional and physical aftereffects of having been raped when she was two and three years old by the family maintenance man, who was like a grandfather to her. She said the abuse involved oral sex on him and vaginal rape. The pain she experienced during the rape was so intense that she fainted, and she remembered that after he raped her she had diarrhea, vomiting, and bleeding. When she told her mother that "Mr. Smith made me sick," her mother responded, "Oh, people don't make you sick! You have the flu." The abuse only stopped when her family moved away.

As a result of this horrific physical and sexual abuse, Claire suffered considerable damage to her reproductive system and urinary tract. In her twenties, she had three surgeries, including urinary tract surgery, a prolapsed uterus with torn ligaments, and a hernia in her groin area. At the time of one surgery, the doctor told her that it looked like she had been gang-raped. Also, she had had frequent yeast and bladder infections since her twenties and a problem with chronic muscle contraction in the area of the urethra.

Claire was referred to me by her physician because of the pelvic pain caused by the chronic contraction of the muscles in the pelvic floor. The physician believed that the muscle contraction was related to the abuse she had suffered as a child and thought EMDR might help her heal.

We began our first EMDR session by *focusing on the muscle contraction in her urethra area.* She closed her eyes and brought her attention to that area, and I asked her what *belief went with that feeling.* After a few moments she replied, *"If I let go, my insides will fall out. . . . I see myself as a little girl with her toes turned in holding onto the wall. I have the sensation that things feel loose and that fear. I tensed all the muscles to keep that from happening. I feel complete turmoil and distress . . .and everyone else is act-ing like things are normal. It's crazy-making."*

From her narration we had all of the target components necessary to begin the processing: the body *sensation* (muscle contraction around the urethra), the *negative cognition* (if I let go my insides will fall out), the *emo-tion* (fear), and the *image* (the little girl trying to hold everything inside).

Before beginning the processing, she chose her safe place with nurturing and protector figures in the four directions—her grandmother in the north, her husband in the south, a wise old woman in the west, and a nurturing maternal figure in the east.

Claire began by contracting her urethra muscles tightly to amplify the physical sensation and focusing her attention in that area. She focused on the image of the little girl holding her insides in and the belief that she had to contract the muscles or her insides would fall out. Her positive cognition was "I can let go safely." Her SUDS was a 10.

The session was very intense with a great deal of somatic processing. She cried and breathed rapidly. She remembered Mr. Smith's kindness and his threatening to kill her and her dog if she ever told. She remembered this "kind" man cutting her little finger to show her he was serious. This piece of the memory was particularly terrifying to her. She struggled with seeing that the same man was both good and evil. This was very difficult for her, but her adult self came in and explained how this was so to her child self.

During the processing Claire experienced letting go of the contractions in her genital and abdominal area. Later in the session she felt pain in her neck and shoulders. This revealed itself to be associated with a memory of forced oral copulation. At one point she felt sick, dissociative, and terrified. It was too much for her child self. When I asked her if she would like to go to her safe place for a break she said "yes" and went there. The maternal figure held Claire in her lap and comforted her. When Claire felt strong enough to continue, she asked to resume the processing.

Claire continued to process the old memories in her mind and body and experienced many energy shifts. As the contractions in her body released, she experienced powerful energy running through her. By the end of the session she felt herself to be powerful and saw Mr. Smith as weak and small. She believed that she no longer needed to hold herself in by contracting her muscles.

The next week she reported that she felt good after the session. When we checked the image of the little girl trying to hold her insides in, she had difficulty getting the picture at all, and the emotions were not there, so we targeted another memory that had arisen associated with the abuse.

The Case of Kate

Many of my clients report a strong feeling of "yuck!" associated with sexual intimacy. Some of them have no conscious memory of having been sexually abused but strongly suspect it. In some cases, I have targeted the feeling of "yuck" because it is the strongest experience they have and they want to work on clearing their aversion to sexual intimacy.

Kate was a woman in her thirties who had a strong aversion to sex with her partner. She believed she might have been sexually abused as a child by her father but had no memories. In fact, she had few memories at all of her childhood. She did know that after her parents were divorced she was made to sleep with her alcoholic father on the weekends when she stayed with him—ostensibly because he did not have an extra bed for her.

In this session she wanted to work on the feeling of sexual aversion. As we explored the feelings and her beliefs about sex she said "I don't need it or want it. All I feel is yuck!"

LP: When you feel yuck, what image comes up for you associated with that?
KATE: I think of my father. It's an image of making love to my father.
LP: What negative belief do you have about yourself?
KATE: I'm helpless, I have no control.
LP: What would you like to believe about yourself?
KATE: I have some control.
LP: How true does that feel to you on a scale of 1 to 7, with 1 not true at all and 7 completely true?
KATE: A 2.
LP: What emotions do you feel?
KATE: Fear, disgust, anger.
LP: Where do you feel that in your body?
KATE: I feel it in my face.
LP: How disturbing does it feel on a scale of 0 to 10, with 0 not disturbing and 10 the most disturbing you can imagine?
KATE: A 10.

We began the eye movements with the image of her father *"making love to her," the feeling of yuck,* and *the sensation in her face.* (The target image was understood to be just an image, and not the truth of something that had actually happened to her. The words "making love" were also her words.)

KATE: ►◄►◄►◄ I'm pushing a person off of my body. ►◄►◄►◄ I got a clear image of a person being drunk, they were lifeless and inebriated and I was pushing them off my body. ►◄►◄►◄ I can't imagine my father doing that—

LP: What are you feeling? *(I am checking to see what else is going on and to help her attend to her body.)*

KATE: Rage! ►◄►◄►◄ I'm feeling mad. I keep seeing a body with its face in the pillow next to me.

LP: Whose body is it?

KATE: A body completely out of it.

LP: How old are you? *(I am trying to get oriented. Where is she and how old is she so I can relate to her historically.)*

KATE: I was around five years old. I don't know who he is. ►◄►◄►◄

Kate continued to process until the end of the session.

TV Shows or Movies as Targets

Images or material in TV shows or movies can trigger emotional responses in clients that feel way out of proportion to the actual content of the shows. As a result, clients may experience anxiety, nightmares, and intrusive images. Many clients have no idea why they have been triggered—they just feel very upset. The client may have seen a special on TV about rape or sexual abuse or a movie with violent scenes.

The image that the client found most distressing in the movie can be used as an EMDR target. The method of developing the target and processing it is very much like working with dreams. One client became very distressed after a rape scene in the movie, "Dead Man Walking." She had nightmares, body memory flashbacks, and an aversion to her partner's touching her. She had no visual memory of having been raped, but her body's reaction seemed to indicate that *something* traumatic had happened to her.

In this case we used the most distressing scene, which was the rape and murder of a woman, as her target. The negative belief was "I'm not safe"; the positive cognition was "I'm safe now"; the VoC was a 2; she felt intense fear (a 10 SUDS); and she felt pressure on her chest and pain in her genital area. She processed the movie scene very much like a dream. She had a lot of body processing and intense abreactions, and it appeared from what transpired during the session that she *had* been raped. By the end of the session she felt calm and we installed "I'm safe now," which also had arisen spontaneously.

Negative Cognitions as Targets

Adults who have been severely abused as children typically have low self-esteem and many self-limiting beliefs. Negative cognitions can be used to develop targets for EMDR processing when clients do not have images or memories they can readily identify as root causes of their current problems. Many clients seek treatment because of the negative self-concepts; they no longer want to believe that they are inherently bad, worthless, and powerless.

I use the following method adapted from the hypnotherapeutic technique called *affect bridging* (Watkins, 1971, 1990) to develop an EMDR target from a negative cognition. I call it the *negative cognition-affect bridge*. Let's say the client believes she is powerless and has no clear idea where this belief came from. Her difficulty manifests in not standing up for herself in her intimate relationships and at work. I would ask her to close her eyes and repeat "I am powerless" to herself and to notice what she feels in her body as she says those words. She might say, "I feel a tightness in my chest and a sick feeling in my stomach." I next ask her to repeat the belief, feel the feeling, and trace the feeling back to another time when she felt that way. I try to get clients to trace the feeling and belief back to the earliest or strongest memory possible. "Notice whatever images pop into your mind; don't censor anything." Usually, I find that an image pops into the client's mind that has a charge. In this example, it might be an image of being a small child being forced to have sex with an adult. The image that emerges might also be a fragment of a scene. The image that emerges becomes the target image.

If the client is unable to come up with anything using the negative cognition-affect bridge, ask her to repeat the negative cognition, feel the feelings in her body, and then begin the bilateral stimulation. While this method is more likely to produce diffuse processing, it can be useful for locating a more defined target such as a memory. If a memory or an image does come up early on in the processing, that memory can be referred back to for full targeting with all components. I have found that the negative cognition-affect bridge method for developing a target creates a more direct route to the primary material to be processed for symptom resolution than beginning with the negative cognition alone. The former produces a specific target, which is more likely to produce complete and thorough processing of a memory.

Chapter 9

The Middle of EMDR Processing Sessions

In this chapter a number of suggestions are provided to aid the therapist in getting the client who is blocked or looping back on track to reprocessing the traumatic memories. Beginning with ways to determine the cause of the blockage, non-interweave and interweave strategies are given and illustrated with case material.

Adults abused as children frequently have difficulty with blocked processing or "looping" during the processing of highly charged emotional material. In addition, sometimes the processing is blocked, or stuck, without a high level of affect and is not progressing for some reason. It seems that, because of the intensity of the childhood trauma, adults abused as children have difficulty accessing their adult selves and consequently require more than usual interaction with the therapist, who employs a number of different techniques for unblocking the processing, including interweaves.

Working with Looping and Stuck Processing

There are four main steps to intervening with blocked processing (also see Figure 9.1):

1. Recognizing that the processing is blocked or incomplete.
2. Identifying the cause.
3. Intervening using non-interweave strategies.
4. Using interweave strategies.

1. RECOGNIZING THAT THE PROCESSING IS BLOCKED OR INCOMPLETE

Clients are looping when the client is not processing information and instead is cycling through the same emotions, sensations, images, or thoughts in successive sets without a change in SUDS level. The emotional intensity remains unchanged. Typically, the client is very distressed but the bilateral stimulation is not able to link up the different memory networks to keep the processing moving along. Looping seems like a broken record repeating over and over the same thoughts, feelings, and emotions without change.

There is not always high affect with looping. Generally, there is a resistance to or blocking of processing. This may take the form of clients' saying "nothing" is happening after several set of eye movements. They simply don't seem to be processing.

Another sign of looping is the client's nearing the end of the session with a high SUDS level. Adults sexually abused as children frequently are not able to complete sessions, especially if there were several abuse incidents. In these cases, therapist-supplied interweaves are very useful for closing the sessions.

2. IDENTIFYING THE CAUSE

There are many possible causes of blocked processing. When you find the client stuck, begin to explore the cause with open questions. The therapist looks at the client's patterns and core issues, as well as the common issues for adult survivors, and suggests a hypothesis. If the client rejects it, he or she tries something else. Working together, the therapist and client look for the cause of the blocked processing. Sometimes it is quite obvious; other times it is not. Following are some potential areas of blockage to explore with the client (see Figure 8.1).

Look for Blocking Beliefs

One of the first things the EMDR therapist does when the client is looping is to look for blocking beliefs. Blocking beliefs are beliefs the client experiences as true on a very deep unconscious level that then block the processing. Beliefs like "I'm not safe," "It was my fault; therefore I am bad," "I am a victim," and "I have no control/choice" are common to adults who were abused. It is helpful for the therapist to be aware of the issues that adults abused as children have in general (see Chapter 2), as well as the issues pertaining to the individual client. Keep these issues in mind as you explore with the client what belief might be impeding processing.

Often, the client is reluctant to express the blocking belief if it evokes feelings of shame, a broken agreement (prohibition against telling, threats of harm), issues of trusting the therapist, or taboo subjects. The therapist can offer suggestions or hypotheses to the client, who accepts or rejects them. Table 8.1 lists typical negative cognitions for adults sexually abused as children.

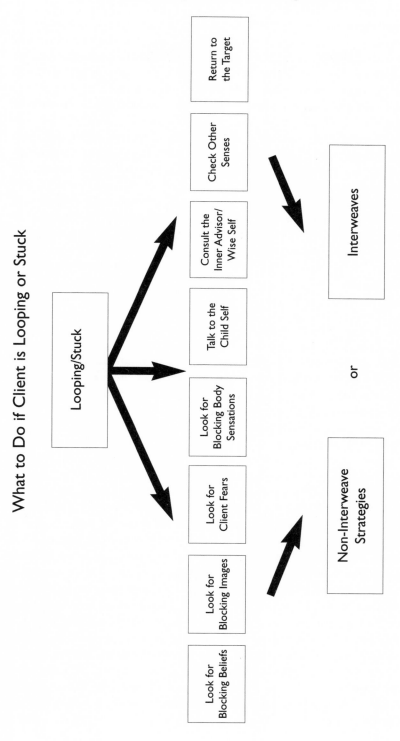

What to Do if Client is Looping or Stuck

FIGURE 9.1

The following are some common blocking beliefs:

- *I am not safe.* The client *feels* that he/she is not safe in the present. The intensity of the fear that is evoked during EMDR processing of an abuse memory can feel very compelling.
- *I am responsible for the abuse and therefore bad.* Almost universally, clients abused as children feel responsible for the abuse they suffered.
- *I am powerless—I have no choices or control.* Clients who have been abused often connect to feelings of being powerless and having no control during the processing of abuse memories. These feelings can be overwhelming. They might also feel that the EMDR process itself is out of their control, which can be frightening. "I am helpless" and "I am a victim" are common negative self-concepts of sexual abuse survivors. During the processing clients may see themselves as victims and the therapist as a victimizer, which can disrupt the processing.
- *I am bad because I felt pleasure.* Clients commonly reexperience arousal during EMDR processing of sexual abuse. This can be very distressing to clients who believe they are perverted or bad because their bodies are responding in this way. They may also be very concerned about the therapist's reaction to them.
- *My therapist will lose respect/regard for me and abandon me if I disclose the nature of the abuse.* Many clients were abandoned or punished for disclosure of their abuse. They may feel repulsed by their own stories and have little self-respect. How can they expect their therapist to maintain regard for them?
- *I can't trust anyone, not even my therapist.* Because of terrible betrayal by the perpetrator(s) and often by other family members and authority figures, it is very hard for adults sexually abused as children to let go and trust anyone. Trusting their therapist feels counterintuitive to them and stimulates the betrayal memory network. Many clients also feel as though they betrayed themselves as children and don't trust their own ability to protect themselves from harm.
- *It's not safe to tell.* Many children are threatened with severe punishment or death if they ever told. This fear comes up frequently and feels very convincing to the child self.
- *It's not OK to feel or express anger.* Many clients grew up with prohibitions against anger, or saw that it was too dangerous in their families to express anger because of the repercussions from the perpetrator. Some clients do not want to feel their anger because they believe it will make them like their abusers. Other clients are overwhelmed by the intensity of their rage and are afraid that it is dangerous.

Look for Client Fears
Some clients may block the processing because they are afraid of getting

better. Secondary gain issues may be blocking the processing. "If I get through these old memories, who will I be? Who will my friends be? What will my life look like?" The current symptoms, though debilitating, are familiar. If identified, these resistances should be discussed with the client. Perhaps the therapy is proceeding too quickly, and the client needs more time to integrate the changes in self-perception and relating to others.

Some clients are afraid of going crazy with the perceived loss of control, the intensity of the images and emotions that are coming up with EMDR processing, and the fantastical, dream-like imagery that may be emerging. Address these fears and reassure the client if necessary. Normalize the reactions: *"So many different things can come up during processing. Just let them pass through. We can always take a break and go to the safe place."*

Because some clients may require help with medication to enable them to better cope with the emotions and anxiety that arise between sessions, having adjunctive psychiatric back-up and support can be very helpful.

When they first begin EMDR processing, many clients are afraid that they're not doing it right. It is important to assure them that you will pay attention to their processing and let them know what to focus on or what to do. Their job is to let whatever is happening happen without censoring it and to report their responses to you.

Clients abused as children commonly fear that in processing the "bad" memories associated with a close family member they will lose the "good memories." I learned a technique for dealing with this from EMDR therapist Landry Wildwind, who recommends having the client imagine putting the good memories in a safe place where they will be kept separate from the "bad" memories. This safe place can be a safe, a file box, or anything the client can imagine where the good memories can be protected. The client then processes the abuse memories while keeping the good memories safe. Later, when the client is ready, the good and bad memories can be integrated.

Look for Blocking Images

Sometimes during EMDR processing an image begins to come into clients' awareness that is extremely distressing. It could be information that is new to them and is so shocking and disruptive to their view of themselves and their past relationships that they try to push it back out of awareness or close the door on it. Clients may feel so distressed by the image—even though they haven't fully "seen" it—that processing becomes blocked and they begin to loop.

If you suspect that there is a blocking image, ask, "What in the picture might be causing the processing to be blocked?" Ask the client to scan the scene for any significant details. If it turns out that there is a very disturbing image, the client may want to stop the processing and talk about it before proceeding.

Look for Blocking Body Sensations

If the client is processing cognitively but not expressing anything about what she feels in her body, you might want to have her bring attention to her body sensations. For clients who have difficulty attending to their bodies, you can direct them to "press the area of the sensation" to amplify it and to make it easier to bring the attention there. Clients can focus on the most pronounced sensation if there are many of them and they can't decide where to focus. Sometimes clients avoid their bodies because they feel sexual arousal—body memories that are being activated by the processing of the old memories. If this is the case, you might need to talk about any blocking beliefs, i.e., "I am bad for feeling this," and possibly do an educative interweave.

Clients can also use movement to emphasize something they are feeling in order to amplify it. They can move their hands or arms or stand up to increase the feeling and to unblock body energy. For instance, a client who is processing a memory of being small and dominated by her abuser may want to stand up and feel her adult size in the present as she confronts the abuser in her imagination. Clients may act out punching, hitting, or even protecting themselves from blows. Movement can effectively activate the somatic memory component, which, with the bilateral stimulation, can increase the effective processing of the traumatic memory.

Encourage clients to speak the unspoken or forbidden words aloud during processing. Often, clients feel a constriction in the mouth or throat. Something wants to be expressed; it may not even be words, but simply sound. Clients can talk to the perpetrator or scream their terror into a pillow as the therapist taps on their hands or knees. Expressing themselves in conjunction with the bilateral stimulation helps to remove the blockage.

Check Other Senses (Smell, Hearing, Taste)

Sometimes the processing is blocked because there is a sound, taste, or smell that has come into the periphery of the client's awareness that is activating a strong emotional response. The smell of a cigarette or the taste of alcohol may be closely associated with the abuser. If the processing is stuck, the therapist can ask the client for other sensory information. Have clients scan the scene. What is happening? What are they hearing? Is there any dialogue in the scene? Are there any sound effects? Do they smell or taste anything? What are they sensing? Try to help them locate themselves in place and time. How old are they? The sensory information can be very helpful in orienting the client and putting the puzzle pieces together.

Talk to the Child Self

If the processing is blocked and the client is in a "child state," talk to the child self in order to find out what might be blocking the processing. It is helpful to use simple language and a gentle tone. If the child is frightened, what is scaring him or her? What is she or he seeing that is distressing? What is happening in the scene? What does the child self need in order to feel safe? This open exploration can lead to a blocking belief or image that the therapist then addresses with an interweave or other intervention.

Consult the Inner Advisor or Wise Self

Sometimes when the client is stuck and neither the therapist or client knows what the problem or the solution is, the client's inner advisor or higher self can be consulted. The client may have already contacted the inner advisor as a resource in the preparation phase of treatment, or some kind of wise self or inner guidance may have emerged spontaneously during EMDR processing sessions. Ask the client to close her eyes and contact this inner advisor, and when she has contacted this part, have her dialogue with it in order to find the source of the problem and the solution. Sometimes the inner advisor will give the client a wise lecture! When the client tells you this advice, install it with the bilateral stimulation or do what has been advised. When I have felt at an impasse and haven't known what to do next, I have called on clients' inner guidance and found it very helpful and empowering.

Return to the Target

One of my general rules when the client is stuck is: When in doubt, return to the target and check it. What is happening now in the picture? Ask the client to scan the picture for visual clues. Ask the client questions to provide more detail about what he or she is seeing or experiencing. Look for any areas of emotional charge or reactivity and target them. Returning to the target in my experience does not derail the processing and provides a sense of comfort to the client that he or she is being closely tracked by his or her therapist.

3. USING NON-INTERWEAVE STRATEGIES TO UNBLOCK PROCESSING

There are a number of non-interweave strategies that therapists can try before using interweaves. Most of these are described in *Eye Movement Desensitization and Reprocessing* (Shapiro 1995).

Change the Eye Movement

If you are using manually directed eye movements with the client, you might want to increase or decrease the speed of the saccades, or change the direction from horizontal to diagonal or vertical. Circular movement can also be helpful for unblocking looping.

Changing the Type of Bilateral Stimulation

Some clients have difficulty moving their eyes back and forth while attending to their inner experience. Others feel self-conscious about crying or expressing feelings in front of the therapist. For these clients, closing their eyes as they listen to bilateral tones or passively having their hands or knees tapped makes processing easier. If I suspect the processing is blocked because of the type of bilateral stimulation being used, I explore this with the client and offer him or her other choices. Some clients who have been sexually abused may feel uncomfortable being touched by the therapist. Auditory processing may be a better choice for them. Others like the contact with the therapist the touch provides as they process frightening experiences. The tapping reassures them that they are not alone. Often, a client will have her eyes closed as she is being tapped and begins to loop. In this case, it may be necessary to change to eye movements or to ask her to keep her eyes open so that she can remain present and aware as she processes the past.

Some clients begin with eye movements, change to tapping in mid-session, and then return to eye movements later in the session. I have found that processing continues with changes in the form of bilateral stimulation.

Alterations

There are a number of ways to alter the target to decrease the intensity, making it easier to process the image for some clients who become stuck.

- *Change the image.* The target image can be manipulated visually to make it less distressing. The image can be made smaller or black and white; it can be transformed into a still photograph or placed at a greater distance from the client. The image can be seen like a video on a TV monitor or as a movie projected on a screen (Shapiro, 1995).
- *Use hierarchy.* Another manipulative technique is taken from Wolpe's desensitization work (Wolpe & Abrams, 1991). The client can place the feared object (e.g., the perpetrator) at a distance during the processing and progressively bring him closer in her imagination. She could also begin by having the perpetrator behind a glass wall and, when she is ready, remove the wall and slowly let him move closer in her imagination as she feels less fearful (Shapiro, 1995).
- *Change the voice.* Clients who have been abused may become very distressed as they hear the sound of the perpetrator's voice in their minds as they process. They freeze in terror. One fun technique is to ask the client to change the perpetrator's voice to something comical like Donald Duck's. "When you hear your father's scary voice in your mind, can you imagine changing it to Donald Duck's voice?" If she says "yes," have her "imagine that" as she moves her eyes back and forth. This technique also works well for clients who have very critical or punitive

inner voices. Changing the voice helps to create distance and disidentification from the voice (Shapiro, 1995).

• *Add a positive statement.* For some clients, adding positive statements like "It's over" and "You're safe now" help them calm and pull out of looping (Shapiro, 1995).

• *Focus on the outcome.* It can be helpful for some clients who are looping or stuck to focus on the outcome of the traumatic experience—*the fact that they did survive.* Sometimes when a traumatic event has been quite shocking, the person becomes stuck in the "I'm going to die" moment, like a broken record repeating over and over "I'm going to die, I'm going to die, I'm going to die." In these cases I have found it helpful to remind the client of the next thing that happened after the moment of terror. It is like picking up the arm of the record player and placing it on the next groove.

For example, Juanita had grown up in a town that had bull fights. When she was three years old, she was at the fair with her grandmother, and a bull escaped from his enclosure and rampaged through the fairgrounds, terrorizing the people. In her memory, she suddenly found herself looking up into the angry red eyes of a giant bull about to gore her. In the next moment her grandmother whisked her away from the bull and pulled her under a table to safety. As this client processed this 10 SUDS memory, she remembered many other things that happened that day, but whenever she brought up the original picture it was still a 10 SUDS with the bull staring down into her three-year-old eyes. It just would not budge. I finally asked her, "Did you survive?" She answered "yes." I then asked her to remember the next scene when her grandmother pulled her away from the bull to safety. She imagined that scene as she moved her eyes back and forth. After the set of eye movements she said that the scene had progressed and connected to the scenes of safety and her grandmother's love for her. When we checked the target image with the bull, it had gone down to a 0 SUDS.

• *Increase the sense of safety in the present.* If a client is looping or stuck because she does not feel safe, it is important to do what you can to increase her sense of safety in the present. You can ask her what would help her to feel safer. You can bring in support people to help her. You can remind her repeatedly during the processing that she is in your office and that she is safe now (Shapiro, 1995).

Spontaneous Interweaves That Arise from the Client's Processing
Often, clients spontaneously connect to inner resources during EMDR processing. According to Anderson (1996), there are five steps that occur, more or less consistently, during the EMDR process for clients who have been sexually abused. She believes that these steps are necessary to complete a full resolution and integration of the abuse. For clients who make

rapid progress, this pattern occurs spontaneously and visually. For clients whose progress is slower, the pattern is absent, unless the therapist uses cognitive interweaves. I have also observed these steps occurring spontaneously with my clients as they process abuse memories. The five steps include:

1. *Distancing.* Usually, by the third set of eye movements, clients remark that they see the target incident at a distance, rather than it happening to them. This appears to be necessary for objectivity and to allow the adult survivor to begin to gain control in the scene.
2. *The Rescue.* The inner or outer resource figures, including the adult self, appear spontaneously and in some way intervene in the abuse and rescue the victim child from the hands of the perpetrator. Often it includes taking the child out of the place of abuse (perhaps to the identified "safe place" with the survivor adult). This results in an amazing sense of control and empowerment for the adult and a sense of protection never before experienced for the child.
3. *Reassurance.* Once the child is safe, the adult reassures the child that she or he is safe, it is over, and it was not her or his fault. This may also include expressing love for the child and other positive feelings as appropriate. This allows the child to receive validation and results in adult self-esteem and acceptance.
4. *Integration.* At this point, clients usually need to be prompted to put their arms around the child, give her a hug, and draw her into the adult's heart, where she remains safe, protected, and valued.
5. *Closure.* Clients are asked to construct a scene whereby they can come to some kind of closure with the perpetrator. They are encouraged to let their imagination "run wild," to do anything they want. (Repressed clients may need to be given some ideas.) Sometimes this involves merely an angry conversation, but often these scenes become quite violent (Anderson, 1996).

Kate (described in Chapter 8) had a session in which she spontaneously connected to inner resources without the need of interweaves. We began the eye movements with the image of her father "making love to her," the feeling of "yuck," and a terrible sensation in her face. At this point she is in the middle of the session and feeling a great deal of rage toward the man on top of her. In order to get oriented, I had just asked her how old she was.

KATE: I was almost five years old. I don't know who he is. ►◄►◄►◄ I was telling him I was going to blow his balls off.
LP: Why is that?
KATE: If anyone were to touch me I'd go into a rage.►◄►◄►◄ I was feeling the adult me talking to him. I handed me to someone else and I annihi-

lated him. *(A spontaneous inner resource emerges. Her adult self has automatically stepped in to rescue her child self. She is openly expressing her rage without holding back.)*

LP: Is the child safe?

KATE: Yes ►◄►◄►◄ I get a clear sense of Don protecting me from my father and my mother. *(Don is a close male friend of hers. This protector figure came to her without my intervention. An outer resource.)*

LP: What do you believe about yourself now?

KATE: I'm OK. ►◄►◄►◄ I have imaginary parents and they are at least protecting me. *(She has spontaneously contacted internal good protective parents as internal resources.)*

LP: How do you feel?

KATE: I feel OK.

LP: Let's go back to the original picture. What comes up for you now?

KATE: I feel like he doesn't have the right to violate me and if he tries it again Don will hurt him. ►◄►◄►◄ I feel protected. ►◄►◄►◄ He had no right to touch me. I am protected now because I'm not that child anymore and I have a right to fight back. *(A spontaneous positive cognition came up for her.)*

She left the session feeling empowered and more able to protect herself.

If the client does not have the resources to create these scenes spontaneously, more help and guidance may be provided through the imaginal and cognitive interweave process (see Figure 9.2). Therapists can guide their clients through these steps by providing general ideas and then encouraging them to create their own personal scenes during the bilateral stimulation.

4. USING IMAGINAL AND COGNITIVE INTERWEAVES

Interweaves are strategies employed by the therapist to unblock block edprocessing by introducing new information or a new perspective to the client in order to weave together memory networks, ego states, or schemas. According to Shapiro (1995), "This proactive version of EMDR deliberately interlaces clinician-generated material, instead of relying solely on the client's spontaneous processing effects" (p. 245). For example, the therapist may want to elicit the adult perspective when the client is stuck in a fearful child state. The therapist may do this by asking the client if she is safe now in the therapist's office. If she answers "yes," bilateral stimulation is added to link the adult self's current information. This linkage causes the old information, "I'm not safe," to lose its power in the present and for the associated level of affect to decrease.

One should allow the natural reprocessing to occur as much as possible

Cognitive and Imaginal Interweaves for Abuse Survivors

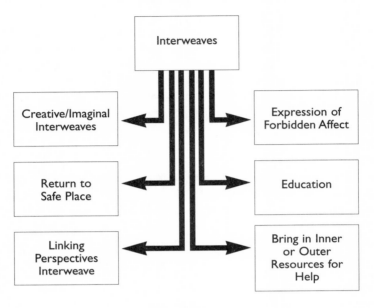

FIGURE 9.2

and use interweaves sparingly. It is best to time interweaves in such a way that they don't feel intrusive or disruptive. When the client indicates that the interweave works for him or her, the therapist guides the client in a set of bilateral stimulation, which links the information together. Interweaves are suggested to clients, who are invited to reject them if they don't fit. Designing interweaves is often a collaborative effort between the therapist and client, who work together to find the key that will unlock the door. Another analogy comes from an experience I had with a train derailment while traveling in Ecuador. During this trip through the Andes, our train derailed three times. After each derailment a group of men would jump off the train and systematically try a number of different methods to get the train back on the track and moving toward our destination. They put rocks on the tracks, grass, leaves, bamboo, and a kind of metal contraption. They'd try one thing and then another. Finally, something would work and the train would again get back on the track, and we'd continue on our trip. The interweaves that the therapist suggests are like the grass, bamboo, rocks, etc. Finally, something works and off you go again toward your destination—the resolution of a disturbing memory.

Many therapists think they have to have the right interweave before they can offer it to the client. Using what you know about the client and the issues being worked on, you can simply make a suggestion. If it works, great; if it doesn't, think of something else! Together, you will come up with something that fits the current problem. Interweaves, like EMDR in general, are collaborative works.

As described earlier, the primary issues that come up for adults physically and sexually abused as children are *safety, responsibility,* and *choice/control. Therapists should listen for these issues and develop the most appropriate interweaves to address them.* Because these issues are associated with different memories or incidents, they come up over and over again in different forms throughout EMDR therapy. Don't be discouraged if it seems like the same issue keeps recurring. It is not an indication that the EMDR is not working. Many different incidents have reinforced clients' negative beliefs about themselves and the world. With persistent EMDR work, clients eventually shift at a deeper level. Current life betrayals or traumas may still activate the old beliefs, but they won't seem as true to the client anymore.

Below are several interweave strategies that you might consider when your client is looping or stuck.

Bring in Inner and Outer Resources

During the preparation phase of treatment, the therapist and client have identified outer resources—people in the client's current life and/or from the past identified as nurturing or protective—and inner resources—nurturing, protective, or wise figures from the person's own psyche that can be summoned when needed.

Inner and outer resources are brought in when the client is looping and is unable to naturally connect with these resources. An example of using outer resources involved a male client who had been severely physically and sexually abused by both of his parents. Joe (described in Chapter 5) had identified his maternal grandmother as someone who had loved and protected him. When he became too overwhelmed by the abuse memories, I would bring her in as an interweave. As he thought of her nurturing and protecting him, while moving his eyes back and forth, his SUDS level went down.

A commonly used inner resource is the adult self, who is deliberately brought in to protect or nurture the child self. For example, if the client is feeling very frightened and cycling in fear, the therapist might ask her if she would like to bring in her adult self to comfort the child and let her know that she is safe now. I try to use the adult self as a nurturer or protector figure *first,* because it reinforces the client's positive view of his or her own capacities. This is not always possible, particularly if the adult self also feels overwhelmed or terrified or the client's inner resources are not strongly developed.

Inner resources from dreams can be used as well. For instance, a 45-year-old woman who had been severely molested as a child, began during EMDR therapy to have dreams in which a wolf appeared. This wolf became an important ally in the work. Whenever she would become overwhelmed and/or stuck during the processing, we would call on him to protect the little girl from the perpetrators. Her SUDS would typically go from a 10 to a 0, and we would install the image of his scaring away the perpetrators and nurturing the little girl, who snuggled on his back. She would say to herself "I am safe now" as she did the eye movements with the imagery. She would even summon his presence before going to sleep at night, which gave her more peaceful sleep.

Sometimes I have brought in more than one resource to aid the client's child self. In one instance, when the client was looping in terror in the middle of an abuse memory, I brought in myself, her adult self, and her power animal to save the child and punish the perpetrator.

A Case Example: Bringing in Inner Resources

Marilyn came to see me because she was suffering the emotional aftereffects of having been physically and sexually abused by her narcissistic, sadistic father throughout her childhood. As a result of the abuse she suffered problems with her weight, difficulties with her sexuality, low self-esteem and self-confidence, and blockages in her creative expression. In this session, which was about three months into her treatment, she wanted to work on a molestation memory.

In the memory she said, "I'm being held down in the bed in my parents' room. I'm feeling suffocated. I'm seeing my father naked and his penis is out.... I feel terrified." I asked her how old she was in the memory and she said "three or four years old." She said she felt like "the devil had come and gotten me. I ended up in the closet."

Her negative belief associated with the memory was "I'm bad and ugly," and the positive cognition was "I'm good and pretty," a VoC of 2. She felt cold terror, was numb, and her SUDS was an 8+. Marilyn was in the middle of processing the memory of being molested by her father when she needed to bring her adult self in as an inner resource to rescue her child self.

LP: Let's go back to the original picture. What comes up for you now?

MARILYN: I want to get her out of there. *(Her adult self has come in and wants to rescue the child.)*

LP: Have your adult self come in and rescue the child in any way you like. *(Inner resource interweave.)* ►◄►◄►◄

MARILYN: I zapped him with a ray gun and froze him and wrapped him up in a cocoon and shoved him into a pit. I told her I'd protect her from any future harm. *(This was a very strong positive response from her adult self.)*

I wanted to also address the child self's belief that she was bad. So I asked Marilyn's adult self if she could tell the little girl that she was good and that her father was bad for harming her. (She is using her adult self as an inner resource.) She readily agreed to tell her this. She moved her eyes back and forth as she talked to her child self.

MARILYN: ▶◀▶◀▶◀ I kept telling her she was good. She's afraid more bad things will happen. What's the protection against people like him?

This was an important question she posed to herself and to me. Her father was a very powerful and destructive man who continued to cause harm to her family members through various means. We discussed this issue for a while and then together we came up with a solution. "I need to recognize my feelings and listen to myself . . . those are the keys to protection. As a child I could see and recognize the danger but I couldn't leave. As an adult I can leave."

MARILYN: ▶◀▶◀▶◀ I can get away from these people. *(She is including others who have harmed her in the past.)* ▶◀▶◀▶◀ I have quit jobs because of harassment. I felt like a failure then. *(She recognizes that she has protected herself in the past, but also sees how she interpreted her self-protection as personal failure. This looks like another area to work on. We were running out of time so I asked her to return to the original picture.)*
MARILYN: It wasn't my fault. It was his fault.
LP: How disturbing does it feel to you on a scale from 0 to 10 with 0 not disturbing and 10 the most?
MARILYN: It feels like a 5 or a 6. I feel angry that no one stopped him and he got away with it. The fear is gone. I feel more calm and tired.

She went to her safe place and connected with her little girl in a nurturing protective way. After debriefing we ended the session, knowing that there was more work to do on this memory.

Return to Safe Place or Conflict-Free Image

Clients can return to the safe place or conflict-free image they identified and developed earlier if they feel overwhelmed and want to take a break from the processing. They can imagine going to the safe place and bringing in their nurturing or protective figures to help calm them down and to increase the sense of safety in the present. When they feel securely in the safe place, the therapist can determine whether or not to install the feeling of safety with bilateral stimulation. The client may choose to remain in the safe place until the end of the session or may decide to return to the processing if he or she feels ready.

Linking Perspectives Interweave

The linking perspectives interweave links two or more memory networks together. The client has all of the needed information in his or her mind but requires help in "merging the two memory files." In many cases, the adult memory network has information that is not connecting with the child self's network. Issues of safety, responsibility, and choice/control commonly arise. Following are techniques for linking perspectives.

"I'm confused" (Shapiro, 1995). This technique is used to link information that the client knows but does not have access to while processing. For example, many adults abused as children blame themselves for the abuse and feel angry at their child self. If during a session the client is stuck feeling angry at the three-year-old child self who was abused by an uncle, the therapist might say the following: "I'm confused. A three-year-old is responsible for the behavior of a 40-year old?" If the client says, "No, that's not true, my uncle was responsible," the therapist then says, "Think about that," and does a set of eye movements to link the information.

"What if your child did it?" (Shapiro, 1995). With this technique the therapist tries to elicit empathy for the child self that the client is blaming for the abuse. If the therapist knows the client has a daughter, niece, or other loved child, he/she seeks to have the client think about the beloved child with sympathy, which then transfers to her own child self. For example, if you know your client has a six-year-old daughter and the stuck part is the client blaming their own six-year-old child self for the abuse, you could ask, "If this were your daughter Mary, would it be her fault?" If the client says no and means it, then follow with a set of eye movements.

Socratic method (Shapiro, 1995). In this method, which can take the form of a single question or a dialogue, the therapist asks the client simply worded questions that elicit answers from the memory network that he or she wants to link to the one that is currently active. The questions the therapist asks lead the client to a logical conclusion. This method is quite powerful, as it enables clients to link what they already know in one memory network to another where it is not known.

Case Example: Linking Perspectives Interweave with the Issue of Responsibility

Connie's processing had become stuck because she was feeling responsible for her teenage cousin's abuse of her when she was five years old.

LP: Who was responsible? *(I am checking to see if the negative cognition has shifted.)*

CONNIE: I'm not sure who was responsible.

(The negative cognition had not fully shifted so I did a linking perspectives interweave. I knew she could empathize with her little daughter, Jill, and would not blame her for any abuse.)

LP: If Gabe had done this to your daughter Jill, would she be responsible? Would it be her fault?

CONNIE: No.

LP: Imagine superimposing your child self on Jill as you think about Jill not being responsible for the abuse. ►◄►◄►◄

CONNIE: I can see the two of us again, but I'm *here* and not *there.*

LP: Who was responsible for the abuse? *(I am checking to see if the negative cognition has changed.)*

CONNIE: He was responsible. *(She said this strongly and clearly.)*

LP: Are you *bad* because of what *he* did?

CONNIE: No. ►◄►◄►◄

We did another set of eye movements to further install the positive cognitions, and she reported feeling calm and peaceful. After several minutes debriefing, she left.

Case Example: Using Linking Perspectives Interweaves with the Negative Cognition "I'm Bad"

Zena, whom I described in the last chapter (p. 126), was processing a flashback memory that was new and distressing to her. In this session I used linking perspective interweaves to help her move through the negative belief that she was "bad." At this point we are in the middle of the session, and she is processing a memory that has emerged in which she is on a bed with an older neighbor boy.

ZENA: We're laying down on his bed and watching TV. He used to rub my back while we watched TV. . . . I liked that, it felt good. ►◄►◄►◄ We did stuff. *(She becomes quiet.)*

LP: What's happening now?

ZENA: It's confusing . . . I liked him, but I didn't want him to touch me. ►◄►◄►◄ *I'm a bad girl. (Her child self is judging her harshly, creating a strongly held negative cognition.)*

LP: Why do you believe you're a bad girl? *(I am trying to ascertain the origins of this belief, so that I can craft an interweave.)*

ZENA: Cause I like him and like being around him and I like some of the things he does and sometimes not other stuff . . . *I liked him but didn't want the touching.* . . . I had a crush on him . . . I guess I was in love with him. . . . We laughed together and watched TV together.

LP: So you wanted love and attention from him but you didn't want the sexual attention? *(Linking perspectives interweave.)*

ZENA: Yes. ►◄►◄►◄ I'm still there. *(She means in the image.)* He would rub my back and kiss me and it felt good. I really liked the attention. Being the youngest in my family, I never got much of that. *(She is realizing why her child self craved attention.)* ►◄►◄►◄ I'm not in the house anymore. It was confusing, I thought I must have been a bad girl because I wanted to see him. I just wanted to be with him . . . I didn't want him to touch me. I didn't go there for sex. ►◄►◄►◄ *(She has an insight that changes her view of responsibility for what happened between them.)* He was the one who was bad. He knew it was wrong . . . He told me not to tell!

At this point we were at the end of our time. She went to her safe place and connected with her child self. She felt calm and in a good place.

Using Educative Interweaves

With the educative interweave the therapist introduces new information to the client. Many people from dysfunctional families did not learn about appropriate behavior. The therapist may offer information about how healthy family members interact with one another. In other cases the therapist may have technical information that can be used in an interweave. For example, a man who had been molested as a child had a compulsive need to wash himself. He showered several times a day because he never felt clean. The therapist asked him if he knew that all of the cells in his body had been replaced and so none of the ones from the time of the molestation remained. When he thought about that with the eye movements, he felt a sense of relief. Later he reported that the need to shower compulsively had disappeared.

Clients sexually abused as children typically believe that they are bad if their bodies experienced pleasure during the abuse. When this came up with a client and she could not shift the negative cognition because neither the child nor the adult had any information to the contrary, I did an educative cognitive interweave. I told her, *"It is normal for the body to experience pleasure when it is touched a certain way. Just like if you stub your toe or bump your knee, the body responds with pain, certain kinds of touch make you feel pleasure. What he did was wrong, bad. You are not bad for your body's natural response."* Both the child and the adult needed this information because it was not in the system. Her SUDS went down and her positive cognition became "My body responded in a normal way. He was bad for doing what he did to me." She felt great relief from the guilt and shame associated with the abuse memories and her body's responses to the stimulation. The perpetrator had told her repeatedly that she was bad because of her sexual stimulation. The cognitive interweave helped to deprogram this negative and harmful message.

Expression of Forbidden Affect

Sometimes strong emotions are locked deep inside because at the time of the abuse it was not safe to express these feelings. The inhibited expression of emotion may manifest as a tightness in the throat or jaw and can block the processing. With EMDR, clients are encouraged to allow the angry thoughts and feelings to be expressed in whatever way is arising in their imaginations. The full expression of anger frees up energy that has been blocked and that has reinforced the feeling of being powerless. With eye movements clients who have been horribly hurt and shamed tell the perpetrators how they feel about what they have done to them. When clients fully express anger and rage at the perpetrator in the safety of the therapist's office, they feel a sense of empowerment and freedom from fear. The anger is then cleared from the system, in many cases eliminating the desire for revenge or need for actual confrontation.

Between the ages of five and ten, Bonnie had been sexually abused by her father. She was a quiet, introverted child who felt quite helpless in her family. In our EMDR sessions she felt tremendous rage toward her father. Her child self would get a bat and beat her father bloody as her adult self restrained him so he couldn't escape. She released her child self completely and expressed the rage she could not express as a child. As a result of being allowed to fully express her rage, albeit in her imagination, she experienced increased openness, playfulness, and empowerment. Consequently, she reestablished a relationship with her elderly father, whom she saw once a year for short visits.

Case Example: Marilyn Gets in Touch with Anger

Marilyn, whom I described earlier, got in touch with unexpressed anger during the processing of a memory of being abused by her father.

MARILYN: I can't talk or make any sound . . . it's like I'm going underground. . . . I'm scared, but I don't feel anything. ►◄►◄►◄ No one to help me, no place to go. . . . It's like he was trying to kill me. . . . I stopped believing in God at that time . . . it got all mixed up with my mother.

LP: What do you believe about yourself?

MARILYN: *I must have been bad if she let the devil come and get me. (A significant negative cognition has come up in response to my question.)* ►◄►◄►◄ God let this happen to me. I also felt like my mother was mad at me. . . . I wasn't a perfect kid. I didn't care about being good anymore . . . I wasn't pretty anymore. . . . I knew that he was evil. . . . I made up a story that he wasn't my father. ►◄►◄►◄ No one believed me. No one would do or say anything, but her [*mother's*] family hated him. They knew but couldn't do anything. ►◄►◄►◄ No one did anything and some people were fooled.

LP: Let's go back to the original scene. Tell me what comes up for you now. *(I wanted to keep it focused so we could try to finish this incident.)*

MARILYN: I now feel angry. *(The emotion has changed from terror to anger, indicating that she is processing the memory.)* ►◄►◄►◄ I was angry and so stopped being the good girl. As an adult it makes sense to be angry. . . . He was trying to destroy me. He was afraid of me. I hated and feared him.

LP: Let yourself express your anger towards your father now in your imagination. It is safe to do that.

(Marilyn expressed her anger loudly as she moved her eyes back and forth for several minutes.)

MARILYN: I feel sorry for him. ►◄►◄►◄ I feel sorry for me because I didn't have a father. He's a fake and he knows it. ►◄►◄►◄ I don't think he'll ever be happy because of his falseness. He couldn't fool me. He could never be trusted, ever.

Creative Imaginal Interweaves

With creative imaginal interweaves the therapist and client work together to find a creative solution to a problem that has come up during EMDR and blocked the processing. The client imagines doing something that solves the problem and then adds the bilateral stimulation. The creative imaginal interweave includes the following interweave strategies described by Shapiro (1995).

Metaphor/analogy. Metaphors, stories, and analogies can be very helpful in unblocking stuck processing. Often the therapist can use images that have come spontaneously from the client during the processing in an interweave. These metaphors, which often take the form of symbolic, dream-like images, can be very powerful.

"Let's pretend." In this method the client is encouraged to imagine saying or doing something that is an alternative to the problem. Through imagery the client is allowed to act out something that may have been forbidden or dangerous at the time. This resembles Gestalt therapy, in that the client is encouraged to talk to family members or parts of him or herself, expressing what has not been expressed before. For example, the client might want to tell the perpetrator how he had hurt the client as a child. The therapist suggests the client imagine doing that and adds the eye movements.

Case Example: Creative Imaginal and Linking Perspective Interweaves

Joan had been suffering from chronic back pain since childhood and was searching for its origins. A nearly crippling lower back condition prevented her from walking more than a short distance and working in her garden. At my urging she went to an orthopedist and began an exercise program.

But the exercises didn't help. During one of our sessions Joan noticed that the back pain got worse during and after EMDR. She had no idea what was causing the pain and the doctor could not find anything wrong with her. When she focused on the lower back pain, Joan became noticeably agitated. Finally, we decided to do EMDR on the back pain.

Using the pain as our target, I asked her what she believed about herself. She believed there was something in her lower back. I told her to go with that belief, along with the sensation, as she moved her eyes back and forth. Joan immediately regressed to her child state and said, echoing her adult belief, "There is something in my back."

JOAN: ►◄►◄►◄ I don't see anything. ►◄►◄►◄

LP: How do you feel?

JOAN: I feel real upset. ►◄►◄►◄ It feels like Uncle Zeb is there and on top of me. . . . I can't get him to go away. ►◄►◄►◄ My back is throbbing but it had gotten better. ►◄►◄►◄ *(She gets very visibly upset and agitated.)* We need to get it out, it doesn't belong in there. *(She has an image of being anally raped and she feels like Uncle Zeb's penis is still in her rectum.)* ►◄►◄►◄ I see a big knife . . . I take it and cut it out . . . but it would hurt me. . . . *(She is attempting to find a solution to the problem of the penis in her back.)* ►◄►◄►◄ I make a hole and get Uncle Zeb's penis out of my back. ►◄►◄►◄ If we used a knife it would hurt me.

> *Joan is looping and is unable to come up with a way to get rid of the penis in her back without hurting herself. We need a creative imaginal interweave to help get the processing back on track. I begin to ask her questions to see if together we can come up with a way to solve this dilemma. We come up with different scenarios, but none seems to fit until I ask her if her trusted gynecologist could remove the penis for her with tweezers and then throw the shriveled thing into the trash. This doctor could remove it in a gentle way. Joan agrees that it is a good idea. I tell her to imagine that removal as she moves her eyes back and forth. (I am interweaving a healing image.)*

JOAN: I'm trying to see the picture of it. . . . It's a good idea. Dr. Martin wouldn't hurt me. I can see a movie of it happening. . . . *(She reports with glee that the doctor has rid her of the ugly atrophied penis and thrown it in the trash. Her agitation and distress decreases and she appears relaxed. The interweave has worked.)* ►◄►◄►◄ *(A new associative channel has opened up with a new negative cognition.)* Bad back, naughty back. *(Her child self is taking responsibility for the abuse.)*

LP: Whose fault was it that this happened? *(Linking perspectives interweave.)*

JOAN: Uncle Zeb's.

LP: Who was bad?

JOAN: Uncle Zeb. ►◄►◄►◄ It was Uncle Zeb who was bad . . . my back is good. . . . I feel a lot better. My back feels better too. It's not healed yet.

LP: Let healing light and warmth stream into the place in your back where you were hurt. ►◄►◄►◄

JOAN: That feels good.

Case Example: Creative Imaginal Interweave that Brings in the Adult to Assess the Child's Safety

Melanie (see Parnell, 1997a) was stuck with the issue of safety and trust because of a seduction molestation by her uncle Bill. Unlike her sadistic aunts, who physically abused her as well, Uncle Bill lured her into his home with candy, cake, and toys of every description. Melanie had repeated nightmares of not being safe. She became very anxious and agitated because she didn't believe she could trust herself or her own judgment because she repeatedly went to Uncle Bill's house. Her dreams were a message from her unconscious mind telling her that she could still be in danger because she could not trust her own judgment. Because Uncle Bill had fooled her and was not scary to her child self, Melanie believed she was still in danger of being hurt by someone.

Assuming that this was her child self's fear and that her adult self would be able to tell that this man's house was not safe, I decided to try a creative imaginal interweave. I asked her to imagine going back to Uncle Bill's house. As she imagined his house she felt fear and her negative cognition was she could not trust herself and so was not safe. As she held those things together in her mind she did a set of eye movements. After the first set she found herself clearly back in her uncle's house. I then asked her to have her adult self join the child in the image. I next asked the adult self to look around and tell me what she saw and recognized as danger signs that the child with less information had not seen as dangerous. What her adult self saw immediately alarmed her! She saw a single, childless man's house full of toys and things for kids. All of the shades were drawn and it was dark inside. The man smelled of alcohol. When she recognized all of these things, it was obvious to the adult Melanie that Uncle Bill's house was not a safe place. With that realization, the adult Melanie took her child self in her arms and ran out the door. We installed this with the eye movements. As a result of this interweave, Melanie realized that she could trust her judgment with men like Uncle Bill in the present and protect herself and her child self from harm.

Case Example: Several Interweave Attempts

Sometimes it takes several attempts to find the interweave that will help the client move out of looping. The following case demonstrates how the therapist sometimes needs to try and fail several times before finding the "right" interweave. This session also demonstrates the installation of resources at the beginning of the session, the use of the safe place in the middle so the client can take a break, and the use of imaginal creative interweaves that use inner and outer resources.

This was a very intense session with Alice, a 40-year-old nurse, early in the middle phase of EMDR therapy. In this session, she was processing being abused by her grandmother, who held Alice under water in the bathtub and locked her in a closet. A number of interweaves and interventions were unsuccessful in lowering the very high level of disturbance. I finally found one that worked—I brought myself and her adult self in to rescue her child self.

Alice came to the session feeling scared, quite anxious, and agitated, without knowing why. We began the session by doing a guided imagery of going down stairs to her safe place. I asked her child self how old she was, and she replied "five years old." She was "scared," and her breathing accelerated. "What are you afraid of?" I asked. She replied, in a child's voice, "I'm afraid of Grandma."

I asked her to imagine a protective boundary around herself and her child that made them safe. Alice was silent for a while and then told me that she had imagined a force field like the one in Star Trek movies, which was invisible but prevented everything from passing. I then asked her to imagine her child self with her in the safe place surrounded by that force field. After a while, she told me that Little Alice liked being held and liked hugs. I told her to give little Alice exactly what she needed. When the feelings of safety and comfort were strongly felt in her body and mind, I installed these feelings with eye movements. I told the child self that she could call on Big Alice to be there for her if she needed her and that they could go to the safe place in the force field together whenever she wanted to.

Alice seemed to feel comfortable with those instructions and was ready to bring up the memory we had worked on the week before that was associated with not feeling safe with Grandma—that of Grandma giving Little Alice a bath. The negative cognition was "I'm different, I'm not like everybody and that's bad. I'm stupid. It's bad to be different from everybody else." She was feeling scared and agitated. Her body began to squirm. I did not get the positive cognition and measurements because she was already abreacting. Her SUDS was obviously quite high.

ALICE: ►◄►◄►◄ She's mad at me . . . she says that the clothes I had on were from her and I got them all dirty. ►◄►◄►◄ She's really mad and hitting me with her hand on my face. . . . She doesn't like it when I cry, she says I'm a baby. . . *there's places for babies. (She is getting more agitated, wringing her hands, her breathing accelerated.)* ►◄►◄►◄ I'm someplace in the bathroom but not the bathtub . . . someplace scary. . . someplace small. *(She has become very upset and frightened. She is overwhelmed. She is*

157

looping and the SUDS is not reducing with the eye movements. She tells me she wants to go to the safe place for a rest.)

LP: Imagine Big Alice taking Little Alice to the safe place. The force field is around the safe place. You are safe now. You can put the scary stuff in a file folder in my office and we can get it later.

She imagined the adult and child selves playing together in a fun place and calmed during the imagery. I told her that she could return to the scary memory if and when she wanted to and continue the processing. After ten to fifteen minutes, she was ready to return to the bathroom scene.

ALICE: ►◄►◄►◄ I'm in a closet on the wall up high. She would put me in there when I was bad . . . and I was small and I couldn't get out. I could die in there and nobody would know I was in there. . . . I have to wait for her to come back and let me out.

(I ask her questions for clarification. Alice is quite upset again.)

ALICE: She leaves her in there a long time. . . *(Her adult self is speaking about her child self, but then changes to a child's voice in the first person.)* It's small and dark in there . . . I can't call for help or it will make her madder.►◄►◄►◄ *(She is getting more upset, very agitated, breathing rapidly, wringing her hands.)* I'm still in there. . . . I can't move. . . . Grandma says the closet on the wall can move and can go down. . . If I cry she'll make it go down. . . . Then it would be really dark there. . . . *I can't cry or move!* ►◄►◄►◄ *I'm still in there. I don't want to be in there anymore!! If I have to stay there any longer I just want to die!!! (She is very upset and looping. She is stuck in the closet and not getting out.)* ►◄►◄►◄

LP: Say what you need to say. *(I try an interweave giving her permission to express verbally unspoken words.)* ►◄►◄►◄

ALICE: *I'm still in there I don't want to be in there anymore. I want to get out !! (She remains extremely upset; my interweave has not worked.)*

LP: Go with "I want to get out."

ALICE: *I'm still in there. I can't get out!!! (She is frantic, and panicking.)*

LP: *(I decide to try a linking perspectives interweave, reminding her that she did eventually get out of the closet, and did survive.)* You did eventually get out of the closet, didn't you?

ALICE: Yes.

LP: Think about that. ►◄►◄►◄

ALICE: *(She's still extremely upset; the interweave has not worked!) I'm still there!!! Get me out!!! (She is pleading with me for help.)*

(At this point my instincts take over and I do an inner and outer resources interweave, bringing in myself and Alice's adult self to rescue

the child self from the confines of the closet. I tell her the following as I keep her eyes moving.)

LP: ►◄►◄►◄ I come into the bathroom along with Big Alice and I break open the closet with an ax and get Little Alice out of the closet. We hold her. . . . You are safe and protected. . . . I then take the ax and destroy the closet, so that you can never be put back in there again. . . . Big Alice and I protect you from Grandma. . . . *(Her distress has dropped, her breathing is calming down, and she is no longer writhing in the chair and wringing her hands. This interweave has worked!)* Big Alice and I take Little Alice to the safe place and put the force field around us. ►◄►◄►◄

ALICE: I feel the force field . . . I feel safe and protected. ►◄►◄►◄

LP: *(I install the positive cognition, "I am safe and protected now.")*

ALICE: The closet is gone, you destroyed it. It's smashed into a million little pieces.►◄►◄►◄ We're both in the force field and we're happy.

By this time Alice had completely calmed. The new image of the destroyed closet had replaced the old one with her trapped inside, and she felt confident that Little Alice could never be put back in there again. She felt deeply moved by my rescue of her and my demonstrated protectiveness. Her SUDS was down to 0, and she was peaceful.

This session deepened the trust between us and gave her new confidence that I would be able to find a way to get her out of the places of terror, even if it meant my coming in and saving her myself. Over the next couple of years of EMDR processing the old image of the closet never returned, and when she thought of the incident she would see the image of the destroyed closet.

As you can see, I did not know what was happening or exactly what to do. I kept offering her suggestions that did not work. Eventually, I found one that did. I believe it is most important for the therapist not to panic when interweaves are not taking; rather, keep trying different things until one does take. It is the client who provides the feedback. If an interweave works, the processing begins to move again, or the SUDS drops. If I hadn't been able to find an interweave that worked, I could have asked her to return to the safe place to calm down and feel safe.

Doing EMDR with adults abused as children can often feel like groping in the dark for a key that will unlock the door. I have learned over time to keep trying different keys until eventually I find the one that works.

Chapter 10

Suggestions for Closing Incomplete Sessions and Helping Clients Manage Between Sessions

This chapter describes many various techniques for lowering the level of distress so that clients can safely transition back into their lives. These include the use of interweaves, positive cognitions, imagery, art, relaxation techniques, and meditation. The chapter closes with suggestions for helping clients manage between sessions.

Closing down the session is a very important step in the EMDR procedure. It is essential that clients feel safe and emotionally contained before they leave the therapist's office. Often it is not possible to complete the processing of a traumatic abuse incident in one 90-minute session. One incident of abuse links into another and then another, making it difficult to reduce the level of distress to one of calm and peace. Even if it means going overtime, EMDR therapists must bring the client to a sense of safety and containment.

Processing to the End

In the standard EMDR protocol, when the therapist believes that the client has fully processed the original target memory, he/she asks the client to bring to mind the original image and report the current degree of disturbance on the SUDS. When the image is reported as no longer distressing (a SUDS of 0 or 1), the client is asked to check his or her original positive cognition and see if it fits with the image. Perhaps a new positive statement fits better. When the client finds the best positive cognition for the image, he or she rates how true the cognition feels to him or her on a scale of 1 to 7, with 1 completely true and 7 completely false. If the positive cognition is rated a VoC of 6 or 7, the positive cognition and image are held together in the client's mind and the positive cognition is installed with bilateral stimulation. After the set of bilateral stimulation, the therapist again measures the VoC to see if it has changed. If it has gotten stronger, more sets of bilateral stimulation can be used.

After the positive cognition has been installed, the body scan is done. The client is instructed to close his or her eyes, concentrate on the incident, and repeat the positive cognition while scanning his or her body for any area of sensation. If a sensation of discomfort is reported, it is reprocessed until the discomfort subsides. After the body scan has been completed, the session is closed with the therapist advising the client that processing may continue after the session and asking them to note what comes up for the following sessions. The therapist and client then debrief the experience of the session.

Closing Incomplete Sessions

An incomplete session is one in which a client's material is still unresolved, i.e., he or she is still obviously upset or the SUDS is above 1 and the VoC less than 6. The following is a suggested procedure for closing down an incomplete session. The purpose is to acknowledge clients for what they have accomplished and to make sure they are well grounded before they leave the office. Be sure to leave sufficient time at the end of the session to close it down—for most people, 10 to 15 minutes.

There are several steps in this procedure:

1. *Ask the client's permission to stop and explain the reason.* "We are almost out of time and we will need to stop soon. How comfortable are you about stopping now?"
2. *Give encouragement and support for the effort made.* "You have done some very good work and I appreciate the effort you have made. How are you feeling?"
3. *Help the client clarify what was gained in the session, or a positive cognition. (Even if the SUDS is not a 0, look for some kind of positive self statement. It can be a process cognition, e.g., I am learning to love myself.)* "What do you want to take away from the hard work you've done today?" or "What was the most important thing you learned today?" "What do you believe about yourself now when you bring up the original picture?" Write down the client's response.
4. *Install the response with a short set of bilateral stimulation.* "Think about 'I'm learning to love myself' and follow my fingers."
5. *Eliminate the body scan.* The body scan is not done because the thera-

pist knows there is still more to process. Time is better spent closing the client down.

6. *Do a relaxation exercise. At this time protector/nurturer resources can be brought in.* "I would like to suggest we do a relaxation exercise before we stop." (The therapist suggests a form of relaxation, e.g., safe place, light stream, visualization, slow vertical or infinity eye movements, etc.) The safe place and positive imagery can be installed with a *short* set of bilateral stimulation.

7. *Containment exercise.* Offer the client the opportunity to leave the distressing material/feelings in an imaginary container until the next time that the two of you meet. Say that the client worked hard in the session and can contain the difficult feelings between sessions. The image of the material in the container can also be installed with a short set of bilateral stimulation. Write down the container image to be used in later sessions.

8. *Closure/Debrief.* "The processing we have done today may continue after the session. You may or may not notice new insights, thoughts, memories, or dreams. If you do, just notice what you are experiencing—take a mental snapshot of it (what you are seeing, feeling, thinking, and the trigger), and keep a log. We can work on this new material next time. If you feel it is necessary, call me."

Spend the remaining time talking with the client about the session, helping him/her begin to digest and integrate the material that has arisen during the session. Make sure the client is grounded in his or her body before he or she leaves your office. Clients may need to splash cold water on their faces and walk around before they get in their cars and drive.

If the client is still too upset to leave your office, go overtime and work with him/her until he or she is in a calm state. Set up an appointment for later in the day or the following day if necessary. Do not leave a client in a distressed state for a week. Make sure the client knows he or she can call you if feeling upset or out of control. EMDR processing causes many clients to regress. An adult regressed to a child state may feel very distressed and unable to function properly. It is important to help the client contact the adult self and feel the adult self functioning and in control.

Below are more detailed descriptions of some closure techniques.

THERAPIST-SUGGESTED INTERWEAVES

Sometimes time runs out before the session is complete and the therapist, by using a strategic interweave, can tie things together for the client in a way that brings rapid closure. During this time the therapist can be more than ordinarily active and directive, helping the client bring in resources and connect disparate memory networks and ego states.

These interweaves can include any of the types described in Chapter 9. Often interweaves that bring in the adult self or protector/nurturer figures to comfort or protect the child are useful in calming down a client who is distressed when the time is running out.

TH: Can you imagine your adult self coming in and protecting your child self?
CL: Yes.
TH: Imagine that. *(Add bilateral stimulation.)*

For a client who is fearful of a perpetrator who is known to be old and feeble, a question eliciting the adult's perspective on present safety can be used.

TH: Where is your uncle now?
CL: He is dead.
TH: Think about that. *(Add bilateral stimulation to link memory networks.)*

For the sorrowful child self, bring in the loving adult self, nurturer figures, or spiritual figures.

TH: Can you imagine your grandmother holding your child self on her lap and telling her that she loves her?
CL: Yes.
TH: Go with that. *(Add bilateral stimulation.)*

A client who is hovering outside of her body because she believes it is not safe to be in her body can be asked, "Is it safe to be in your body *now?*" If she replies "yes," add the bilateral stimulation to complete the interweave.

INSTALLING A POSITIVE COGNITION OR IMAGE

Another modification to the standard protocol is to always install a positive cognition, statement, or image at the end of EMDR processing sessions. You can ask the client "What do you believe about yourself now when you bring up the original image?" Install what he or she reports. The client may have a process-oriented positive cognition (Wildwind, 1993), one that shows movement in the direction of positive change—for example, "I am learning to love myself" or "I can heal this in a safe way."

If the target issue is still quite unresolved at the end of the session and a positive cognition cannot be found, the therapist might ask, "What did you learn from today's session?" When the client reports to the therapist what he learned, the therapist applies the bilateral stimulation to install it. Some clients may ask the therapist to help them review the session using the therapist's notes. The areas of insight or nuggets of wisdom that came from the client can be repeated to him or her along with the bilateral stimulation for installation.

The therapist may want to guide the client to his or her safe place and install images and statements about safety. It is crucial that something positive be installed and that the client feel like he or she has gotten something from the session. This installation of something positive or constructive feels very good to clients. It helps them to feel contained, cared for, and empowered, and that they are moving in the direction of healing.

IMAGERY AS A CLOSING TECHNIQUE

When it is time to close down a session, whether or not it is complete, I often ask clients to return to their safe place, imagine their adult self holding their child self, and feel as strongly as possible the feelings of safety and security. I might also ask them to bring in the nurturer, protector, and spiritual resources. Either I, or their imagined resources, repeat positive cognitions discovered during the EMDR processing, along with beneficial affirmations. Often the positive statements are related to the issues of safety, responsibility, and choice: "You are safe now," "you were a little girl who was hurt by a mean, angry grown-up, it wasn't your fault," "you didn't have a choice then as a little boy, but you do now as an adult," etc. Use process positive cognitions that express movement toward health, such as, "I'm beginning to heal," "the hurt is beginning to lighten," "I can change." When clients report feeling calm, peaceful, and safe, install the image, cognitions, and feelings with a short set of bilateral stimulation.

Here is an example of a therapist-directed closure using resources the client had developed earlier.

Tн: OK, now imagine going to your safe place, along with your child self. . . . Imagine putting up that protective shield. . . . Imagine bringing in Bear to protect and nurture both the adult and child. Feel his warm fur and his large presence. Imagine Jesus there with you, too, with his warmth and love. You are safe now. Imagine holding the child and telling her that she's safe with you now . . . that she's a good girl . . . that you love her. . . . Let me know when you feel calm and peaceful. . . . Good. Now follow my fingers with your eyes. ►◄►►◄►◄ Good. How are you feeling now?

Sometimes I ask the adult self to soothe the child self with caring words. Sometimes the nurturers, protectors, or spiritual figures are called upon to do the comforting. It depends upon the client and his or her needs at the time.

There are times when healing imagery is helpful. After clients have processed a very intense memory of having been assaulted, their bodies reverberate with the aftermath of the remembered abuse. They often feel raw and wounded. The therapist can suggest to a client that she *"imagine healing light flowing down through the top of your head and down into all of the places of pain . . . the light gently heals these places with warmth and love. . . . Slowly the wounds are beginning to heal. . . . Feel the warmth and healing. . . . The healing light moves to all of the places of pain bringing new life and renewal to all of those places."*

Use the words and images that you believe will work best for particular clients and give them permission to create imagery that works best for them. It can be helpful to develop imagery with the client for this visualization. One woman chose to imagine herself under a beautiful waterfall of crystal-clear water that cleansed her body of pain from past assaults. We installed the imagery and feeling with knee taps. She was later able to imagine the waterfall when she took showers to continue the feeling of healing and renewal.

Imagery may also be used during closing sessions for *containing the unfinished material.* Since there are many different imagery techniques, it is a good idea to make some choices with the client ahead of time. Some clients like to imagine leaving their unfinished material in a file folder in the therapist's office until their next session. Other clients like to put the material in an imaginary locked vault or safe.

A colleague of mine asks her clients to leave whatever feels uncontainable someplace in her office. Many clients choose a basket. She then asks them to "imagine all of the unfinished images, feelings, body sensations, tastes, and smells and put them into the basket." As they do this, she asks them to do a short set of eye movements or other bilateral stimulation. After the image and feeling of containment have been installed, she tells the clients that, if they choose, they can continue to work on the contained material when they come back the next week.

Another colleague uses the following imagery to close incomplete EMDR sessions. Clients are asked to imagine the traumatic scene as if they were viewing it on a movie screen. The therapist then asks them to imagine the scene becoming miniaturized. Next clients are asked to imagine putting the scene in a chest that is a very strong container. They then imagine dumping the chest out of a boat so it sinks out of sight; yet they know they can retrieve it whenever they like. After the visualization clients are asked to go to their inner sanctuary or safe place, gathering around them whatever guides or resources they might need. The resultant sense of safety may be installed with a short set of eye movements or other bilateral stimulation.

Another method of containment is to have clients imagine that the remaining traumatic material is on a video that they can edit or eject and store until they want to replay it at a later time. Most people can readily imagine using a VCR, and this gives them a sense of control over the material.

Some clients feel the need to do something physically symbolic to increase the sense of safety and containment. One woman, upon completing an EMDR session processing an abuse incident, still felt a sense of contamination in her current life from the perpetrator. After exploring various solutions to this problem, we came up with the idea of her physically destroying all of the gifts the perpetrator had given her. She felt these gifts were contaminating her in the present because they represented ties to the perpetrator. This woman systematically searched her home for every gift and then smashed all of them with a sledge hammer until they were broken into tiny pieces. She burned what could be burned in a liberating fire in her fireplace.

ART AS A CLOSING TECHNIQUE

Art can be a useful tool for closing EMDR sessions. The physical act of drawing or sculpting something is grounding, and the product is a concrete representation of the client's inner experience. Clients can draw the new image, belief, or feeling that they have at the end of the session. The drawing gives form to what has been privately held inside, and it can be shared with the therapist. If the client began the session with a drawing, the drawing at the end provides a comparison and a sense of movement. The drawings give a concrete sense that change has occurred during the session, as well as information about work yet to be done.

Clients can also draw the containment image. For example, the client who has imagined his distressing material in a chest at the bottom of the ocean might be asked to draw the scene. The drawing further reinforces the sense of containment.

One woman who had been sexually abused as a child by her grandfather was afraid the good memories of her grandfather would be contaminated by the bad ones. Just imagining the separation of the memories was not sufficient for her. After exploring various potential solutions with her therapist, she found a large box with a lid, placed physical representations of the distressing images inside it, and firmly closed the lid. She left this box in her therapist's office, where she felt it would be safe.

Clients can also reinforce the feeling of safety at the end of the session by drawing the safe place with their adult and child selves and nurturing and protecting figures. After drawing the safe place image, clients can take it home if they wish, as a reminder of their safety in the present.

GROUNDED BREATHING AND LOVINGKINDNESS MEDITATIONS

I first learned Metta or Lovingkindness meditation from Sharon Salzberg at a Vipassana meditaton course she was co-teaching with Joseph Goldstein in 1976. Since then I have practiced and taught this meditation and have found it very helpful for developing compassion for oneself and for others. Adults who have been abused as children suffer from broken hearts. Those whom they loved and depended on hurt them. The physical wounds may be long healed, but their hearts remain damaged. Lovingkindness meditation in conjunction with EMDR can bring healing to the heart. I have used this meditation as a closing technique for many clients. It allows them to focus on loving themselves, further reinforcing the healing of the shame and self-hate so many adult survivors feel. I believe that the development of compassion for oneself is an essential aspect of healing from childhood abuse. The more we as therapists can offer and reinforce compassion through our nonjudgmental caring for our clients, the better for their healing.

As I mentioned earlier, for two years I led a meditation group for women who had been sexually abused as children. In this group I taught grounded breathing, Vipassana meditation, and lovingkindness meditation. I adapted these practices to the needs of the women, making the meditations shorter and offering more guidance. In the lovingkindness meditation, we focused on sending compassion to their child selves whom they imagined in the safety of their loving hearts. Many of the women could barely manage sending love to their child selves, but they insisted on doing the meditation each time and wanted to begin and end the sitting period with it. They added words and phrases they wanted me to say like "May I have compassion for my closed heart," "May I be safe," and "May I be free from fear."

What follows is a grounded breathing meditation, which I learned from Jean Klein, whose yoga and meditation seminars I attended for several years, and lovingkindness meditation (Salzberg & Kabat-Zinn, 1997). These can be done together or separately. Sometimes you might want to go right into the lovingkindness meditation after the EMDR work. These practices can be done for five minutes to thirty minutes or longer. You might choose to teach clients these practices before using them at the end of a session. Some clients also do these practices at home between sessions. You can make a tape for clients, or they can purchase any of the available commercial tapes.

Both meditations require that the client find a quiet, undisturbed place to sit, disconnect the phone, and insure that there will be no interruptions during the time of the meditation. The person can sit cross-legged on a cushion or in a chair with the feet on the floor. It is important that he or she be comfortable and sit in an upright position.

Grounding Breathing Meditation

*Close your eyes and feel yourself sitting. Be aware of the places of contact
... your bottom on the cushion and your feet on the floor. Be aware of your
breathing. In and out. Feel the breath in the body. Let yourself relax into the
present moment.*

*Now take a deep breath, drawing the air up from the earth, filling your
abdomen ... then filling your chest ... and filling your throat ... and then
slowly exhale back down deep into the earth, ... from the throat ... chest ...
and then abdomen. ... Now again breathe up from the earth, slowly filling
the abdomen ... chest ... and ...throat ... then slowly exhale back down into
the earth ... from the throat ... chest ... and abdomen. ... Let the breath be
deep, full, and smooth. Feel yourself present moment to moment, one with
the breath.*

The expansion of the breath should be as full as possible. Deep full
breaths. Breathing in from the earth, and exhaling slowly back down into
the earth. Repeat the breathing and instructions for a several minutes. This
breathing helps to calm, center, and ground. It is useful preparation for the
lovingkindness meditation. This breathing can be followed by a guided
imagery to the safe place, putting a protective boundary around the person
and bringing in nurturers or protectors if needed. The lovingkindness meditation can then be done within the "safe place."

Inner Child Lovingkindness Meditation

*Now bring your attention to the area of your heart. Breathe in and out from
your heart. ... Let the breath be gentle and natural. In and out ... in and out
... feel your heart becoming soft and warm. Breathing in and out of your
loving heart. Now imagine your inner child in your heart. Your loving heart
is a safe place for your tender child. Begin to send lovingkindness to this
child self.* (Repeat in a soft, gentle voice, with pauses between phrases:) *May
you be peaceful. May you be happy. May you be filled with lovingkindness.
May you be free from fear. May you be free from suffering. May you be joy-
ful. May you feel free. May you love and be loved. Use the words that work
for you. Repeat them silently to yourself as you send lovingkindness to your
child self. May you be peaceful. May you be happy. May you be free from
suffering. May you be free from fear. May you be safe.*

Continue in this way, repeating words of lovingkindness to the child self.
Clients may want to imagine their adult self holding the child in their lap
as they repeat the loving phrases, and other nurturer or protector resources
may also send lovingkindness. The meditation can focus completely on the
child self or it can expand to include others.

Imagine in front of you someone you love very much. Imagine sending lov-ingkindness to him or her. Just as I want to be happy, may you be happy. Just as I want to be peaceful, may you be peaceful. Just as I want to be free from suffering, may you be free from suffering. Just as I want to be free from fear, may you be free from fear. (The person can continue to repeat words that work for him or her, sending lovingkindness to the loved one.)

The meditation can be expanded to include others the person loves and then expanded again to include family members and friends. It can be expanded to include the person's community, town, state, country, conti-nent, world—finally, the whole universe. You can have clients imagine sending lovingkindness to all of the plants and animals as well as people. At the end of the meditation the person can imagine sending lovingkind-ness to all sentient beings in the universe. *May all beings everywhere be happy, peaceful, and free from suffering.*

Instead of focusing on the child self, the person can begin the meditation by sending love to him or herself. *May I be peaceful. May I be happy. May I be free from suffering.* The idea is to generate a feeling of warmth and ten-derness toward oneself. This is very difficult for many people. You can add, "May I have compassion for my closed heart" for those who have difficul-ty feeling compassion for themselves. This meditation can be adapted as you feel fit. Lovingkindness can even be extended to people who have caused harm. Some people do this spontaneously. Use discretion with this part because premature forgiveness can cover over the deeper layers of woundedness that should be processed for full healing.

Suggestions for Helping Clients Manage Between Sessions

HOMEWORK

Clients can be encouraged to take walks in nature, meditate, do yoga or tai chi, or try other things to reduce stress and connect more with themselves. Attention should be paid to a healthy diet, regular exercise, and getting enough restful sleep. Some clients may benefit from group work or a course in self-defense or model mugging. As clients experience stress with the EMDR processing of painful memories, they should be reminded not to drink alcohol or take drugs. If it appears that the client is in need of antianxiety or antidepressant medication, a referral to a psychiatrist for a medication evaluation should be made.

There are many things clients can do between sessions to help with con-tainment or facilitate processing, depending on what is in their best interest.

Journal writing helps clients continue to process and integrate material. Many clients find poetry an important outlet for feelings that cannot be expressed easily in prose.

Clients can also be encouraged to express feelings and images that arise in art such as drawing, painting, collage work, and sculpting. Artwork is very integrative and empowering. The focus should be on the expression, not the product. Let whatever wants to be expressed come out in whatever form it takes. Creative expression can be spiritual and enlivening, helping clients experience themselves beyond the victim identity.

TRANSITIONAL OBJECTS

Many clients who have been abused as children have a difficult time with object constancy, especially if the abuse was by a parent or someone close to them. Consequently, it is hard for them to carry the therapist inside as a positive inner representation for any length of time. They have a hard time remembering that their therapist continues to exist and cares about them between sessions. For this reason it can be helpful for clients to have what Winnicott called transitional objects that represent the therapist and the nurturing/healing environment. These transitional objects can take a variety of different forms. Some clients are given small objects of their choosing as a reminder of the therapist and the office as a safe place. For instance, one client would become very distraught when I took vacations, so I gave her a quartz crystal from my office as a reminder of me and our work.

Tapes of relaxation exercises and of the invocation of the safe place and inner and outer resources can bridge the time between sessions. In these guided imageries, designed for each individual, the therapist speaks directly to the client and uses the client's name. These tapes can be very comforting. Clients can play the tapes to help them sleep at night or to relax. If they feel disconnected from the therapist, they can play the tapes as a reminder of the relationship. The tapes can be particularly helpful when therapists take vacations and clients need regular reminders of the reality of the therapeutic relationship.

Clients need to know that their therapists hold them in their hearts between sessions. Some clients leave objects that represent aspects of themselves with the therapist in the healing space, for example, artwork, poetry, special objects, and childhood photographs. Sometimes they are gifts, and sometimes they are "lent" to the therapist for a time. I realize that there are various opinions about this issue and different ways of working with it, depending upon one's theoretical orientation. I do not interpret the gifts, because I feel that would create an empathic break. Usually, there is an unspoken understanding of their meaning. I feel honored to be trusted enough to be asked to hold these things for my clients and do so until they request their return.

Part IV

. . . .

Cases

Chapter 11

Case Sessions Demonstrating Various Techniques

In this chapter I describe EMDR processing sessions from three cases to illustrate some of the techniques described in the previous chapters, including developing targets, facilitating processing, working with abreactions, unblocking blocked processing, and closing sessions.

The Case of Anya: Working with Powerful Somatosensory Abreactions

Anya desired EMDR therapy because she felt stuck sexually. She had been with her partner for four years in a loving relationship but had not been able to be sexual with him for two years. She had worked on this issue with another therapist but the feelings of repulsion only got worse. At this time she did not even want to cuddle with her partner.

Anya was born in Southeast Asia while her father, who was a career military officer, was stationed there. His career necessitated moving frequently all over the world. Anya's mother became pregnant with Anya soon after her marriage, and Anya's brother was born two years after Anya. Her parents were heavy partyers and drinkers who did not have a close marital relationship. When Anya was in her late teens, her mother told her that her father was impotent, an excuse her mother used for justifying her affairs. Anya's father also had affairs.

Anya had very poor recall of her childhood. She believed that her father had sexually abused her when she was around seven but was not sure and did not have any clear visual memories. She sensed another figure in her childhood bedroom, which elicited sexual feelings in her body and deep discomfort and fear. She had dreams that made her feel that she had been sex-

173

ually abused. She feared groups of men and wondered if something had happened related to that. She felt she had been sexually assaulted in different settings. Nothing was clear, and there was no family collaboration. Four years ago, with the support of a survivor group, she raised the incest suspicions with her mother, who was surprised but supportive of her. Anya then confronted her father, who denied it. The confrontation triggered panic attacks and what she called "body-memory flashbacks."

Anya always had friends, even though she was shy. She had her first boyfriend when she was 16, a relationship that was nonsexual the entire nine months they were together. The one time he wanted to be sexual, she became hysterical, even though he was, in her words, quite sweet and gentle.

She grew up feeling unworthy. Her low self-esteem and fear of intimacy caused her to choose emotionally unavailable men in relationships. Most of her relationships did not last beyond a year—with the exception of a relationship in her twenties that lasted four years and her current relationship. In all of them, she stopped having sex as they became closer over time.

In our second session, Anya and I talked about her negative self beliefs and about issues, themes, and dreams that could be targets for EMDR sessions. We listed them:

1. My body and sexuality is dirty and disgusting.
2. If I'm sexual, I'm bad.
3. Sex is OK in short-term relationships but not in long-term ones. Sex is OK in the beginning of a relationship but not later. (She believed this related to her parents' attitudes and behaviors.)
4. It is dangerous to feel out of control. Feelings, including sexual feelings, are dangerous.
5. I want to be seen and heard, but it's scary to be seen and heard. It is hard to find my voice, to speak up in a group. I have problems with my throat.
6. Fear of not being able to breathe. She had a history of panic attacks and sleep problems. Related to this issue, Anya recounted a recent dream: "I'm a little girl in another century. I'm remembering I had been strangled to death. I was about to be strangled. I was trying to comfort myself. In the dream I was scared and I was sobbing."
7. If I get close I'll be abandoned. She related this belief to emotional abandonment from both of her parents and her mother's not protecting her from her father.
8. She had recurrent dreams about being pregnant and having an abortion, which she had no conscious memory of ever having. She did not know what this meant.
9. For many years she had dreams of being chased by something evil.

10. Disturbing dreams that were very violent and bloody. One involved burying body parts.

Despite the intensity of Anya's inner life, she appeared very calm and grounded in relating to me. She was bright, articulate, and insightful. She had done quite a lot of work on herself over the years, which helped prepare her for EMDR. She seemed to know herself well—as well as could be expected after traditional talk therapies—but she had not unlocked the mystery of the bizarre dreams and aversive feelings about sex. She had a good support system, which included close friends and her partner. She practiced Vipassana meditation, so she was more able to witness her experience and maintain a broader perspective. She also connected with something larger than herself in nature.

In the second session we did a safe place exercise and inner child guided imagery. She was able to find a safe place, a lovely garden. In the garden her child self connected with her adult self. They were able to play together and the child felt comfortable sitting on the adult self's lap. This was significant information. She had strong inner resources that were easily accessible. I could use the adult self, as well as her partner and friends, as a resource for the child. This information, along with her stability, connection with me, and willingness to explore the unknown origins of her current problems, gave me confidence to begin the EMDR processing in the next session.

For our first EMDR session we decided to target her aversion to sex with her partner. Because she did not know what it was associated to, we used the memory of being in bed with her partner recently when she felt disturbed. In exploring this memory with her eyes closed, she told me "I don't want any part of my lower body to touch him. . . . I'm wearing underwear, but he isn't. I let our legs touch and I feel discomfort with our skin touching because we'll get sweaty, which is yucky. I don't want his genitals to touch me. My palms get sweaty and the bottoms of my feet get sweaty. I associate sweat with fear, and that makes me cringe and want to get away. It's scary to be that close. I am disgusted by bodies, secretions, and odors. I feel dirty and he is dirty. Sex is dirty, bodies are dirty."

The negative cognition she chose for the image was "bodies/sex are dirty and scary." The positive cognition was bodies and sex are fine, which she rated a VOC of 1–2. The emotions were fear, repulsion, disgust, and "yuckiness." Her SUDS was a 7. The body sensations were disturbance in her lower abdomen, tension in her shoulders and neck, and nausea in her throat. When she was ready we began the eye movements using the light bar.

ANYA: ►◄►◄►◄ What if this doesn't work for me?
LP: What are you feeling?

ANYA: Calmer.
LP: Go with that. ►◄►◄►◄

> *(Anya began a very strong abreaction. Her body was jerking spasmod-ically from the waist, and she was making strange strangling sounds from her throat. She kept moving her eyes and I encouraged her to keep going.)*

ANYA: I feel calmer and woozy. Something is getting stuck here. It feels familiar.
LP: What are you feeling in your body?
ANYA: My throat is tight and so is my chest. ►◄►◄►◄

> *(She again began to abreact with her body jerking, causing her to lurch forward on the couch. This time she was coughing and gagging. It looked like something was taking over her body.)*

ANYA: My chest and stomach aches; there's tension in my head. Something is happening. ►◄►◄►◄
(More abreactions, choking, coughing, jerking, lurching forward.)
ANYA: The tension has moved to my left side. The feelings and thoughts are disconnected from the body sensations.

> *(She and I had no idea what was happening. I asked her to return to the original picture and tell me what came up for her.)*

ANYA: Flickerings of feelings of sadness.
LP: What beliefs do you have now?
ANYA: It's wrong, it's wrong. *(She isn't aware of what she is referring to.)*
LP: Go with that. ►◄►◄►◄
ANYA: During the eye movements I was feeling numb. There was no sad-ness. I'm not feeling anything. I'm feeling sad about the disconnection and numbness. I couldn't let myself feel or think. ►◄►◄►◄

> *(Anya began to sob during the eye movements. I gently encouraged her to stay with it, saying that she was doing a good job. We continued the eye movements until she stopped crying.)*

ANYA: I feel a little better. It hurts though. ►◄►◄►◄ I flashed to an earlier thought. I look ugly when I cry. Where did that come from? *(She was curious.)*

> *(She seemed off the processing track so I asked her to again return to the original picture and check it.)*

ANYA: It seems less powerful. There is a little tightness in my stomach. There is slight warmth in my throat and chest. ►◄►◄►◄ There is still tightness in my abdominal area from my body contracting. ►◄►◄►◄ I was thinking about how sensitive I've been with hands there. I feel the possibility of having been pregnant. The contractions, and pushing that happened, are like what happens when you give birth. I'm not trusting my thinking. ►◄►◄►◄ More thinking. Why not . . . your thinking is fine. The upset stomach started to go away a little bit. I'm amazed. ►◄►◄►◄ My body and stomach is relaxed, possibly as relaxed as it can get.

LP: Let's go back to the original picture again.

ANYA: It's hard to bring it up. It's not clear. The feelings are gone—neutral, distant.

LP: What do you believe about yourself now?

ANYA: I'm kind of OK. I'm OK—there's some distrust.

LP: Go with the feeling of distrust. ►◄►◄►◄

ANYA: A part of me says don't trust it.

> *(I wanted to explore what this was about if I could with her. I asked her to imagine being in bed naked with her partner. What comes up for you?)*

ANYA: I feel calm and relaxed. . . . I have a glimpse of being OK.

LP: Go with that. ►◄►◄►◄

ANYA: There is inner chatter in my head. I'm testing it out in my imagination. I had some soothing images. It might possibly be OK. ►◄►◄►◄ I can be OK with the images in my head, but I don't trust real life.

> *(I had the sense that there was a blocking belief involved here. So I asked her.)*

LP: What belief would you have to let go of to feel OK?

ANYA: *(She had a response to this question.)* People don't have sex in long-term relationships. To get closer I risk being left. . . . I am afraid of the pain of loss.

> *(I could see that she did not experience her parents as having a sexual relationship. I decided to try a linking perspectives interweave, linking information from her present life to the child's memory of her parents' relationship.*

LP: Can you think of people you know who are in loving long-term relationships who have an active sexual relationship?

ANYA: Yes.

LP: Can you think about them—they have solid relationships, they're married, vital, and alive people, and they have a good sex life. Can you imagine them as a good model? *(I am actively trying to counter her old view with more up-to-date information. She did know people who contradicted the old belief.)*

ANYA: Yes.

LP: Think about that. ►◄►◄►◄

ANYA: I feel OK and content.

LP: Imagine bringing this sense of a loving long-term relationship that is sexual into your current relationship. *(This is an imaginal interweave that allows her to try out this new information in her imagination.)* ►◄►◄►◄

ANYA: It feels good.

We ended the session by debriefing and talking about what had come up for her. She felt calm and peaceful when she left.

During the next session she told me that she had felt worse the day after our session, then much better. She then had a number of what she called "flashbacks" with no images. "I can feel them coming. . . . I feel uncomfortable in my body, then these convulsive movements come on, like in the session. They get worse, and I feel fearful, I begin to cry and have a terror feeling, and want to get really small in a fetal position. My mouth will open and I start to scream over and over again and I can't breathe—it felt like my air supply was cut off—then I could breathe again. These flashbacks came at night. It feels like I'm dying . . . I feel a lot of shame."

In addition to the flashbacks, she was feeling rage come up in her relationship with her partner around the issue of not being seen accurately. She also had a number of intense dreams—some frightening and some very positive and spiritual with symbols of transformation. We decided to focus our EMDR work on the rage and the issue of not feeling seen by her partner. We began with an image of her with her partner and her feeling rejected. The negative cognition was "I'm not deserving of attention unless it is sexual." She felt rage and a tightness in her stomach.

During this session she had very intense body abreactions. She jerked, coughed, screamed, hyperventilated, shook, and convulsed during the eye movements. At one point she had a flash of a girl screaming in a self-protective gesture. "I can almost hear her screams." From her body movements and emotional releases it looked like she was reliving a terrifying sexual assault. At another point in the processing she said she was "begging them not to do it . . . . What was happening was hurting me inside and felt unbearable—like rape. I want to get out of my body."

Later she felt rage toward those who were hurting her and imagined being violent toward them. By the end of the session her SUDS was between a 1 and 2 and she said "It is OK to say no to sexual attention. I can say no and feel increasingly comfortable." She reported feeling some discomfort in her abdomen. During the debriefing she said she still did not know what had happened to her, but it appeared to have been a gang rape. She left the session feeling more empowered.

At the next session she said she had felt less volatile but had had a flashback experience after a social gathering. During the flashback she said she felt like she was being touched and she began to gurgle and scream. She had also had a nightmare during the week about being held hostage by two violent men. In the dream her only way to escape was by agreeing to have sex with one of the men. She said she felt like she was a "slut" for agreeing and felt disgust and sadness. The dream became the target for our EMDR session, which was very intense. The convulsive spasms returned with screaming and choking. At one point she said, "Something black is coming out my mouth . . . something gross is in my throat." She expressed both rage and terror during the processing but had no visual memories. At one time a nightmare from the past came to her mind of a dog with its flesh pulled off. She let out a blood-curdling scream and sobbed for several minutes. The image was absolutely horrifying. She felt so sorry for the dog, and somehow responsible. She was overwhelmed by the sense of seeing horrifying things and experienced intense abreactions. She said it felt like she was looking at something with complete terror. This linked to another dream about witnessing something beyond horror and perversity and being speechless. During the session I kept her eyes moving and encouraged her to keep moving through it. She was able to maintain a witness awareness despite the intensity of the somatosensory and emotional reactions. I felt overwhelmed at times but could see that she was moving through the material, whatever it was. By the end of the session she was calm enough to close it down and go to her safe place.

When she came in for the next session she said that after our last session she had a dream followed by a flashback and that she was experiencing a lot of rage. She said that in the flashback she was raped by a group of young men in Asia. We focused our EMDR session on the dream.

Anya described the dream and its aftermath: *"I'm close to a beach. A car drove by—it's my brother, he pulled into the parking lot. He's in a van. It turned into a plush hotel suite. . . . I and my brother and other people from the van are checking it out. I felt embarrassed to put on a bathing suit. Then there is a prolonged series of scenes of being chased by a short, chubby, balding man. No matter what I do he's right there and I can't shake him. I get into a cab and take off. He gets into a car behind me. I fire a gun at him but the bullets don't have any effect. Now I'm caught. He ties me up with the nylon wire. He straps my hands and arms across my body and tapes my mouth shut. I'm terrified and helpless. I see three dogs . . . he's going to have the dogs fuck me. . . . I feel utter helplessness. How do I dissociate?*

"At that point I woke up. The dogs were like stupid kids. I felt real sadness and then had a flashback. Why would anybody do this to me? I cried and sobbed. Then I started suffocating myself. It was very scary. I couldn't breathe. I felt tremendous shame and told my partner. I then felt so angry. During the week I had terrible fights with my partner. I didn't feel cared about. The dream triggered feelings that my partner didn't care about my feelings. I felt hurt and angry. There was so much grief coming up. I sobbed and also felt rage. I haven't been sleeping."

Despite this intense processing, Anya was functioning well in her life. She felt basically solid and understood that what was coming up for her was somehow connected to the past and needed to be processed. She was eager to continue with EMDR processing.

We decided to target the dream. She had no clear memory of being gang raped other than the flashbacks and nightmares. In order to process the dream I asked her what the worst part of the dream was.

ANYA: I am all tied up and helpless . . .there's nothing I can do . . . I'm going to be raped by the dogs!

LP: What do you believe about yourself? *(the negative cognition)*

ANYA: I am helpless.

LP: What would you like to believe about yourself?

ANYA: I have power.

LP: How true does "I have power" feel to you on a scale from 1 to 7 with 1 completely false and 7 completely true?

ANYA: A 2.

LP: What emotions are you feeling?

ANYA: Terror, fear, and rage.

LP: On a scale from 0 to 10, how disturbing is it to you?

ANYA: A 9.

LP: Where do you feel that in your body?

ANYA: All in the center of my body.

LP: Bring up the image, the belief "I'm helpless," the emotions and feelings in your body, and follow the lights with your eyes. ►◄►◄►◄

(Her body began to jerk convulsively, her breathing was rapid and loud. She looked terrified. At one point she let out a blood curdling scream. It looked like something terrible was happening to her. I kept encouraging her to move through it, it was old stuff, etc. This extremely intense abre-action lasted several minutes. Then it seemed to subside, as though a gigantic wave had passed by.)

LP: What's happening now?

ANYA: I'm feeling sad and hot . . . nauseous. ►◄►◄►◄ *(The jerking spasms began again, but not as intensively.)*

LP: What's happening now?

ANYA: I'm feeling some relief . . . that part being over . . .

LP: What was happening? *(I want to know what she was experiencing.)*

ANYA: I think I was being raped.

LP: Let's go back to the original picture. What do you get now?

ANYA: It's harder to bring up . . . . The dogs are different. They are unsure . . . . growling, not doing anything. I feel something around my throat. ►◄►◄►◄ I got images of throwing up something . . . . There is a scarf around my neck. *(She shows no affect here.)*

(Because there seems to be no emotional charge, I ask her again to return to the dream image we started with.)

ANYA: It has changed again. I'm up in the air and they are down below and can't get at me . . . they're barking at me.

LP: How do you feel?

ANYA: I feel OK . . . out of danger, they can't get me. ►◄►◄►◄ I feel some relief . . . I'm out of danger. Then a dream image came up . . . an old boyfriend sweating. He's happy to see me, but I feel repulsed. ►◄►◄►◄ I went back to my first boyfriend, and then my father and brother . . . I don't like sweat, but sweat's not dangerous.

(This was a significant insight for her because she had had a strong aversion to sweat and it had been a trigger for flashbacks and emotional distress that she had not understood. I wanted to keep making sure she cleared the charge from the dream and did not wander too far from the target so I asked her to check the original picture again.)

ANYA: The dogs are disappearing . . . there is a black hole where they were . . . . I'm aware of the nylon wire string around my arms and chest. ►◄►◄►◄ I don't feel as confined. The wires have gone away. I feel free of the wire . . . . I feel angry . . . . They unraveled themselves and fell down.

LP: When you go back to the original picture, what do you get now?

ANYA: There's no danger, no dogs, no wire. . . . I'm dancing! It feels good!!

LP: *(The image had changed considerably and had lost its charge. I want to go back and check the rest of the dream for charge.)* Go back to the beginning of the dream and run through it and look for any disturbance.

ANYA: It's not really disturbing. . . . What's my brother doing in the dream?! ►◄►◄►◄ I had two other dreams with my brother. . . . He has a friend I hate . . . greasy and slimy. I feel very angry at my brother in one of them. I also feel anger toward the greasy guy. My stomach is starting to hurt. ►◄►◄►◄ I felt very calm. I focused my anger at him. My anger in my eyes and upper body. He's the scum of the earth. ►◄►◄►◄ Piece of shit, loser, not worth my time. He isn't worth my time.

LP: How are you feeling?

ANYA: I have a headache, I've had it all day.

LP: Let's go back to the dream. What do you get now?

ANYA: The man isn't the threat that he was. I'm kicking him around ... he's more of a joke. He's a shape with no substance. I'm tying him up around his neck and humiliating him by having the dogs pee on him. ►◄►◄►◄ The image disappeared ... and the dogs are dancing on their hind legs .... the can-can. *(She is laughing and is obviously delighted with the new image.)*

(I ask her to scan through the dream once again and look for any charge. She said there was none.)

LP: What do you believe about yourself now in this image? (I am checking the positive cognition.)

ANYA: I am strong and powerful. (We do an installation of the positive cognition.) ►◄►◄►◄ I can take care of myself. (Here is another positive cognition, which we install.) ►◄►◄►◄

(We debriefed the session and talked about what had come up for her during the processing. She felt very strongly that she had processed a rape by gang of adolescent boys. She still did not remember what had happened, but felt a great deal of relief.)

The next session Anya said that she felt a big shift after the last session. She felt much better. She had had no new nightmares or flashbacks and said she felt like we had "cleared it out." She again said she felt it was the memory of a rape experience and that in some way it was connected to her brother. She also said she was feeling closer to her partner, but still felt blocked sexually.

I continued to work with Anya for several months, focusing on dreams and symptoms. Her processing continued to be primarily somatosensory with large abreactions and few visual memories. The lack of clear visual memories did not impede her recovery and the reduction of her symptoms. By the end of our work together she was feeling close to her partner. She enjoyed kissing and cuddling with him and was not avoiding intimacy. She felt increasingly comfortable with her own sexuality and enjoyment of her body—she was able to be sexual with her partner and enjoy it. She was no longer seized by terror and rage, nightmares, or flashbacks. Her internal state had calmed down considerably. She ended treatment with me feeling as though she had completed an important piece of work and could return at a later time if she wanted.

Gina's Sessions: Putting the Pieces Together

Gina came to therapy because she had suffered from bulimia for ten years. She told me in our first session that she had had issues around food all of her life. She also suffered from low self-esteem, aversion to sex, and chaotic unsatisfactory relationships with men. She tried to avoid sex with her partner, whom she loved, but would "give in" and then resent it. She believed that "I can't say no, I have to serve."

Gina also had fears at night and terrible anxiety that she related to being molested by the family gardener when she was a little girl. He would come into her room when her parents were not around and sexually "play" with her and make her play with him. She never told her parents, but her mother fired him a year later for unknown reasons.

Gina was born in an Eastern European country and sent to an orphanage by her unwed mother until she was adopted at the age of four by an American couple. Her younger sister was also adopted. Gina had virtually no memories of her life in the orphanage except that she had often been hungry.

In our first EMDR session, Gina related a recent nightmare involving the childhood gardener that was very frightening to her. I asked her for a memory that related to the dream and she gave me the following:

GINA: I was four or five years old. I was lying in bed; my parents were gone. It was not really dark. He was standing on my left-hand side. I could see him and know it was him. He would take his huge genital out and he took my hands and had me touch him—and then he touched me in my private parts—he didn't get into the bed and didn't penetrate me. My sister was in the other bed. He was very big and tall. He got fired and it stopped then.

LP: OK, before we begin the EMDR I think it is important for you to find a safe place. This is a place in your imagination where you feel totally safe and protected. Can you close your eyes and find a place like that? When you have found it let me know. *(Gina closes her eyes, appears relaxed, and is silent for a few minutes.)*

GINA: My safe place is swimming in the water with a mother and baby dolphin circling around me. I can feel the life energy in everything. This feels very safe and protected to me.

LP: OK, good. Gina, you can stop the processing anytime you want and return to your safe place. Just let me know. We are going to start the set-up for the EMDR now. Can you tell me what image represents the worst part of the memory?

GINA: The huge genital in front of me. I want to run away and I can't.

LP: What do you believe about yourself?

GINA: Men can do that and I can't do anything about it.

LP: What would you like to believe about yourself?

GINA: I am in control now.

LP: How are you feeling?

GINA: I'm feeling anxious, feeling helpless. I feel it in my lower part—in my genitals, my stomach. There is energy there. I feel disgust. *(I omitted the ratings because I knew Gina had low self-esteem and thought performance anxiety would get in the way of her processing the target memory.)*

LP: OK Gina, I want you to bring up the image, the emotions, body sensations, and think "Men can do that and I can't do anything about it," and follow my fingers with your eyes. Let whatever comes up come up without censoring it. ►◄►◄►◄ OK, close your eyes take a deep breath, tell me what is happening.

GINA: I feel like I'm somewhere else. I don't see him, or hear him, it's like I'm totally somewhere else—feeling empty like I'm not feeling anything.

LP: Go with that. ►◄►◄►◄

GINA: *(She begins to cry very hard for several minutes, I keep encouraging her to continue, it's old stuff.)* It's dark, I feel scared. ►◄►◄►◄

LP: What's happening now?

GINA: It's dark, churning and whirling, I feel paralyzed.

LP: Go with the sensations. ►◄►◄►◄

GINA: *(Crying and abreacting again as she moves her eyes back and forth for several minutes.)* ►◄►◄►◄

LP: What's happening now?

GINA: *(She's crying as she speaks.)* It's an image like he was on top of me—but it's like I'm not there. I can see his face. There were other images. I'm in a dark room and I never see anyone. The door opens and shuts. The two images are overlapping together. There is a feeling of emptiness. I am sitting on the floor, and it's empty. I'm not crying, there's no feeling.

LP: Go with the images and empty feeling. ►◄►◄►◄

GINA: I'm going deeper and deeper into a void like I'm cramped up in a box. I can't move or do anything. There is nothing there or out there. *(At this point I am feeling lost. I don't know what Gina is processing. For this reason I ask her to return to the original picture to see if the original image has changed.)*

LP: When you bring up the original image you started with, what comes up for you now?

GINA: I feel scared and he's constantly putting his fingers to his lips not to make a sound and he continues playing with me.

LP: What beliefs do you have about yourself now? *(I am checking for the cognitive component to see what is happening there.)*

GINA: I have my body, I don't like my body.

LP: OK, go with the image and the beliefs and we'll do some more eye movements. ►◄►◄►◄

GINA: He's humping me and suffocating me. I want him to go. ►◄►◄►◄ I'm floating again and it's dark like there is nothing. *(It sounds like she is dissociating, either in memory or in reaction to the memory.)*

LP: What are you feeling? *(I am trying to help her get into her body.)*

GINA: I like it. *(The floating outside of her body feeling.)*

LP: Why is that?

GINA: There's nothing I have to do—it just feels good. *(At this point I again bring her back to the target to assess where she is.)*

LP: What do you get now when you bring up the original image?

GINA: I feel a resistance in me. I have a headache.

LP: *(I have no idea what is going on, the processing is lacking images or cognitions so I ask her what she now believes about herself.)*

GINA: I am nothing. I don't know who I am. (She then has a realization.) In order to survive I became nothing.

LP: Go with that. ►◄►◄►◄

GINA: She's crying. *(Gina, who is crying, is referring now to her child self who is crying in Gina's imagery.)* She's in bed crying. I want to reach out to her but I can't—I feel emptiness around my heart. *(At this point I feel the need to do an inner or outer resource interweave and bring in nurturing resources for Gina's child self because Gina's adult self is not able to do it.)*

LP: Who could comfort the little girl?

GINA: *(She responded immediately.)* Susan, my good friend Susan could.

LP: Go with that. ►◄►◄►◄

GINA: I see Susan holding her and she starts crying. It feels like I can't be with her—I want to but I can't.

LP: Why can't you?

GINA: I can't help her yet. *(Her adult self is not yet ready to nurture the child self, but the potential is there.)* . . . She's sleeping now. ►◄►◄►◄ It's like I'm looking down on the picture with Susan holding her and I feel a sense of peace. I feel like I'm in heaven and I'm looking down. I'm very often out of my body. *(Gina has an insight.)* I had to cut off so I didn't have to feel, because I couldn't say anything. ►◄►◄►◄ I couldn't express myself then, because I was a little girl and I was threatened by a big man, but I can express myself now! *(Spontaneous positive cognition)* ►◄►◄►◄ I feel power coming back even in my heart area and the tension is gone. I feel energy moving up into my heart and expanding.

It was nearly time to end the session. Gina was feeling great. She was back in her body. The session had been very powerful for her. When we discussed what she had gotten from the session, Gina realized that she had left her body all of her life and the absence from her body caused her to panic, which she believed led to her bingeing and purging. The memory of the gardener on top of her was new to her and helped explain why she hated her partner to be on top of her during their lovemaking.

This session was very intense and at the same time vague. That was why I brought her back to target as often as I did to check. This kept her focused and better able to handle what arose for her during the processing. Some of the vague body memories that arose for her in this session became more vivid in the next, with the associated visual memories eventually emerging also.

The following week Gina spoke at length about her relationship with her partner. She said she was making connections between her present behavior and the past event as a result of the previous EMDR session. She talked about her feelings of insecurity around people. She had difficulty feeling OK about herself and felt a need to prove herself. She found it much easier to give to others than to receive.

I asked her to picture the scene with the gardener that we had worked on the week before and to tell me what came up for her. She said, "Now I see the gardener standing there. I can't see myself. There is darkness . . . he's gone. I'm feeling an emptiness in my upper chest area. There is a heaviness and no energy there." This sounded to me like some kind of body memory. I asked her what she believed about herself. She replied, still in the picture, "I am nothing." We then began the eye movements. (I omitted the rest of the set-up because the memory network was evoked and I was concerned that the positive cognition and ratings would take her out of the experience.)

GINA: ►◄►◄►◄ It's still very dark—I'm being crushed and I can't move. It feels like I'm in something confined and I can't really breathe very well. I feel paralyzed. I feel like I'm going to explode. I need some air. *(It seems that another memory has come up that is linked to the other one. This is primarily a body memory; there is as yet no image. Neither of us knows what is happening or when it occurred. We are both in the dark.)* ►◄►◄►◄ Now it's like I'm outdoors and it's dark and I hear sounds and I think I'm lost and I'm hurting. *I'm scared. (Gina begins to cry, from the sound of her voice she is in a young child memory network.)* ►◄►◄►◄ All these noises and I have to be very quiet because they can get me and I don't want them to get me . . . . They do hurt me. They're people and they're going to hurt me. *(She sounds very frightened.)*

LP: How old are you? *(I am trying to get oriented and get a sense of what is happening and when in her history.)*

GINA: I'm very tiny. ►◄►◄►◄

(Gina begins a very intense abreaction. She is crying, breathing rapidly and she begins to cough and throw up. I gently encourage her to let it go, it's old stuff, as she continues to move her eyes.)

GINA: There were boys holding me down and they were hurting me really badly. One was holding a hand over her mouth and they were sexually assaulting her. ►◄►◄►◄ *(She begins to cry and abreact again and then she stops.)* I feel like I'm going somewhere now—I'm floating. *(She is dissociating—either a memory of doing it or she is doing it in the session as a defense against the intensity of the feeling.)* ►◄►◄►◄ I feel myself floating . . . no pain . . . . it feels good. I want to stay there, I like it.

LP: Let's go back to the original picture. Tell me what comes up for you now.

GINA: It feels like I'm going to die. I'm gone.

LP: What happened?

GINA: I died.

LP: What do you mean?

GINA: Everything died.

LP: Can you tell me what you mean by that? *(I am trying to understand what is going on.)*

GINA: The little girl died.

LP: Are you sure she is dead?

GINA: It's like she's in a box and she can't move—she's trying to get out and she can't get out.

(At this point I can see that she is looping and is stuck. The little girl is trapped in some kind of a box. The blocking belief is that she is trapped and there is no way out. She needs an inner or outer resource interweave to get her out of the box.)

LP: Who can get you out of the box? *(She immediately came out with her response.)*

GINA: My sister can get me out!

LP: Think about that. ►◄►◄►◄

GINA: I can breathe!!! The heaviness is gone. *(She takes several deep breaths.)* ►◄►◄►◄ I feel lighter too. My body muscles feel sore from the tension.

LP: What do you believe about yourself now?

GINA: She was very scared and shut down. There's so much holding back. Her whole body was totally tense trying to hold back the cry and screams because it would get worse if she expressed her feelings—she'd be hurt more. They punched as well.

(We are almost out of time, and I want to begin to close the session. It is important to bring in the safety of being able to express herself in the present time, so that she will no longer hold the old view, which associates expression with punishment. For that reason I decide to do a link-

ing perspectives interweave. Her adult self knows that she is safe in the present to express herself and that it wasn't safe in the past.)

LP: Tell me, Gina, is it true that it wasn't safe to express yourself then, but that it is safe to express yourself now?

GINA: Yes, that's true.

LP: Think about that. ►◄►◄►◄

GINA: That feels good.

She said she felt in a good place to stop. She felt calm and strong. During the debriefing, Gina explained to me what she remembered during the EMDR processing. The memories were from the time in the orphanage. There were few adults there to supervise the many children so they left the older boys in charge at night. These boys physically and sexually abused the younger children. She remembered that they would put her in a trunk as punishment. When she wet the bed they would put her outside in the freezing cold. One of the memories that came up was of being held down outside by several boys. She managed to get away and ran and hid. She had to be quiet and make no noise or they would find her. These memories felt like missing pieces of her life and helped to explain many of her symptoms and self beliefs.

Theresa: Two Sessions Demonstrating the Use of Interweaves

Theresa came into treatment because of serious problems with her husband. She was projecting hate onto him and avoiding intimacy, behavior she attributed to early childhood incest. She suffered from anxiety and phobias and feared working on the incest memories, which she had avoided for years. Theresa was stable emotionally and had a good job, close friendships with women, and no history of drug or alcohol abuse.

Theresa grew up in a large, chaotic, and unstable Catholic family. Her alcoholic father molested several of the children, including two of her older brothers. One of these brothers molested her when he was 15 and she was around three. Theresa described her mother as an overwhelmed victim who was not able to properly care for all of her children. With so many children in the family and all of the chaos, Theresa grew up feeling unnoticed and invisible. She did feel loved by her mother and by an aunt and uncle with whom she stayed in the summers.

Theresa had a number of themes she wanted to work on with me. These included not feeling safe in relation to the incest, feelings of violations around her boundaries and the hurt and anger it engendered, and the feeling of invisibility and being an object.

Following are two EMDR sessions we did that demonstrate the use of interweaves. In the prior sessions, we had been working on her molestation by her brother. The target for many of our EMDR sessions was a scene in the basement where he would take her to molest her. He molested her many times there, so the scene she chose was a composite that represented all of the times he assaulted her. As she processed, elements from different incidents would emerge, but the theme, emotions, body sensations, and thoughts were very much the same with each occurrence.

To begin the EMDR I asked Theresa to bring up the scene in the basement where her brother is molesting her.

LP: What do you feel?

THERESA: Yuck, a little like I'm bad. I hate sex and I think it's gross and used to hurt people. It's selfish. The whole body feeling is yuck. I feel sick. I don't have any sexuality. I don't want that or need that, it's bad.

> *(Theresa was very self-conscious and tended to have difficulty connecting with me or her feelings. I did not elicit the positive cognition and measurements because I was concerned it would disrupt the processing and harm our therapeutic alliance. The trauma memory network was evoked with the image, negative cognition, emotions, and body sensations. We begin the eye movements using the light bar.)*

THERESA: ►◄►◄►◄ I felt my internal being contract and defend. ►◄►◄►◄ I felt my stomach clench. ►◄►◄►◄ It went away. My stomach feels queasy. ►◄►◄►◄ I remember being really little. I'm so little I don't want to do this. . . . I want to please him because he's my big brother. ►◄►◄►◄ I feel hot.

LP: Let's go back to the original picture. What comes up for you now?

THERESA: I feel less attached to it. I feel how my brother was a boy. ►◄►◄►◄ What he looked like and fear of his taking his clothes off. I have body feelings. ►◄►◄►◄

THERESA: My body feels hot. ►◄►◄►◄ *(Theresa becomes visibly distressed.)* I have the feeling like I was being crushed. Am I still alive? ►◄►◄►◄ I feel the weight on me. I left my body and come back and wonder if I was still there I feel like I am dying. *(Her little body was being crushed by her brother's as he humped her, causing her to leave her body.)* ►◄►◄►◄ I felt relief. I am impenetrable. You can't get me and I'm not here. I felt so happy that I could leave. ►◄►◄►◄ It's not safe to be here. *(In the body)* ►◄►◄►◄ Vague, him telling me not to tell anyone.

LP: What do you believe about yourself?

THERESA: I'm invisible and powerless. I must be invisible, that's the only reason he could do this to me. . . . I don't exist.

(I can see that these negative cognitions are not changing and are very convincing to her. She has lost the adult perspective and is caught in the child's. She is clearly not distressed but that is because she is not in her body. I can't let her leave the session out of her body and believing she is invisible. In situations in which the client has dissociated, the SUDS reading is meaningless to determine the session's completion. We are near the end of our time so I do a linking perspectives cognitive interweave to unblock the blocked processing.)

LP: You weren't invisible, you were *treated* like you were invisible. It wasn't safe to be in your body *then,* but it is *now.*
THERESA: That's true. That feels right.

(I need to know if this is true for her. What if she still believes it isn't safe to be in her body? If that were the case, I would have to look for something else that is true for her.)

LP: Think about "I wasn't invisible, I was *treated* like I was invisible," and "It wasn't safe to be in my body *then,* but it is *now*." ►◄►◄►◄
THERESA: I can feel myself in my body for the first time! . . . I didn't know I wasn't in my body before. ►◄►◄►◄ It feels very intense to be in my body. *(She has a look of astonishment on her face.)*

Theresa was amazed to be in her body. It was as if she had been hovering over her body and popped back in. We debriefed and then I asked her to check in with her child self and see how she was. She then imagined holding her in her safe place and making sure she felt safe. Theresa left the session feeling astounded at her embodiment and excited to see how it would affect her life.

When Theresa came in the following week, she was very excited to tell me about all of the changes that had happened since our session. She felt different physically and felt more present with people. "I felt different in my body, more centered and there with myself. . . . I felt less invisible and more solid. . . . I was able to deal with people more assertively. . . . I am more forgiving towards myself and I feel more real." She reported that she had dreams of being safe and powerful. She was also much more aware of her bodily functions. Prior to our session, she would go all day without going to the bathroom or eating. As a result of being embodied, she was taking more care of herself, eating regularly, and going to the bathroom according to her body's needs. Her partner told her that he noticed a release in her.

To begin the EMDR session, we checked the picture from the last session of her being in the basement with her brother molesting her. She told me "I feel distant from it. . . . It feels flat, less charged . . . more gray than color." When I asked her what she felt in her body, she said she still felt some fear in her stomach and chest. I decided to continue the processing of the scene with her brother, focusing on her remaining body sensations.

THERESA: ►◄►◄►◄ I feel tight and racy. ►◄►◄►◄ My stomach feels like it's burning, and my chest is tight. I distrust that the feelings are related to what happened to her. *(She's referring to her child self.)* ►◄►◄►◄ The feelings are starting to dissipate a little bit. *(She begins to tell me that she and her husband had tried to make love this weekend for the first time in two years, but she was tight and held back. It hurt so they stopped. She wasn't ready yet.)* I'm holding myself back. ►◄►◄►◄ This is how I hold myself. It is familiar. It's not safe. Would it ever be safe to let go of the psychic holding?

LP: Imagine letting go of the psychic holding. *(This is an imaginal interweave to give her permission to check out what something might be like.)* ►◄►◄►◄

THERESA: I feel sad and tentative—it might be possible to do that.

LP: What are you feeling in your body now?

THERESA: I feel contracted inside.

LP: Go with that. ►◄►◄►◄

THERESA: I feel like I could feel myself become very contracted and I had a memory of feeling that as a little girl—pulled up inside. I have a memory of being safer when I am alone. I have an image of a little girl walking in the grass, she's not contracted. ►◄►◄►◄ Feeling very self-conscious around other people. When I was little I was not relaxed, I felt I was bad. There's something wrong with me . . . at the same time I don't believe it. *(pause)* When I'm alone I feel better. ►◄►◄►◄ Wanting to distract and comfort myself from feeling feelings. . . . I used food as a kid, and getting away from other people, to cope with the feeling there isn't enough for me, there's no one taking care of me. . . . I'm not going to have what I need. ►◄►◄►◄

(During that set of eye movements, Theresa began to abreact. Her breathing accelerated and she looked distressed. It was obvious that her SUDS had gone up. Her emotions had changed from sadness to terror.)

THERESA: I feel fear of being caught. I feel terror in the situation with my brother and the possibility of someone seeing me. I feel responsible like I'm bad for doing this.

(At this point I feel the need to do a linking perspectives interweave to bring in what her adult self knows to be true with the child self's distorted perspective. The child self is taking inappropriate responsibility for the actions of the older brother.)

LP: How old are you?

THERESA: Two, three, and four years old

LP: How old was he? *(I am trying to help her see that he was much older than she was and so should have been the one responsible. Her adult self knew this but her child self did not.)*

THERESA: He was 12, 13, 14.

LP: Who should know better?

THERESA: He should. *(She makes the link between the adult and child memory networks and realizes that her brother was the responsible one.)*

LP: Think about that. ►◄►◄►◄ *(We add the eye movements here to connect the two memory networks.)*

THERESA: I can feel myself sink into my body. He was also a victim of my father. ►◄►◄►◄ My dad was such a mess and his dad—a whole lineage of victims and perpetrators, it was handed down. That's sad and hopeless and we're a mess. In relationship to my brother and dad it's sad. *(She is recalling that her brother was molested by her father. His emotional injury then contributed to his abuse of her. She could see a long chain of abusers and victims in her family history.)* ►◄►◄►◄ My legs feel hot, and my stomach feels weird.

LP: Who was responsible for the sex abuse? *(I want to make it very clear to her that the child was not responsible for the abuse.)*

THERESA: My brother and dad.►◄►◄►◄ And I think my mom. Part of me feels like they had no business having kids. It wasn't my fault they were overwhelmed and not getting their needs met. It's not my fault and *(speaking to her parents)* fuck you for having me! ►◄►◄►◄ I feel hot and mad. What a bunch of shit I went through because they were so unconscious. I hardly ever let myself feel angry at them. ►◄►◄►◄ I keep feeling like wanting to tell them to wake up, look at what you're doing! This sucks! ►◄►◄►◄ I feel heat coming on me . . . body sensation. As a little girl I feel surprised that I can feel. ►◄►◄►◄ I felt my anger get really hot and come to a peak and dissipate. I'm so amazed I can ride the feeling out.

LP: Stay with "I can ride the feeling out."*(I want to reinforce and further install this positive cognition.)* ►◄►◄►◄

THERESA: It's still dissipating.

LP: What do you feel in your body now? *(I am bringing her back to attend to her body to give us a possible focus for processing.)*

THERESA: I still feel a little bit hot, tingly, and tired.

LP: What do you believe about yourself as a kid?

THERESA: I really got a raw deal. I was in a situation where people didn't want me and weren't ready for me and didn't appreciate me and didn't have enough for me. I deserved better than that. . . . There's a part of me that believes that I helped create it.

LP: How?

THERESA: Our soul needs to go through it . . . I picked them for some reason.

LP: Go with that. ►◄►◄►◄

THERESA: I think that, but I think it's not so simple as that.... I see the word *innocent*. I am innocent and I was. *(A spontaneous positive cognition)* ►◄►◄►◄ A couple of memories at different ages came up. First at four years old—that little girl was innocent, and as little as one-and-a-half or two. I have a strong pain in my heart knowing that the little girl was innocent.

> *(Because it is near the end of our time and I do not want to leave her feeling so small and vulnerable, I do a positive cognitive interweave. I offer her another linking perspectives interweave with the theme of control, so she can leave the session feeling more adult and empowered.)*

LP: You didn't have control over your body or what others did to you then, as a child, but you do now, don't you?

THERESA: Yes. That's true.

LP: Think about that. ►◄►◄►◄

THERESA: I feel a little bit of fear around David [her husband] and don't want him to leave me because I don't do what he wants. I want to do what I want to do. I want to find out what I want to do and honor it. I want to have control.

Theresa left the session feeling embodied and empowered. Her adult self was feeling more in control with more choices about what she did in her life.

The next week Theresa came in feeling much happier, lighter, yet more grounded. She felt more in her body and was eating when she was hungry and going to the bathroom when she needed to. People were noticing the difference. She felt more present and connected to her body.

Another change was most likely a result of the installation of the spontaneous positive cognition "I can ride the feeling out," from the previous session. She said, "I'd be OK if David and I split up. I can go through the feelings and be OK." She felt a new confidence that she could go through whatever happened in her life, that she could go through the emotions, letting them pass through, including getting through the grief of the loss of David. "I'm not as afraid to be alone anymore." We continued our work for several months, working on issues around the sexual abuse and parental neglect.

Chapter 12

Christina

This final chapter focuses on a single, complex case history that illustrates many of the treatment issues raised and techniques described in the previous chapters.

Christina came to see me because she was feeling "stuck" in her life and full of unprocessed anger, which she often directed at her children. She told me that deep inside she didn't feel safe and protected; instead, she felt anxious, frantic, and hypervigilant. She felt she was "not OK" and was deeply unhappy because of her self-loathing. Feeling "shackled by some unknown force" she couldn't move forward in her life. Emphatically, she told me that she had felt much happier until a year ago, when she was the victim of a freak accident that seriously injured her and shattered her sense of well-being. Since then she had hit "rock bottom." The accident triggered early feelings of being betrayed by God and of being punished because she was "bad." Christina believed the problems that were triggered were related to her father's sexual abuse of her when she was a little girl.

Christina was an attractive woman in her mid-forties who was quite intelligent and articulate and had benefited from past therapy. Because of that, she had a good ability to introspect and describe her inner experience. Christina was distressed about what she called a "split" in herself. Although she did not have dissociative identity disorder, she did have a number of different parts, or ego states. She described different parts of herself that were at odds with one another. One part was the "special kid" who was Daddy's favorite; another was the "bad self" who believed she was not OK. A third part was angry, vindictive, and destructive. These ego states were unintegrated and seemed to act autonomously from one another.

Christina related a recent dream she thought was relevant. "My mother died and she's coming towards me with a knife. She says to me, 'I have to kill you because you're the only one who remembers.'"

Christina told me that her father abused her when she was five years old but that her memories were very vague. She feared she'd "blow apart" if she got to it. Her memory was of sitting on the stairs in the family home waiting to get into a room where her father was when he was through with his work. Something about this memory felt sexual and bad and made her head spin. Thinking about that scene made her want to shut down emotionally and cognitively; she felt unsafe and like she wasn't OK. She hadn't remembered being sexually abused until she saw a film about the subject that caused her to sob and sob. Later, with a therapist, she did a sand-tray with the theme of "betrayal." She had an EMDR session years ago with an inexperienced therapist who opened her up and did not close her down properly. That scared her so much she did not return. She said the fear that was evoked in that session lasted for a year and left her feeling like a little kid.

Christina was the second child of six in a lower-middle-class Greek Orthodox family. She described her father as having a "type A personality," being "inappropriate sexually," and "always hitting on women." Her mother told her that she was her father's "favorite." Christina always felt like the other woman with her "Daddy" and that they had a "special" relationship. Her mother was so busy taking care of all of her brothers and sisters that Christina became the surrogate wife. Christina adored her father and saw him as "God." Her relationship with her mother was more "strained." She did not get very much attention from her busy mother. Both of her parents were very emotional.

As an extroverted young woman Christina was popular in high school. When she became pregnant by her long-term boyfriend, an event which greatly disrupted her life, she was forced by her parents to go to a home for unwed mothers in another state and became quite isolated. After the birth of her child, she gave him up for adoption and returned home. She finished her schooling at another school and made a new start, but the splitting began then—she had a secret self unknown to her new friends, she was a young woman who had had a baby. Christina spent her early adult years moving to different places and having children with different men. Thirteen years ago she had settled down, and concentrated on raising her children. Recently she had started school to complete a higher education. She had a good support system in the community where she lived, was close to her sisters, and had many deep and satisfying friendships. She had not had a long-term intimate relationship with a man in many years and longed for one.

Christina and I spent several sessions talking about her early history and her current situation. Along with the history-taking, I prepared her for EMDR processing by identifying and developing inner and outer resources. We talked about people she was close to in her current and early life, as well as her spirituality, and we developed a safe place—a beautiful spot by the ocean where she felt peaceful and protected. We did inner child guided imagery to assess the adult self-child self relationship. Since she had a good relationship with her inner child, her adult self could be an inner resource for her during EMDR processing of her childhood abuse. She chose Jesus as her inner nurturer and protector and felt a close relationship with him. She could call on him as necessary.

Christina seemed to trust me and we developed good rapport very quickly. She appeared to have sufficient ego strength for EMDR, and her life and financial situation were stable. She was committed to her own growth and healing, although she was afraid of the intensity of the EMDR process and the feelings it might arouse. She seemed to know herself well and to have insight into her current difficulties, but her emotions were feeling out of control. She felt blocked in every area of her life.

When she and I both felt she was ready to do EMDR, we scheduled a double EMDR session. In this first EMDR session, after checking in, she went to her safe place by the ocean; then she brought Jesus in as her guide and protector. I told her she could stop at anytime and return to her safe place. From her safe place I asked her to connect with the feeling that was disturbing her the most. It was fear that was located in her chest and gut. "I can't survive," she said. "My father hurt me, he won't let me go." The image that came to her mind was, "I'm in the room with the metal door as a child. I'm floating up to the ceiling. I feel like I'm on the ceiling looking down. There is a tightness in my stomach. *(pause)* I hear choking. I feel like I'm choking." She believed, "I'm going to die." The positive cognition was "I'm safe now," a VoC of 3.

We began the eye movements at that point with the image, negative cognition, emotions, and body sensations activated.

CHRISTINA: ►◄►◄►◄ I'm in the room but hiding. It's real quiet and still, like it's a game of hide and seek. ►◄►◄►◄ *(She begins to abreact, crying. Her respiration rate has increased, and she looks visibly upset.)* Daddy, Daddy don't make me do that. I'm saying it inside, not saying it out loud. I feel like I want to run out the door but I *can't!* I can't do what I want to do. It's a life theme for me. ►◄►◄►◄ He has me pinned down on my stomach but I feel like I'm in my body now. I feel a lot of resistance. *(pause)* I feel like I want to beat the shit out of him. I feel *angry.* ►◄►◄►◄ I'm pinned down, I feel really helpless. It's presented as a kind of game. *(She has an image of her father pinning her down and beginning to molest her but he is doing it in a way that confuses her. Like it is something that is supposed to be fun.)* Part of me is saying I'm crazy for making it all up. *(She is doubting what is coming up for her.)*

LP: What are you feeling now?

CHRISTINA: Sadness. He's laughing. I feel scared on the inside but I don't show it. I can't act how I feel.

LP: Why is that? *(I am asking her to bring to awareness what she knows instinctively. The information she provides will help continue the process of linking the child and adult perspectives.)*

CHRISTINA: If I show how I feel, he'll get angry . . . now it's play.►◄►◄►◄ I feel like I'm trying to get out of my body—so I won't feel this stuff. Now if I can watch it I can get through it. *(She's referring to the dual awareness she has now.)*

LP: What are you feeling now? *(I am trying to have her attend to her body to decrease dissociation.)*

CHRISTINA: I have a detached feeling—like I'm a separate non-person. ►◄►◄►◄ My spirit feels really heavy.

LP: Where do you feel that in your body?

CHRISTINA: In my brain.

LP: What do you believe about yourself now? *(I am trying to activate the cognitive component and see what is happening there.)*

CHRISTINA: I am nothing. *(This is a very powerful core negative cognition that is probably an underlying cause for her depression. She is surprised at the words that came out of her mouth in response to my question.)* ►◄►◄►◄ I'm going to die. There is an incongruence going on between what's going on inside and what I am showing on the outside. On the inside I'm struggling to get away from my father, and on the outside I'm just laying there. Inside I'm frantic! I want to scream and yell and get away. ►◄►◄►◄

CHRISTINA: I want to kill him—stab him in the heart.

LP: Let yourself imagine that. *(I am giving her permission to safely express in fantasy some of the anger that she has held inside nearly all of her life.)* ►◄►◄►◄

CHRISTINA: I felt a lot of rage . . . and I feel removed, dissociated . . . outside of my body.

LP: What do you believe now?

CHRISTINA: If I don't feel it, I can survive it. *(Another core belief has emerged, one that has operated for much of her life, causing her to shut herself off to feelings. The processing of this negative cognition brings new insights to her.)* ►◄►◄►◄ I'm aware of feeling two different things. One is null and void of feelings. It is cold. The other is a strong feeling of wanting to hurt my father. I want to see his penis hurting. *(pause)* I'm trying to protect my father from myself. It's not acceptable to think about hurting my father, so I end up not feeling—I shut down. This feels so familiar. ►◄►◄►◄ I have an image of burying my head in the sand. Also of telling my father I hate him. ►◄►◄►◄ Image of slapping somebody. I feel a tremendous amount of rage. I want to strangle him. . . . It's like he holds the key. I'm afraid I'll be stuck here forever between life and death. *(She is commenting on her inner process of holding back her feelings and as a result not living fully.)*

(At this point the time is running low in the session and I want to see if we can bring some sort of closure to it. I want to see how much processing she has done on the original image so I ask her to return to it and tell me what comes up for her.)

CHRISTINA: I'm totally confined. . . . I can't move. . . . . There is a heaviness in my chest. *(She is having a body memory.)*

LP: *(I want to see what is happening in the cognitive channel to help me in focusing my interventions.)* What do you believe about yourself?

CHRISTINA: It's safer not to feel.

LP: Go with that. ►◄►◄►◄

Christina: Fear he would kill me. I'm being ultimately threatened. *(She is realizing more fully how she felt as a child. She was aware of an aggressiveness under the "game" her father wanted her to play.)* ►◄►◄►◄ I want to kill my father . . . castrate him. I'm stabbing him. I feel split—passive or violent. *(She then has thoughts about the anger she has directed toward her children. She can see it is displaced anger and has nothing to do with them.)* ►◄►◄►◄ I'm aware of my anger turned inward—a voice saying "you're trapped."

(We are running out of time, and I can see that she is stuck, so I again ask her to return to the original picture.

CHRISTINA: I don't understand why he's doing this to me. He's vindictive.

LP: What do you believe about yourself now? *(I am trying to find out what has happened in the cognitive channel. What are the blocking beliefs?)*

CHRISTINA: I don't deserve to be free. It's my fault; therefore I don't deserve to live. . . . I should die. *(The child self is taking responsibility for her adult father's actions.)*

LP: How old are you? *(I want to know who has these beliefs, the child or adult so that I can adjust my next intervention accordingly.)*

CHRISTINA: I'm five years old.

LP: Who is responsible, a five-year-old or a 40-year-old?

CHRISTINA: The 40-year-old.

LP: Think about that. ►◄►◄►◄

CHRISTINA: I feel trapped.

(The interweave appears to work because the processing becomes unblocked—it goes down another channel. However, the interweave does not help her come closer to closing the session. Because we need to close the session, I do an imaginal interweave. I ask Christina to go with

her child self to her safe place at the beach and bring in Jesus for pro-tection. She imagines going there and does a short set of eye movements. She returns to a state of calm and peace. She tells me that during the set of eye movements she imagined her adult self playing ball with her child self at the beach. The two had fun together!)

We ended the session by debriefing and talking about what came up for her. I reminded her to be easy with herself because she had opened up old painful material, to keep a log of her dreams and thoughts, and to call me if she needed to.

The next week Christina told me she had had a dream related to the work we had done the previous week. "I am sitting in a movie theater and a huge fat lady came in and sat against me and leaned against me. I pushed her forward and she apologized. It felt like a weight was pushing on me from the outside."

From what she related in the dream, it seemed as if things were moving internally. She set a boundary in the dream, and the person who intruded on her boundary took appropriate responsibility and apologized. However, there was something unprocessed about the body sensation.

I asked her to bring up the image we worked on the week before and to tell me what came up for her now. She said, "It is an image of my father on top of me. I feel a lot of sorrow." I asked her what she believed about her-self now in the picture. She replied, "I don't count. I don't matter." Her positive cognition was "I do matter," and VoC of 2. Her SUDS was 8. We began with that target.

During the first set of eye movements, she began to cry. She reported that she felt betrayed by her youngest child's father who was not helping the boy when he was in need. She was angry.

CHRISTINA: ►◄►◄►◄ I have a sense of powerlessness, I feel the need to be aggressive.... I feel angry at the betrayal. ►◄►◄►◄ I don't deserve happiness. I feel anger and rage. I feel shaky. *(I wasn't sure what was happening for her and what she was seeing so I asked her to return to the original picture to check.)* Get off, you fucking asshole....What are you doing to me? ►◄►◄►◄ I hate you, I hate you!!! ►◄►◄►◄ Something's in my throat ... oral sex ... "Daddy's candy." ►◄►◄►◄

(Christina cries and is full of rage toward her father. She feels like throw-ing up, and I have a wastebasket ready. She is caught between fully feel-ing and expressing her rage toward her father and protecting him. Because she is looping, I do an imaginal interweave, bringing in present safety and a linking perspectives interweave, linking her adult's present-day perspective with the old childhood perspective. I tell her that she is

safe in the present, that there is a protective boundary around us here now, and that the daddy that was hurting her as a child is the daddy from the past and not him now. She says, yes, that is true, and then does another set of eye movements. The interweaves work, and the processing begins to move again.

CHRISTINA: I feel for the innocent child. ►◄►◄►◄ I feel things in my body . . . in my stomach, head, and neck. It is like my neck is in a vice, contracted. . . . I feel sick to my stomach. *(She has now opened a somatic channel and is processing body memories.)* ►◄►◄►◄ I feel sick to my stomach.

LP: What do you believe about yourself? *(I am checking the cognitive component because the somatic channel seems blocked.)*

CHRISTINA: I'm never going to amount to anything. There is tightness in my throat and the back of my neck. It's like someone beat me up. Like it's residual of something really traumatic. ►◄►◄►◄ I don't want to be in my body. It feels too bad.

LP: What is happening in the picture? *(I want to know what she is seeing that is disturbing her so much and to bring more of the pieces together for her conscious mind.)*

CHRISTINA: My father's standing exposed with a hard-on. I'm standing also. I'm a little girl. I don't want to believe this is happening. ►◄►◄►◄ I feel sadness. I can see the generational effect on my kids . . . my problem being present. *(She realizes that her denial of what happened with her father at the time affects her ability to be present with her children now. She then got in touch with her rage at him and began to call him names like "slimy bastard.")* ►◄►◄►◄ I'm not going to let you get away anymore. I'm not going to protect you anymore. I'm taking the power back. I see what I've passed onto my sons.

LP: Let's go back to the original picture. What comes up for you now? *(I want to keep the processing contained for the time we have left and I want to check her progress in processing the original memory.)*

Christina: I'm in front of him. His penis is in my mouth. My stomach is sick. ►◄►◄►◄ Don't make me do that Daddy. Over and over again I repeat that. I remember a man I went out with told me I had problems because I didn't like oral sex.

(She takes time out to talk about some of the connections she is making related to the rising information. "I was always a rebel, resisting anybody making me do anything. Now it is time to be an adult. I haven't felt like a mature adult because I am small and I have believed I have less value." She then does another set of eye movements.)

CHRISTINA: I had the thought "I hope I can get through this," and then the words "You have power and might" came to me. ►◄►◄►◄ I am feeling increasingly positive. Power and might. *I am presence, I am!* This is a spiritual feeling. *(During this spontaneous spiritual experience, Christina is speaking with a kind of awe.)* ►◄►◄►◄ I feel cleared out in my body. I feel calm and spiritual. *I am free, I am present. I am intact.* . . . The abuse experience is overlaid on top of this.

(We are close to the end of the session, so I ask her to return to the original picture and tell me what comes up for her.)

CHRISTINA: I am an adult now. I have the resources to handle what comes my way. I have the resources to manage my life.

(We install that positive cognition with the eye movements, and she feels calm, peaceful, and empowered. We debrief and talk about what has come up for her during the session. She is greatly moved by what has arisen at the end. Her wise inner voice in this session becomes more prominent and defined in following sessions and develops into a strong ally for her in EMDR processing.)

I saw Christina a couple of weeks later for another double EMDR processing session. During our check-in she told me she felt energetic but fragmented and that her anger was coming out more. She talked about her relationships with men and a theme of being taken advantage of. She said, "I don't trust anyone," adding that it had been three years since she had had a relationship with a man. The last relationship had ended after she had vacationed in Greece with her partner. On this trip she "met the Goddess" in a spiritual epiphany and no longer felt subservient to her partner. She began to challenge him. We talked about the terrible accident she had been in a year earlier and the emotional aftereffects.

Christina chose to use this session to focus on her feelings of being blocked in her life. She was struggling to complete her school work and felt "stuck." She believed, "I'm not capable." To develop the target more fully, I asked her to close her eyes and locate the blocked feeling in her body. Then, I asked her to say, "I'm not capable" while paying attention to the feeling. I asked her to trace it back, paying attention to whatever thoughts and images came to her. A memory arose of her father verbally demeaning her when she was a little girl, seven or eight years old. She was showing her father some artwork she had done that she really liked. He responded, 'You call that art? That's a piece of shit!' and then showed me *his* stuff." As she continued, she told me she remembered feeling excited about sharing her picture with him—and then deflated. Her negative cognition was "I'm not good enough." Her positive cognition as "I am good enough," a VoC of 3.

Christina preferred my tapping on her knees because she was better able to stay focused on her inner experience when she had her eyes closed. Because she had stimulated the memory network, I began to tap on her knees as she focused on the memory of her father demeaning her and her negative cognition, "I'm not good enough."

CHRISTINA: ►◄►◄►◄ There is tension in my throat, stomach, and chest. *(She is speaking in a high-pitched child's voice.)* I can't do this, I'm scared. I'm scared. Don't make me do this. *(She is processing an earlier memory with her father—I'm guessing the same one from the previous sessions— and not the one where he demeans her.)* ►◄►◄►◄ I'm so sorry, I'm so sorry that I wasn't there for myself . . .that there wasn't anyone there for me. ►◄►◄►◄ My spirit guide took over. *(The voice she heard last time has now come in as a protector figure for her. She refers to her as a "shaman.")* My father came towards me and she told him to leave me alone. She treated him like a child. She took control . . . . He's in his place. ►◄►◄►◄ You can't hurt me now. *(She's talking out loud to her father.)* I'm in control. . . . That's a scary thought. ►◄►◄►◄ I need to relinquish control to my sacred self, otherwise I lose sensitivity and mow people down. . . . It's the opposite of paralysis. ►◄►◄►◄ Take a deep breath. . . . There is nothing to be threatened by. *(This is probably the "shaman" talking. Then she changes to the first person.)* I have a fear that there won't be enough for me. . . . I don't deserve to have what I want. *(She then remembers the doll she loved who was like a protector figure for her, and how her mother took the doll from her and gave it to her three-year-old sister, who destroyed it. This experience was very painful for her and rein- forced the belief that she was undeserving.)* ►◄►◄►◄ The image of the shaman is stronger. "I'll take care of you. I'm here for you now." I feel a definite presence of beautiful feminine energy that is strong and defined. . . . It is fairy-like as well as otherworldly. . . . It is comforting.

(I want to see where she was in the processing, so I ask her to recall the original picture and tell me what comes up for her. When she brings up the picture it has completely changed. She is no longer a child with her father. Rather an image of the Sphinx at Delos, Greece, appears. She hears the words—and speaks them aloud to me—"The beauty is within you . . . no matter what someone tells you. It is from the inside out that counts, not the outside." Her voice is filled with awe, and she is clearly moved by what she is experiencing and the truth of what she is saying. This is clearly a transpersonal experience, one that she will call on for strength at later times. I begin to tap on her knees again.)

CHRISTINA: The Sphinx guards the temple. I can censor what comes in and out if I'm conscious to guard the temple. I don't have to let in what I don't want to come in. ►◄►◄►◄ The Sphinx is protecting me from my anxious self. Inside is the princess. . . . I'm very anxious to contact part of myself. . . . *(Christina has an insight.)* I need the anxiety to keep me going.

(We are running low on time so I ask Christina to return to the original picture.)

CHRISTINA: He's nodding . . . not demeaning. I feel a sense of safe place now. . . . He's in the past. *I* like it. *(She's referring to her childhood artwork.)* It only matters what I think and I'm my own person.
LP: What do you feel now?
CHRISTINA: I feel a sense of peace and composure.

(We install the positive cognition and peaceful feelings with a short set of tapping. Christina talks about the power of this session during the debriefing. She feels better about herself and has a more objective view of her father. The sense of awe she experienced with the contact with the feminine shaman and the Delos Sphinx is very strong.)

The next week Christina said she was feeling good and reported that "an immense amount of energy had opened up." She was excited about school and had a new job. She felt more "integrated" and able to channel her energy creatively. When we went back and checked the picture from the last session, of her father demeaning her childhood artwork, she reported, "I feel equal to my father. He's a person. He was driven. I feel it's a wonderful life."

This confirmed that the work from the last session was done and that her associated negative feelings and self beliefs had shifted. I then asked her to check the picture we had worked on in the other sessions, the one in the room with her father. With closed eyes, she brought the image to mind. At first she said, "The reality is that I survived it. I feel like I'm on the other side of it." But anger stirred as she kept the image in her mind's eye. "Don't take advantage of me!" she said aloud to her imagined father. Strong feelings of anger, sorrow, and deep betrayal were arising.

I asked her what she believed about herself now, in that image. She answered, "You have to make sacrifices for the family. I sacrificed my soul. I have to sacrifice my soul for the betterment of the family." This was clearly the negative cognition. She was in the memory and feeling the emotions. I did not want to go back and ask for the positive cognition and measurements because I felt it would derail her processing. We had sufficient information for EMDR processing—the memory network was lit up. She said she was ready to begin the tapping and, with her eyes closed, immersed herself in her childhood experience.

CHRISTINA: ►◄►◄►◄ It feels like the charge has lifted. I felt fear . . . then it was in the past. The power comes from within me, not from without me . . . inside out, not right side in. ►◄►◄►◄ I feel like I was caught under my father's wing. Now I'm in the world. I'm my sacred self. He doesn't have me anymore. I'm with my sacred self. Now I can fly! ►◄►◄►◄ Take it around . . . life is circular . . . not linear . . . don't get caught anyplace. There's nothing to fear. I don't have to prove myself. I was the holder of the secret. . . . I was bad. . . . It was my father's fault, not my responsibility. *(She is spontaneously realizing who was responsible for the abuse.)* ►◄►◄►◄ It is all about feeling safe. The greatest loss was not feeling safe. I couldn't trust anybody, not even myself. ►◄►◄►◄ *(She receives an auditory message from her inner shaman.)* "We can transcend our limitations. Once we're aware of them we can work through them." ►◄►◄►◄ I want to be free—to be liberated, whole and integrated, and at peace. The cynic comes in and says "This isn't real." What's real? I withdraw into a little ball. A part of me says "You can't be all that you're meant to be." ►◄►◄►◄ The little girl has come home. The sacred self is in the garden with the little girl. I want to be like her. *(She is referring to her unintegrated sacred self.)* It didn't feel safe to be that gracious person. ►◄►◄►◄ I'm feeling comforted by my sacred self. She's commiserating with me. "I'm here now." I feel her nurturing, real, consoling presence. There's no one to fix.

> *(Christina is angry as she remembers a woman telling her, "It isn't so bad" as she lay in the hospital bed in terrible pain after her devastating accident. She imagines telling the woman, "Get out of my face!" I tell Christina to "go with that" and begin to tap again).*

CHRISTINA: I feel a desire to be present with people.
LP: Imagine doing this for yourself. ►◄►◄

> *(As I am tapping, Christina is talking aloud. She tells herself, "It's OK to feel how you feel, and it is OK to relinquish control. I am here for you." After I finish tapping she feels "peaceful and relaxed.")*

The next week Christina came in feeling irritated and agitated. She was angry, unhappy, and felt resentful about "bailing everybody out." She had had a fight with her large teenage son and punched him. (He was in no physical danger from his diminutive mother, and she was aware that her behavior was clearly not acceptable.) We had scheduled a 50-minute session due to time and financial constraints. Based on her demonstrated capacity to stay with the processing of strong affect and upsetting memories and her ability to close incomplete sessions, I believed that she had the inner resources to contain and close down a shorter session if she needed to. During this session, she wanted to return to using eye movements.

We decided to work directly on the incident with her son. When she brought up the worst part, when she punched him, she said, *"Shut up and stop complaining! Why can't you appreciate what you have?!!"* She felt angry and resentful. She began the eye movements and went directly to the earlier incident with her father. Her neck felt as if it were in a vice and her stomach felt sick. A great deal of rage came out, and the physical fight with her son became a physical fight with her father. She was both angry and sad remembering her father's abuse of her. We ended the incomplete session with her going to her safe place and being comforted by her feminine shaman.

After this session we had a month break due to our summer vacations. In the session following the break, Christina reported feeling much better. "I feel increasingly accountable for my life." She was focused on her school work and moving forward again. She reported feeling more relaxed, adding "life is good." She felt good being alone, comfortable with herself. Her initial distressing split when we began our work now felt "integrated. "Her inner shaman now gave her a sense of peace and empowerment, and Christina felt a change in her ability to set limits and boundaries in her relationships. "I can have healthy boundaries," she said with a smile. She was open to the possibility of an intimate relationship with a man, and had met a man who stirred her interest. However, she was aware of negative feelings about her body, and she wished to explore these feelings during this session. Sexuality surfaced as her focus.

I asked her to close her eyes and bring up the image of the man she was interested in, along with the feelings that came up with the image. When she had done that, I asked her what belief accompanied the uncomfortable feeling. "My body is not appealing," she said and then told me an image came up of her having to hide. There was tightness in her throat, a restriction in her stomach, and her neck was tight. In this session she wanted to use tapping. With her eyes closed, her inner attention on the image of hiding along with the sensations in her body and the thought "my body is not appealing," I began to tap on her knees.

CHRISTINA: I feel him with an inviting energy. I want to be who I am in a relationship. ►◄►◄►◄ A voice saying I have to be free at all costs. I don't have to be with someone. ►◄►◄►◄ A real stillness and peace. *(She has apparently completed a channel.)*

LP: Let's return to the original picture. Tell me what comes up for you now.

CHRISTINA: I flashed to hiding behind the shaman. My father's coming toward me.

LP: What are you feeling?

CHRISTINA: A wave of sadness. ►◄►◄►◄ I see this guy again and I tell him I need him for something. If I give him the impression I need him it will bring him close. *(She is aware of old conditioning.)* ►◄►◄►◄ Really deep peace with a flash of franticness. I feel a tightness in my throat. *(It sounds like the oral sex body memory arising for her.)* ►◄►◄►◄ I felt like gagging, like I was going to throw up. I have been feeling this for a couple of weeks. ►◄►◄►◄ Image of someone out to get me. Then there is the image of the shaman and the girl hiding behind her. I'm being protected but I can hardly believe it. It is challenged when someone moves closer to me. *(She's speaking about the new possible romantic interest.)* ►◄►◄►◄ Nothing can hurt you unless you let it. . . . I'm afraid of exposure. ►◄►◄►◄ I want to be seen. *(When her father abused her he did not see her and treated her like an object.)*

(We need to close the session. She feels calm and able to end the session. We briefly talk about what has come up for her. She needs to be seen in relationships. Part of the damage done to her by her father was not being seen by him.)

In the session two weeks later Christina wanted to continue to work on issues related to her body and intimate relationships. I could feel that the intensity of the earlier sessions had diminished. She was reporting fewer symptoms, seemed happy in her life, and was engaged in several creative pursuits. Her earlier blockages seemed to have been lifted and were no longer brought up as issues. She had to dig deeper to come up with things to work on. They weren't jumping out at her as they had been in the earlier sessions.

We explored the issue of her blocked sexuality. "Can I feel sexual pleasure?" She believed that she needed to be perfect and to keep herself in perfect shape. Her mother was overweight, and Christina believed this caused her father to cheat on her, which then caused her emotional pain, which Christina believed killed her mother at an early age. As a result, Christina believed that she had to be perfect or the man she loved would leave her and she would die.

I wanted to assess how Christina's child self was doing as a result of the work we had done. This assessment would help me decide what direction to take. When Christina closed her eyes and contacted her child self, she saw that she was protected by the shaman. I asked how she felt, and she answered that she felt protected and knew she wouldn't be hurt. I asked her to bring the child, shaman, and adult self together. After a long pause, she told me, "They are holding hands . . . they are coming toward me, and they are stepping into my body." She appeared to be spontaneously integrating these disparate ego states. I asked her to begin doing eye movements to install this integration.

CHRISTINA: ►◄►◄►◄ I feel joy with the integration! I can be whole! *(Then doubt arises.)* Can I really be free? ►◄►◄►◄ It all matters, but I am a spirit-being. I want my emphasis there. I want to be unshackled. ►◄►◄►◄ I feel a real yearning to be true to myself and respect myself. *I want to see me.* ►◄►◄►◄ I want to seek more of the mystical truths. *(She then describes a feeling and image of her sexuality opening. She has a beautiful image of a lotus flower blossoming that she understands to be symbolic of her unfolding sexuality.)* ►◄►◄►◄ Can I trust myself in relationships to keep myself safe? ►◄►◄►◄ I need to be true to myself . . . my own person . . . listen to the beat of my own drummer.

LP: Christina, can you go back and check and see how you feel about your sexuality? *(I wanted to see if anything had changed here.)*

CHRISTINA: I'm remembering a message I got from a man in an old relationship. "I'm oversexed." ►◄►◄►◄ I can set appropriate boundaries with people. *(This is a good positive cognition. I ask her to think about that and do another set of eye movements.)* ►◄►◄►◄ I was dancing and moving and feeling how liberating that is.

> *(Christina has been very involved in an imagery and energy experience in which she is moving and dancing and expressing herself freely. Energy is moving in her body. She says, "I'm accepting of my body image.")*

LP: Open to the energy and sensation and imagery of your body expressing in movement your sexuality. ►◄►◄►◄

CHRISTINA: I feel a lot of peace and quietness. I don't have to push or make anything happen.

> *(Christina feels good about ending the EMDR processing at this point as it feels complete. After debriefing, we spend the remaining part of the session talking about the issues she wants to work on in the future. There are a number of things she still wants to work on, including the belief that she is a "nonperson.")*

At this point Christina wanted to take a break from therapy because she felt she had accomplished what she had most urgently desired to do. She was no longer depressed or stuck. She felt much more integrated. Her connection to her spiritual self was deep and empowering. She felt better about herself and her ability to set appropriate boundaries and take care of herself. She felt at peace and was no longer so angry. She wanted to focus her energies and money on her physical recovery from the accident and to work on integrating some of the work we had done using art and movement. We agreed to take a break. She knew she could return when she wished in the future. She appeared to be in a very good place. Our EMDR work together had facilitated her healing process in a profound and beautiful way.

References

Acierno, R., Van Hasselt, V.B., Tremont, G., & Meuser, K.T. (1994). Review of validation and dissemination of eye-movement desentitization and reprocessing: A
scientific and ethical dilemma. *Clinical Psychology Review, 14,* 287–299.

Anderson, C. (1996, June). Visualization for survivors of molest. *EMDRIA
Newsletter. 1.*

Baker, N., & McBride, B. (1991, August). *Clinical applications of EMDR in a law
enforcement environment: Observations of the Psychological Service Unit of the
L.A. County Sheriff's Department.* Paper presented at the Police Psychology
(Division 18, Police & Public Safety Sub-Section) mini-convention at the APA
annual convention, San Francisco, CA.

Bass, E., & Davis, L. (1988). *The courage to heal: A guide for women survivors of
child sexual abuse.* New York: Harper & Row.

Bernstein, C., & Putnam, F. (1986). Development, reliability, and validity of a dissociation scale. *Journal of Nervous and Mental Disease, 174,* 727–735.

Boudewyns, P.A., Stwertka, S.A., Hyer, L.A., Albrecht, J.W., & Sperr, E.V. (1993).
Eye movement desensitization and reprocessing: A pilot study. *Behavior Therapy,
16,* 30–33.

Bresler, D.E. (1990). Meeting an inner advisor. In D.C. Hammond (Ed.), *Handbook
of hypnotic suggestions and metaphors* (pp. 318–320). New York: Norton.

Briere, J (1995). *Trauma Symptom Inventory professional manual.* Odessa, FL:
Psychological Assessment Resources.

Carlson, E.B., & Putnam, F.W. (1992). *Manual for the dissociative experiences scale.*
Available from the first author.

Carlson, E.B., & Putnam, F.W. (1993). An update on the dissociative experiences
scale. *Dissociation, 6,* 16–27.

Carlson, J.G., Chemtob, C.M., Rusnak, K., Hedlund, N.L., & Muraoka, M.Y. (1998).
Eye movement dessensitization and reprocessing for combat-related posttraumatic stress disorder. *Journal of traumatic stress. 11,* 3–24.

Chambless, D.L., Baker, M.J., Baucom, D.H., Beutler, L.E., Calhoun, K.S., Crits-
Christoph, P., Daiuto, A., DeRubeis, R., Detweiler, J., Haaga, D.A.F., Bennett
Johnson, S., McCurry, S., Mueser, K.T., Pope, K.S., Sanderson, W.C., Shoham, V.,
Stickle, T., Williams, D.A., & Woody, S.R. (1998). Update on empirically validated
therapies, *The Clincial Psychologist, 51,* 3–16.

Cohen, B.M., & Cox, C.T. (1995). *Telling without talking: A window into the world of
multiple personality.* New York: Norton.

Cohn, L. (1993a). Art psychotherapy and the new eye movement desensitization and reprocessing (EMD/R) method, an integrated approach. In Evelyne Dishup (Ed.), *California art therapy trends.* Chicago, IL: Magnolia Street Publisher.

Cohn, L. (1993b). *Art therapy and EMDR.* Workshop presentation. EMDR Conference. Sunnyvale, California.

Daniels, N., Lipke, H., Richardson, R., & Silver, S. (1992, October). *Vietnam veterans' treatment programs using eye movement desensitization and reprocessing.* Symposium presented at the International Society for Traumatic Stress Studies annual convention, Los Angeles, CA.

Datta, P.C., & Wallace, J. (1996, November) *Enhancement of victim empathy along with reduction of anxiety and increase of positive cognition of sex offenders after treatment with EMDR.* Paper presented at the EMDR Special Interest Group at the Annual Convention of the Association for the Advancement of Behavior Therapy, New York.

Davis, L. (1990). *The courage to heal workbook.* New York: Harper & Row.

Douglass, F. (1941). *The life and times of Frederick Douglass.* New York: Pathway Press.

Erickson, M.H., & Rossi, E.L. (1976). Two level communication and the microdynamics of trance and suggestion. *American Journal of Clinical Hypnosis, 18,* 153–171.

Feske, U. (1998). Eye movement desensitization and reprocessing treatment for posttraumatic stress disorder. *Clinical Psychology: Science and Practice, 5,* 171–181.

Foster, S., & Lendl, J. (1996). Eye movement desensitization and reprocessing: Four case studies of a new tool for executive coaching and restoring employee performance after setbacks. *Consulting Psychology Journal: Practice and Research, 48,* (3), 155–161.

Goldstein, A. (1992, August). *Treatment of panic and agoraphobia with EMDR: Preliminary data of the Agoraphobia and Anxiety Treatment Center, Temple University.* Paper presented at the fourth World Congress on Behavior Therapy, Queensland, Australia.

Goldstein, A., & Feske, U. (1994). Eye movement desensitization and reprocessing for panic disorder: A case series. *Journal of Anxiety Disorders. 8,* 351–362.

Goldstein, J. (1976) *The experience of insight.* Boulder, CO: Shambala.

Greenwald, R. (1994). Applying eye movement desensitization and reprocessing to the treatment of traumatized children: Five case studies. *Anxiety Disorders Practice Journal, 1* 83–97.

Harner, M. (1980). *The way of the Shaman.* New York: Bantam.

Herbert, J.D., & Meuser, K. T. (1992). Eye movement desensitization: A critique of the evidence. *Journal of Behavior Therapy and Experimental Psychiatry, 23,* 169–174.

Herman, J.L. (1992). *Trauma and recovery.* New York: Basic Books.

Kabat-Zinn, J. (1990). *Full catastrople living: Using the wisdom of your body and mind to face stress, pain, and illness.* New York: Dell.

Klein, J. (1988).*Who am I?* Longmead, Shaftesbury, Dorset: Element Books.

Kleinknecht, R. (1992). Treatment of post-traumatic stress disorder with eye movement desensitization and reprocessing. *Journal of Behavior Therapy and Experimental Psychiatry, 23,* 43–50.

Kleinknecht, R. (1993). Rapid treatment of blood and injection phobias with eye movement desensitization. *Journal of Behavior Therapy and Experimental Psychiatry, 24,* 211–217.

Kluft, R.P. (1985). The natural history of multiple personality discorder. In R.P. Kluft (Ed.), *The childhood antecedents of multiple personality.* Washington, DC: American Psychiatric Press, Inc.

References

Kluft, R.P. (1987) First-rank symptoms as a diagnostic clue to multiple personality disorder. *American Journal of Psychiatry, 144,* 293–298.

Korn, D. (1997). *Clinical application of EMDR in treating survivors of sexual abuse.* Workshop presentation. EMDR International Association Conference, San Francisco, CA.

Kornfield, J. (1993). *A path with heart: A guide through the perils and promises of spiritual life.* New York: Bantam.

Leeds, A.M. (1997, July 13) I*n the eye of the beholder: Reflections on shame, dissociation, and transference in complex posttraumatic stress and attachment related disorders. Principles of case formulation for EMDR treatment planning and the use of resource installation.* Unpublished paper presented at the EMDR International Association Conference, San Francisco. Available from <ALeeds@concentric.net>

Leeds, A.M. (1998). Lifting the burdern of shame: Using EMDR resource installation to resolve a therapeutic impasse. In P. Manfield (Ed.), *Extending EMDR: A casebook of innovative applications* (pp. 256–281). New York: Norton.

Leeds, A.M., & Korn, D. (1998). *Clinical applications of EMDR in the treatment of adult survivors of childhood abuse and neglect.* Workshop presentation. EMDR International Association Conference, Baltimore, MD.

Leeds, A.M., & Shapiro, F. (in press). EMDR and resource installation: Principles and procedures to enhance current functioning and resolve traumatic experiences. In J. Carlson & L. Sperry (Eds.), *Brief therapy strategies with individuals and couples.* Phoenix: Zeig, Tucker.

Lendl, J., & Foster, S. (1997). *EMDR performance enhancement for the workplace: A practitioners' manual.* Self published manual. Inquiries to: Sandra Foster, Ph.D., 220 Montgomery St., Suite 315, San Francisco, California 94104. E-mail: samrolf@aol.com.

Levin, C. (1993, July/August). The enigma of EMDR. *Family Therapy Networker,* 75–83.

Levin, C., Grainger, R.K., Allen-Byrd, L., & Fulcher, G. (1994, August). *Efficacy of eye movement desensitization and reprocessing (EMDR) for survivors of Hurricane Andrew: A comparative study.* Paper presented at the American Psychological Association conference, Los Angeles, CA.

Levine, S. (1987). *Healing into life and death.* New York: Anchor/Doubleday.

Linehan, M. (1993a). *Cognitive-behavioral treatment of the borderline personality disorder.* New York: Guilford.

Linehan, M. (1993b). *Skills training manual for treating borderline personality disorder.* New York: Guilford.

Lipke, H. (1994, August). *Survey of practitioners trained in eye movement desensitization and reprocessing.* Paper presented at the American Psychological Association annual convention, Los Angeles, CA.

Lipke, H., & Botkin, A. (1992). Brief case studies of eye movement desensitization and reprocessing with chronic post-traumatic stress disorder. *Psychotherapy, 29,* 591–595.

Loewenstein, R.J. (1991). An office mental status examination for complex, chronic dissociative symptoms and multiple personality disorder. *Psychiatric Clinics of North America, 14,* 567–604.

Loewenstein, R.J. (1993). Posttraumatic and dissociative aspects of transference and countertransference in the treatment of multiple personality disorder. In R. P. Kluft & C.G. Fine. (Eds.), *Clinical perspectives on multiple personality disorder* (pp. 51–86). Washington, DC: American Psychiatric Press.

Lohr, J. M., Kleinknecht, R.A., Conley, A.T., dal Cerro, S., Schmidt, J., & Sonntag, M.E. (1992). A methodological critique of the current status of eye movement desensitization (EMD). *Journal of Behavior Therapy and Experimental Psychiatry, 23,* 159–167.

Lovett, J. (1999). *Small wonders: Healing childhood trauma with EMDR.* New York: Free Press.

Maltz, W. (1991). *The sexual healing journey.* New York: HarperPerennial.

Marcus, S., Marquis, P., & Sakai, C. (1997). Controlled study of treatment of PTSD using EMDR in an HMO setting. *Psychotherapy, 34,* 307–315.

Marquis, J. (1991). A report on seventy-eight cases treated by eye movement desensitization. *Journal of Behavior Therapy and Experimental Psychiatry, 22,* 187–192.

McCann, D.L. (1992). Post-traumatic stress disorder due to devastating burns overcome by a single session of eye movement desensitization. *Journal of Behavior Therapy and Experimental Psychiatry, 23,* 319–323.

McCann, I.L., & Pearlman, L.A. (1990). *Psychological trauma and the adult survivor: Theory, therapy, and transformation.* New York: Brunner/Mazel.

McFarlane, A.C., Weber, D.L., & Clark, C.R. (1993). Abnormal stimulus processing in PTSD. *Biological Psychiatry, 34,* 311–320.

McNeal, S., & Frederick, C. (1993). Inner strength and other techniques for ego-strengthening. *American Journal of Clinical Hypnosis, 35,* 170–178.

Miller, E. (1996). *Letting go of stress.* Source Cassette Learning Systems, Inc.

Ogden, T.H. (1994). *Subjects of analysis.* Northvale, NJ; Aronson.

Page, A.C., & Crino, R.D. (1993). Eye-movement desensitization: A simple treatment for post-traumatic stress disorder? *Australian and New Zealand Journal of Psychiatry, 27,* 288–293.

Parnell, L. (1994, August). *Treatment of sexual abuse survivors with EMDR: Two case reports.* Paper presented at the 102nd annual meeting of the American Psychological Association, Los Angeles, CA.

Parnell, L. (1995–1998). *EMDR in the treatment of sexual abuse survivors.* EMDR Institute: Level II Specialty Presentations.

Parnell, L. (1995, June).*The use of imaginal and cognitive interweaves with sexual abuse survivors.* Workshop presesentation. EMDR International Association Conference. Santa Monica, CA.

Parnell, L. (1996a). Eye movement desensitization and reprocessing (EMDR) and spiritual unfolding. *Journal of Transpersonal Psychology, 28,*129–153.

Parnell, L. (1996b, August). *From trauma to transformation: EMDR and spiritual unfoldment.* Association for Transpersonal Psychology Annual Conference.

Parnell, L. (1997a). *Transforming Trauma: EMDR.* New York: Norton.

Parnell, L. (1997b, July). *Beyond recovery: EMDR and transpersonal experiences.* EMDR International Association Conference, San Francisco, CA.

Parnell, L. (1998a, July). *Transforming sexual abuse trauma with EMDR.* Workshop presentation. EMDR International Association Conference, Baltimore, MD.

Parnell, L. (1998b) Post-partum depression: Helping a new mother to bond. In P. Manfield (Ed.), *Extending EMDR: A casebook of innovative applications* (pp. 37–64). New York: Norton.

Parnell, L., & Cohn, L. (1995). *Innovations in the use of EMDR, imagery, and art.* EMDR regional network meeting.

Paulsen, S., Vogelmann-Sine, S. Lazrove, S., & Young, W. (1993, October). *Eye movement desensitization and reprocessing: Its role in the treatment of dissociative disorders.* 10th Annual Conference of ISSMPD, Chicago.

Phillips, M. (1997a, July). *The importance of ego strengthening with EMDR.* EMDRIA Conference. San Francisco, CA.

Phillips, M. (1997b, November). *The importance of ego strengthening with dissociative disorder patients.* Fourteenth international fall conference of the International Society for the Study of Dissociation. Montreal, Canada.

Phillips, M. (in press). Hypnosis, EMDR, and ego strengthening. *American Journal of Clinical Hypnosis.*

Phillips, M., & Frederick, C. (1995) *Healing the divided self.* New York: Norton.

References

Pitman, R.K., Orr, S.P., Altman, B., Longpre, R.E., Poire, R.E., & Macklin, M.L., 1996). Emotional processing during eye-movement desensitization and reprocessing therapy of Vietnam veterans with chronic post-traumatic stress disorder. *Comprehensive Psychiatry, 37,* 419–429.

Popky, A.J. (1997). *EMDR integrative addiction treatment model.* EMDR Institute: Level II Specialty Presentation, San Francisco, CA.

Puffer, M.K., Greenwald, R., & Elrod, D.E. (in press). A single session EMDR study with twenty traumatized children and adolescents. *Traumatology.*

Puk, G. (1991). Treating traumatic memories: A case report on the eye movement desensitization procedure. *Journal of Behavior Therapy and Experimental Psychiatry. 22,* 149–151.

Puk, G. (1999). In F. Shapiro, *EMDR Institute manual.* Pacific Grove, CA: EMDR Institute.

Putnam, F.W. (1989). *Diagnosis and treatment of multiple personality disorder.* New York: Guilford.

Putnam, F.W., Guroff, J.J., Silberman, E.K., Barban, L., & Post, R.M. (1986). The clinical phenomenology of multiple personality disorder. *Journal of Clinical Psychiatry, 47,* 285–293.

Pynoos, R. S., Steinberg, A., & Goenjian, A. (1996). Traumatic stress in childhood and adolescence: Recent developments and current controversies. In B. van der Kolk, A. C. McFarlane, & L. Weisaeth (Eds.), *Traumatic stress.* New York: Guilford.

Ross, C.A.(1989). *Multiple personality disorder.* New York: Wiley.

Ross, C.A. (1995). Diagnosis of dissociative identity disorder. In L. Cohen, J. Berzoff, & M. Elin (Eds.), *Dissociative Identity disorder.* Northvale, NJ: Aronson.

Ross, C.A., Herber, S., Norton, G.R., Anderson, G., & Garchet, P. (1989). The Dissociative Disorders Interview Schedule: A structured interview. *Dissociation, 2,* 169–189.

Ross, C.A., Miller, S.D., Reagor, R., Bjornson, L., Fraser, G.A., & Anderson, G. (1990) Schneiderian symptoms in multiple personality disorder and schizophrenia. *Comprehensive Psychiatry, 31,* 111–118.

Rossman, M.L. (1987). *Healing yourself: A step-by-step program for better health through imagery.* New York: Walker.

Rothbaum, B.O. (1997). A controlled study of eye movement desensitization and reprocessing for posttraumatic stress disordered sexual assault victims. *Bulletin of the Menninger Clinic, 61,* 317–334.

Salzberg, S. (1996). *Loving-kindness meditation—Learning to love through insight meditation* (audio cassette).

Salzberg, S., & Kabat-Zinn, J. (1997) *Loving kindness: The revolutionary art of happiness.* Berkeley: Shambala.

Scheck, M.M., Schaeffer, J.A., & Gillette, C.S. (1998). Brief psychological intervention with traumatized young women: The efficacy of eye movement dessensitization and reprocessing. *Journal of Traumatic Stress, 11*(1), 25–44.

Schore, A.N. (1994). *Affect regulation and the origin of the self: The neurobiology of emotional development.* Hillsdale, NJ: Erlbaum.

Schore, A. N. (1998, January 31). *Memory, brain process and development, part I.* Understanding and Treating Trauma: Developmental and Neurobiological Approaches: Lifespan Learning Institute Conference, Los Angeles, CA.

Shapiro, F. (1989a). Efficacy of the eye movement desensitization procedure in the treatment of traumatic memories. *Journal of Traumatic Stress Studies, 2,* 199–223.

Shapiro, F. (1989b). Eye movement desensitization: A new treatment for post-traumatic stress disorder. *Journal of Behavior Therapy and Experimental Psychiatry,, 20,* 211–217.

Shapiro, F. (1995). *Eye movement desensitization and reprocessing.* New York: Guilford.

Shapiro, F. (in press). Eye movement desensitization and reprocessing (EMDR) and the anxiety disorders: Clinical and research implications of an integrated psychotherapy treatment. *Journal of Anxiety Disorders.*

Siegel, D. (1998, February). *Memory, brain process and development, part II.* Understanding and Treating Trauma: Developmental and Neurobiological Approaches: Lifespan Learning Institute Conference, Los Angeles, CA.

Silver, S.M., Brooks, A., & Obenchain, J. (1995). Eye movement desensitization and reprocessing treatment of Vietnam war veterans with PTSD: Comparative effects with biofeedback and relaxation training. *Journal of Traumatic Stress, 8,* 337–342.

Solomon, R., & Kaufman, T. (1992, October). *Eye movement desensitization and reprocessing: An effective addition to critical incident treatment protocols.* Preliminary results presented at the International Society for Traumatic Stress Studies annual conference, Los Angeles, CA.

Solomon R., & Shapiro, F. (1997). Eye movement desensitization and reprocessing: An effective therapeutic tool for trauma and grief. In C. Figley, B. Bride, & N. Mazza (Eds.), *Death and trauma.* London: Taylor & Francis.

Spector, J., & Huthwaite, M. (1993). Eye-movement desensitization to overcome post-traumatic stress disorder. *British Journal of Psychiatry, 163,* 106–108.

Spector, J., & Reade, J. (in press.) The current status of eye movement desensitization and reprocessing—EMDR. *Clinical Psychology and Psychotherapy.*

Spiegel, D. (1993). Multiple posttraumatic personality disorder. In R.P. Kluft & C.G. Fine (Eds.), *Clinical perspectives on multiple personality disorder.* Washington, DC: American Psychiatric Press, Inc.

Steinberg, M. (1995). *Handbook for the assessment of dissociation: A clinical guide.* Washington, DC: American Psychiatric Press, Inc.

Taylor, C. (1991). *The inner child workbook.* Los Angeles: Tarcher.

Thompson, J., Cohn, L., & Parnell, L. (1996, June). *Beyond the cognitive interweave: The use of dreams, art, and imagery in EMDR.* EMDR International Conference, Denver, CO.

Tinker, R., & Wilson, S. (1999). *Through the eyes of a child: EMDR with children.* New York: Norton.

van Etten, M.L., & Taylor, S. (1998). Comparative efficacy of treatments for post-traumatic stress disorder: A meta-analysis. *Journal of Clinical Psychology and Psychotherapy, 5,* 126–144.

van der Kolk, B. (1998, January 31). *Social and neurobiological dimensions of the compulsion to forget and re-enact trauma.* Understanding and Treating Trauma: Developmental and Neurobiological Approaches Lifespan Learning Institute Conference. Los Angeles, CA.

van der Kolk, B. (1996). The complexity of adaptation to trauma: Self-regulation, stimulus discrimination, and characterological development. In B. van der Kolk, A.C. McFarlane, & L.Weisaeth (Eds.), *Traumatic stress.* New York: Guilford.

van der Kolk, B. (1994). The body keeps the score: Memory and the evolving psychobiology of posttraumatic stress. *Harvard Review Psychiatry, 1:* 253–265.

van der Kolk, B., Burbridge, J.A., & Suzuki, J. (1997). The psychobiology of traumatic memory: Clinical implications of neuroimaging studies. In R. Yehuda & A.C. McFarlane (Eds.), *Annals of the New York Academy of Sciences (Vol. 821): Psychobiology of Posttraumatic Stress Disorder.* New York: New York Academy of Sciences.

van der Kolk, B., & Fisler, R. (1995). Dissociation and the fragmentary nature of traumatic memories: Overview and exploratory study. *Journal of Traumatic Stress. 8,*(4), 505–525.

References

van der Kolk, B., McFarlane, A.C., & Weisaeth, L. (Eds.). (1996). *Traumatic stress.* New York: Guilford.

van der Kolk, B.A., Perry, C., & Herman, J.L. (1991). Childhood origins of self-destructive behavior. *American Journal of Psychiatry, 148,* 1665–1671.

Watkins, J.G. (1971). The affect bridge: A hypnoanalytic technique. *International Journal of Clinical and Experimental Hypnosis, 19,* 21–27.

Watkins, J.G. (1990). Watkins' affect or somatic bridge. In D.C. Hammond (Ed.), *Handbook of hypnotic suggestions and metaphors* (pp. 523–524). New York: Norton.

Wernick, U. (1993). The role of the traumatic component in the etiology of sexual dysfunctions and its treatment with eye movement desensitization procedure. *Journal of Sex Education and Therapy, 19,* 212–222.

Wildwind, L. (1993). *Chronic depression.* Workshop presentation. EMDR Conference, Sunnyvale, CA.

Wilson, D., Covi, W., Foster, S., & Silver, S.M. (1993, April). *Eye movement desensitization and reprocessing and ANS correlates in the treatment of PTSD.* Paper presented at the California Psychological Association annual convention, San Francisco, CA.

Wilson, S.A., Becker, L.A., & Tinker, R.H. (1995). Eye movement desensitization and reprocessing (EMDR) method treatment for psychologically traumatized individuals. *Journal of Consulting and Clinical Psychology, 63,* 928–937.

Wilson, S.A., Becker, L.A., & Tinker, R.H.(1997) Fifteen-month follow-up of eye movement desensitization and reprocessing (EMDR) treatment for PTSD and psyschological trauma. *Journal of Consulting and Clinical Psychology, 65,* 1047–1056.

Wolpe, J. (1991). *The practice of behavior therapy* (4th ed.). New York: Pergamon.

Wolpe, J., & Abrams, J. (1991). Post-traumatic stress disorder overcome by eye movement desensitization: A case report. *Journal of Behavior Therapy and Experimental Psychiatry, 22,* 39–43.

Yeshe, Lama T. (1995). *The tantric path of purification.* Boston: Wisdom Publications.

Young, W. (1994). EMDR treatment of phobic symptoms in multiple personality. *Dissociation, 7,* 129–133.

Index